THIS LAND

FAITH READER

A literary chronicle of the struggle between power and passion

Selections from *This Land* magazine, 2010–2016

THIS LAND

Vincent LoVoi, *Publisher*

www.ThisLandPress.com

Printed in the United States of America

First Edition

ISBN 978-0-9962516-3-1

THIS LAND

FAITH READER

A literary chronicle of the struggle between power and passion

Selections from *This Land* magazine, 2010–2016

CONTENTS

by Kathryn Parkman

WHAT WE TALK ABOUT WHEN WE TALK ABOUT GOD

For six years This Land Press collected stories, ambitiously chronicling life and culture in the middle of America from an independent perspective, untethered by denominational obligations or political affiliations. Many of these stories directly or indirectly relate to faith and show different faces of God told by different voices from different perspectives and different places.

One tells us that 47 percent of our neighbors worship a God like the God that Charles Fox Parham found in Kansas at the end of the 20th century. This God is a personal God; He rips "through your viscera like an electric current and make your religious conviction dynamically manifest" when you emerge from a sacred baptismal, writes contributor Mike Mariani in "Tongues of Fire in Kansas."

The "Strange Love of Billy James Hargis" by the late Lee Roy Chapman and Michael Mason shows how the Christian Crusade, which Hargis founded in Tulsa, Oklahoma, in the 1950s, brought this God into millions of homes. His Okie-flavored rhetoric gripped the country as he preached that the civil rights movement was a godless communist plot. And Hargis begat the American Christian right.

Dear God.

"God is a GOOD God," Oral Roberts promised. Roberts' God only wants to heal, not punish. In "The Gospel of John," Lindsey Neal Kuykendall dug through Oral Roberts University's ephemera for the letter ex-Beatle John Lennon wrote to Roberts in a moment of desperation. Lennon was searching for forgiveness and through Roberts, the story goes, found it.

"The ability to forgive and forget is divine," said Pastor Bob Yandian, formerly of Grace Fellowship, in defending the church's handling of a pedophilia scandal to Kiera Feldman, who wrote "Grace in Broken Arrow." Pastor Bob's God always forgives.

God damn.

We find more bad men in the City of God. Chapman and Joshua Kline traveled to the Oklahoma-Arkansas border—where white separatists and fringe militia types flock to worship and, some say, conspire to dismantle the "Zionist-occupied government"—to find out "Who's Afraid of Elohim City?"

Oh, for God's sake.

Life is America has always been intertwined with faith, and we publish the Faith Reader to give some insight to the spiritual landscape of Middle America today. This anthology, made up of investigations and reportage and inspired by personal experience and historical archives, represents the best deconstructions of, investigations into, and meditations on faith and spirituality that we've had the privilege to publish.

God bless.

Originally published
November 2011

by Sheilah Bright

JUST AS I WAS

Confessions of a fallen Southern Baptist

I sprang from a deep well of Southern Baptist blood—crimson, of course. One of my most frightful childhood memories involves waking up to find a strange man standing in the living room of our tiny two-bedroom house in Prattville. He was raining sweat as he tried to angrily force "Just As I Am" out of some black-and-white crying lap dog.

Later, too much later, I learned he was a visiting preacher man. The wailing animal was an accordion.

I freaked out again when someone on *The Gospel Singing Jubilee* television show (it might have been one of those bouncy Happy Goodmans) belted out "I Saw the Light," and I fled into my bedroom, where I saw a glowing midget with wings. Chances are it was a cough-syrup induced hallucination or some kind of flashback from that flying monkey scene in *The Wizard of Oz*. Back then, it was interpreted as a divine sign, an angel encounter, perhaps gifted from my deceased Baptist tent revival grandfather. If the Holy Ghost had anything to do with it, I hoped he was the smiling Casper kind instead of those convulsion-laden spirits rumored to be flying around the Pentecostal church near my school.

So now you know why angels, accordions, and some Pentecostals creep me out. It is also why I am scared as hell that, if I keep babbling about religion like this, I am going to get struck down by God's middle finger and not get into Heaven where most of my family now resides.

Confession chagrin: (Touching the pages of an ancient family Bible just saved me from Pharisee paranoia at this midnight hour, so I'm going to keep writing, with y'all's blessing.)

My paternal grandfather felt the call at an early age and spent most of his life stomping across Oklahoma and Arkansas, spreading the word in tent camps and tiny churches, where he was paid in pecans, cantaloupes, and the occasional chicken. The fact that he, the preacher man, married my grandmother, an unwed mother, made me love him even though he died several months before I was born. His heart was crushed by the steering wheel of his Volkswagen beetle when he couldn't stop at an icy intersection and was hit by a car.

"If your grandfather were alive, you wouldn't be wearing cutoffs."

"Grandpa wouldn't have anything to do with you crimping those eyelashes. And mascara? Forget it, sister."

"The birth control pill? Lord, have mercy."

Here is what my teenage self used to think: *Thank God, he isn't alive. I wouldn't get to do anything with him around.* I hate to admit this because I have grown fond of this preacher man. Many of his books were given to me and, from the sermon notes penned in the margins, I learned much about the self-educated minister who quoted Paul but also read Plato. In a funeral sermon preached in the latter years of his life, he wrote, "Falling leaves are but nature's sermon," and, "There will be a smell of varnish in the house when the casket is brought, and then the procession will slowly move toward the city of sighs and tears." It was read again at his funeral in 1961 and at my father's funeral in 1997. A few years ago, I read it at my uncle's service, and I suspect it might get read again when his last surviving child leaves us.

I spend a lot of time at the pulpit these days because so many of my family members are dying. Apparently, I give good eulogy. Capturing and conveying a person's life with words is what some in the family call my spiritual gift. Sometimes, it feels like a blessing. Other times, it's more like a curse.

Baptists love a little dramatic reading at a funeral. It helps explain the wailing and gnashing of teeth. I have never heard anyone say they were saved at a funeral, but there is usually an altar call thrown in at the end. By this point of a funeral service, you're wanting the whole thing to be over, and secretly I think most of the crowd is hoping no one walks forward to drag this thing out any longer.

Confession chagrin: (Verily, verily I say unto thee: The burden of this religious angst is weighing heavy on me so I have to lighten up before I sink too low.)

Operators Are Standing By

Vacation Bible School always lifted my spirits. It might have been the cross-shaped cookies or the Bible cakes. On the giant, felt boards used for story hour, it seemed so fun to dump all the felt people into one big pile and then grab-bag it so that baby Moses and Noah could spend time together in the same boat. The sad-sack Job looked perkier when you stood him next to the Wise Men in a manger populated by the shepherds, one of Daniel's lions, and that hunk of a man, Goliath. There were a lot of snakes, and for some reason our teacher insisted that Eve's serpent stayed in Eden. It was the '60s.

I loved the language of the Old Testament characters, always crying "Alas" and "Behold," but I couldn't memorize a Bible verse to save my soul. If the words sounded awkward or not prophetic enough, I simply reworked them, ensuring that the Bible Bowl championship would never be in my future. The songs were fairly lively and lyrical except for "Onward Christian Soldier," which caused me to stiffen. "Marching as to war" was the last thing I wanted to do. For some reason, "I'm in the Lord's Army" caused no alarm because acting like you were riding a horse to "ride in the cavalry, shoot the artillery" made it seem less violent than it sounded. The warm fuzzy of religion felt better: "Joy in my heart" and "Jesus loves the little children."

Many years later, I would think about those innocent songs when one of my sons visited Africa on a mission trip and heard children happily singing, "Telephone to Jesus, telephone to Jesus, every day." "Talk to Jesus" had probably been the original message, but they were so happy singing the mixed-up version that, thankfully, no one corrected them.

I walked the aisle at a church camp in the Kiamichi Mountains, and it stirred something deep inside me. Honestly, it may have been the preacher, who looked a lot like Robert Redford. You got a hug and his autograph in a Bible for "going forward." Everyone wanted to know when I would take the next step, which involved letting someone hold you under water while the congregation held its collective breath.

My cousin's baptism gathered us onto the rocky shores of a lake in southeastern Oklahoma. We clasped hands and beheld her gentle backbend into the same murky water where we caught catfish. She emerged a cleansed soul with a mud-stained robe, and everyone applauded then sang a personal favorite, "Shall We Gather at the River." I had trepidation about this kind of immersion because those sacred waters were also home to cottonmouths and turtles big enough to remove your toes.

I opted for the citified baptism, although there was some doubt whether the church water was any cleaner. No one had ever seen the baptistry changed out. The organ mood music and dim lights were the most sacred selling points for me. They gave that "this is a Broadway show and you are the star" kinda quality to the ceremony. The bonus was that the church ladies always made special desserts out of Cool Whip and pudding mix for the after-party in the fellowship hall. People shook your hand and hugged you. If you were lucky enough to be the solo baptism act, you got all the glory.

My luminous moment lost its glow before the crowd even finished the second verse of the first congregational song. That's when I realized I had forgotten an extra change of clothes to wear at the reception. Thinking the baptismal robe would cover my "what nots," I stripped down to my underwear and tossed the holy cloth over my head.

Like many times in my life, I overlooked some important details. I forgot to hold my nose so I sputtered and coughed spastically onto the preacher as I surfaced the frigid water. And for some ungodly reason, likely rooted in a clearance sale at Froug's or TG&Y, I was sporting a hot-pink training bra under the white robe. Jesus may have turned water into wine, but my holy experience turned a cotton cloak into sheer humiliation. People gasped as my fluorescent breastlets rose from the spiritual dunk tank. One of the church ladies nearly fell in as she tried to scoop me up into a scratchy towel. At the time, it felt like the Rapture.

Stop, in the Name of Love

I rededicated my life often during my teen years. There is no doubt that our youth ministry program kept us busy and guilty-minded enough to dissuade a lot of bad decisions. It didn't stop me from doing things before I should have, but an internal moral compass pulled me away from some things that could have been my downfall. At least that's what the youth leader said.

Confession chagrin: (Dear God, Can I still seek forgiveness for that incident back in '77 when I told my mom that I was helping paint the church youth room? I was really drinking beer and possibly smoking pot at Estill Park. Sorry. I think I did give double to the Lottie Moon Fund on that next Sunday.)

In the 1990s, when the Southern Baptists began

kicking up their heels over abortion and gay rights, I began backsliding from my home church. Then my dad died, and all I could think about during Sunday morning service was how his casket had been sitting right there. Invitation songs made me burst into tears. The offering plates kept getting deeper. The contemporary praise music put me in a bad mood. I usually stayed out late on Saturday night, so getting up in time for Sunday service bummed me out. People started wearing pajama pants and shorts to worship the Lord. Excuses, don't get me started.

After we survived the millennium, it seemed like Baptists started spending way too much time bashing the culture instead of nurturing the congregation. It was the dawn of multimedia presentations, where snippets of television sitcoms might pop up on the big screen that electronically rolled down over the rugged cross of Jesus. Country-and-western song lyrics, news clips, and product commercials became launching pads for parables about how liberal sinners were dragging the country down into Gomorrohland.

Someone who once taught my Sunday school class tried hard to convince me that Oprah was the Antichrist. My homosexual friends were being asked to admit their sins or find another place to worship. Meanwhile back at a church that I once attended, a deacon had slipped out of town with a pocketful of building fund money and his arms around another man's wife. He was at the top of the prayer list.

One Sunday, I snuck into another house of prayer expecting to rediscover "Showers of Blessings" or a "Sweet Sweet Spirit" in my heart. I walked out about 10 minutes later because the congregation was celebrating something called "Abortion Sunday: Free the Babies." The propaganda machine churning during the presidential elections made me want to speak in tongues filled with curse words.

The pastor at my home church was kind, but I couldn't hear the goodness for all the Southern Baptist badness swirling around. So I stopped going to church.

Slip-Sliding Away

On a certain shelf in my library, there is a dedicated shrine of Bibles and religious books, including an old green one entitled *The Blood of the Lamb*. I'd like to say they get pulled from the shelf every day, or week, or month, and read, but it would be a lie. I pray. I believe in God. I sing hymns sometimes when I am walking. Becoming one of those "you don't have to go to church to worship" kind of folks was never in my master plan. It may not last forever.

In my travels abroad, I have spent a fair amount of time in mosques and monasteries. It makes my Baptist family really nervous when I say things like, "I think I should have been a Buddhist," or, "What they believe and what we believe isn't that different." The characters are just mixed up and wear different names. Just like on that Bible school felt board.

Last year in Morocco, I became somewhat addicted to a certain imam's call to prayer. Unexpectedly soothing and so unlike what we hear on televisions, the public broadcasts lulled us to sleep and nudged us to awake.

"What is he saying?" I finally asked the Muslim guide. "Come to pray," he said. "Praying is better than eating or sleeping."

I told that story once to broaden the mind of a rigid Republicanostal. She made some nasty comment about how "those" people always tried to make everything about religion, and that we don't do that here in the United States.

Really? Check out the "Agape" or "Trinity" listings in a Tulsa phone book. (Under hair salon listings, roofers, you name it.) A few years back in our Sand Springs Christmas parade, a group of kids were marching with a banner that read "Twirling for Jesus." Does Christ want people twirling in his name? Is that what it means to carry the baton of God? Wouldn't it be better to say "Feeding the Homeless for Jesus?" In India, a young guy who was driving me back to the airport asked if I was Catholic, and when I said that I grew up Baptist, he replied, "Why do you Baptists make such mean signs?" It took me a few questions to realize that he had seen news coverage of that warped Westboro Baptist Church and their funeral protests.

Nobody every promised that this religion thing was going to be easy. Some days, I think I might become Methodist or Presbyterian or Unitarian, but it just takes too much mental energy to start anew and learn all those dos and do nots. Quakers sound nice. My memory skills aren't good enough to be Catholic. People are always making fun of Lutherans. Non-denominational sounds like you're chickening out on commitment. I don't like the clothes or hairstyles worn by the Pentecostals. A back-sliding Baptist is likely my destiny.

From the moment I learned about Lot's wife turning into a pillar of salt for trying to catch one longing last glimpse of sin-laden Sodom, I knew faith was going to test my life. The best that I can do for now is to see more of the good than the bad in people and their religions.

I'm hell-bent to try to be one of the good ones.

Originally published
January 2012

by Holly Wall

THE ODDITIES OF EVANGELISM

Exploring the strange collection of T.L. Osborn

After he slew his enemy—a warrior in another tribe who killed his brother and was, according to ritual, justly punished—the Jivaro Indian removed his victim's head and then retreated into the seclusion of his hut to do his work.

After boiling the head so that its skin was supple and pliable, he sliced into the back of the man's neck, gliding his knife along its nape, from the decapitation wound to the crown of the head, pulling skin away from skull and removing the hard white shell that encapsulated the man's brain. That, too, was removed, along with everything else that once served to give the man life, and the Jivaro then filled the cavity with hot sand and pebbles, slowly and persistently rotating the head to ensure even drying, He repeated the process for days, until the head was completely dry and had shrunk about five times its normal size, until it was no bigger than the Jivaro's fist—though its features remained remarkably intact.

He used cotton to sew the head's eyes and lips shut. When he'd finished, he presented his trophy to his tribe, and his people celebrated his victory with a bountiful ceremony of dancing, drink, and orgy. He displayed the head in his hut until a buyer—some Westerner fascinated with his tribe's headhunting tradition—offered him a musket in exchange.

Eventually, the trophy—and others like it—would find itself on a shelf in Tulsa, in a museum owned by a world-traveling evangelist. Children visiting the museum on school field trips would wander its halls, oohing and aahing at the thousands of artifacts on display, but invariably they would return to the three shrunken heads. They'd stare collectively in grotesque wonderment, unsure if the faces were real or manufactured for the explicit purpose of scaring the hell out of them.

. . .

Tommy Lee "T.L." Osborn opened The World Museum in 1963 to display the art and artifacts he'd spent 15 years collecting while on mission trips in other worlds, where he preached the gospel and healed the sick by the thousands. Housed in the T.L. Osborn Evangelistic Association's headquarters—a white, domed structure that stood just east of Peoria Avenue and south of Skelly Drive until 2007, when it was torn down to make way for the Highway 44 expansion—the Worlditorium displayed Asian and New Guinean tribal art, African and Native-American tribal art, Oriental art, European porcelain, collectors' cars, and European and American furniture, clocks, and musical instruments.

The building had seven arched alcoves; inside each was a map of a continent, composed of faces of people from that land, and a collection of artifacts associated with that place.

The center's lobby contained, at the time, the "world's largest vinyl carpet," according to a *Tulsa World* article, which represented the Earth's surface and carried the message: "Go ye into all the world and preach the Gospel to all creatures." It was what Osborn had done nearly his entire life.

Born in 1923, Osborn was one of 13 children raised by poor parents near Pawnee. Born again at 12, he hit the road three years later with evangelist E.M. Dillard, eventually landing in California, where he met a woman with a similar background. Daisy Washburn, one of 11 children born to poor California fruit farmers, received her salvation at a young age. The two married on Easter Sunday 1942—he was 18, she 17—and they began traveling the American West preaching the gospel of Jesus Christ.

In Portland, the Osborns met a missionary who told them of the great need for the gospel in India, and so they sold all their possessions and moved there, determined to win Indian souls for Christ.

"They were not prepared," said LaDonna Osborn, their daughter, an evangelist who followed in her parents' footsteps. "They didn't have a clue about India. They thought India was full of pagans, and that's the last thing that's in India. It's a nation of devoutly religious people; we know that today. They went and had a very disappointing experience. They were doing all they were taught to do: praying, fasting, loud preaching. And nothing worked, and they did not know how to convince people of other faiths that the Bible really was the word of God, that Jesus really was the son of God and that he gave his life purposefully for the sins of people and that he's alive today to continue his work through believers.

"So my father and mother did a very smart thing. They came home."

They continued their U.S. ministry until they met a missionary who inspired them to return overseas, this time to Jamaica, where they spent 17 weeks preaching and praying. The Osborns healed 90 blind people and cured countless others from deafness, deformation, cancer, and other diseases, LaDonna said. She was nine months old then, traveling with her parents and older brother from country to country.

Their philosophy was simple: "Just teach the people the promises of God, explain to them why they can expect to be healed, and pray for them—and let Jesus do the rest."

The native missionaries they supported were so grateful that they would bestow on the family their most precious art and artifacts—and Osborn would use his "collector's DNA" to purchase and commission art.

"I think he had such a eye for art—he's a real artist. He has lots of talents in that way," LaDonna said. "I think, because of that, many of the things that were given to us were really quality. In later years, they would purchase things that needed restoration."

One of Osborn's commissions still stands in LaDonna's office at the ministry's current headquarters near Fifth Street and Memorial Drive in Tulsa. The statue is life-size and standing on a pedestal and depicts a man with a wood bit in his mouth, held in place by chains wrapped around his head. Even more chains entangle his hands and feet, and he wears no clothing save a loincloth.

"The purpose of this was to typify humanity in the bondage of sin if they do not have Christ," she said. "Now, I can tell you that when I have African-American friends who come here, that is very offensive. I need to put a plaque on it or something. We are not affirming slavery. We are making a spiritual statement."

• • •

Osborn expanded his museum in 1972, adding a second floor, thousands more artifacts, and renaming it The World Museum/Art Centre. Oklahoma Governor David Hall and Tulsa Mayor Robert LaFortune spoke at the facility's ribbon cutting. The 50,000-square-foot museum housed more than 5,000 artifacts from 100 nations.

A *Tulsa Tribune* reporter called its contents "a collector's fantasy of global memorabilia" that included "totems, gongs, swords, drums, fetishes, talismans, graven images, idols, and grotesques; music boxes from Bavaria, Black Forest mechanical villages, monster African and Burmese statues carved from trees."

"And temple lions with rose quartz eyes, and instruments for a Siamese orchestra Compleat, and chandeliers from palaces in Spain; a faun discovered in the rubble of Pompeiis [sic]."

There were also boats—a 57-foot-long New Guinean war canoe and a 37-foot New Guinean banana fleet boat—that required partial dismantling of the museum to get inside the upstairs gallery.

Each artifact was accompanied by a placard that described it and its origin and also included some tidbit that, LaDonna said, "would inform people about the cultures of the world or about the religions

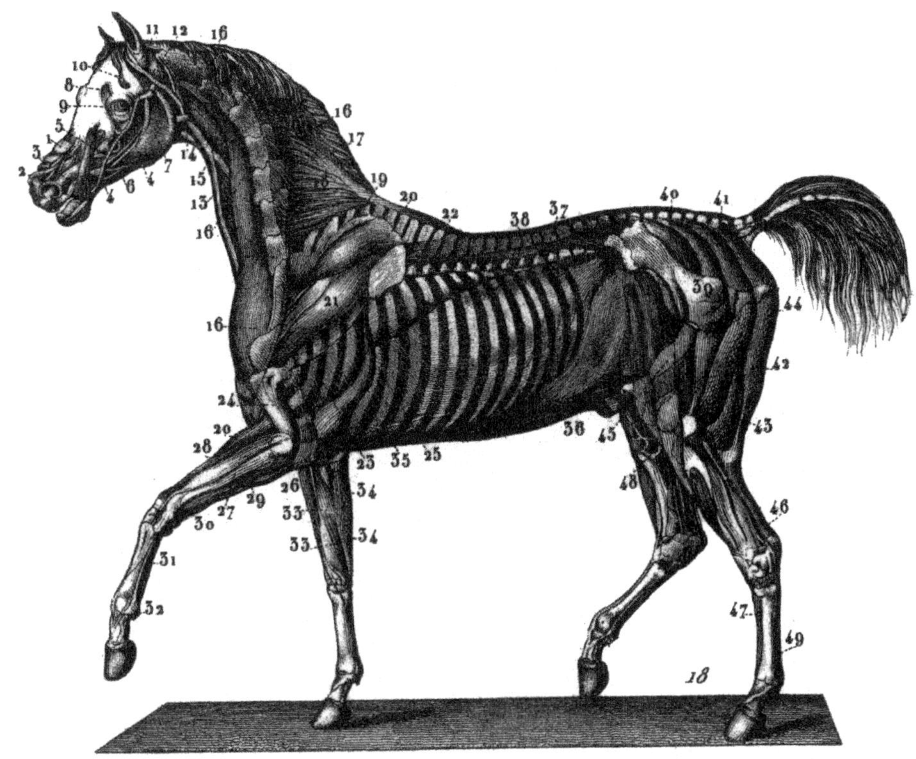

of the world or about the need for help, for hope, for rescue."

Osborn told the *Tulsa World* before the opening: "It has long been our contention that many of the world's fears and prejudices among people of different nationalities could be alleviated, if not eliminated, by bringing artifacts from the different cultures of the world together, so that we might study them and learn to understand and sympathize with people who have outlooks and backgrounds different from our American and European heritage."

The museum received 6,000 visitors a month, but its founders, and the ministry that made them jet setters, remained a mystery to most Tulsans. Osborn, though comfortable in leading thousands of foreigners to Christ, remained a recluse in his hometown, often refusing media interviews.

"It was a paradox to have such an amazing collection in the hands of simple missionary kind of people," LaDonna said. "The art community could not understand how we got ahold of these things, how we were able to restore them and present them in such a way."

She remembered visiting France with her family and wandering the courtyards outside of the museums, where her parents would find "marble statues that were cracked or growing moss" and buy them at a "reasonable" price, restore them and display them in Tulsa.

"Now, coincidentally, after the museum was liquidated, France actually passed laws disallowing the export of their fine-art pieces. They came and took a lot of their things back."

But she said the family never ran into any legal issues when exporting or importing fine art or artifacts—including the shrunken heads and ivory tusks so huge "you couldn't believe that an elephant could be big enough to carry them around."

LaDonna said the purpose of the museum was to endow the ministry. "In my father and mother's logic, in times to come it might be difficult to finance the evangelism programs or to make payroll or to add on to a building—to do anything necessary, so they thought, we could sell a piece of art. So that was a good idea at the time."

The ministry was—and is—financed through private donations, which were, until the late 1980s, solicited through a magazine the Osborns published titled *Faith Digest*.

But T.L. was always tight-lipped about his ministry's finances. In 1977, two *Tulsa Tribune* reporters wrote: "Not even Osborn and his associates claim to know how much the museum and its displays are worth. They do know, however, how much money is

solicited by the foundation. But they refuse to make that figure public. In fact, due to the foundation's 'church' status, not even the Internal Revenue Service can find out. Osborn's foundation has been estimated to receive $6 million–$8 million per year, but officials would not confirm that figure."

"We've never had debt; we've never gone into debt for anything," LaDonna said. "We have survived. I should say, 'Thank you, Jesus.' I believe if you do what God wants done, he helps you."

• • •

In 1981, T.L. Osborn closed The World Museum and liquidated most of its assets. The museum had become more than just a set of curios inside ministry headquarters; it had a full-time staff, guards, guides, and a curator. It was a major tourist attraction for the region and had garnered notable national attention from folks in the art world.

"One day my mother and father had lunch with the head of the Oklahoma Tourism Council—whatever the proper term is—and she was just commending the museum, expressing what an attraction it had become in Oklahoma, and that it was the finest collection west of the Mississippi—next to the Smithsonian, the finest world art collection. And she looked at my father and she said, 'You have spent this portion of your life collecting these amazing artifacts; now you must give the rest of your life guarding and preserving it.'"

Deciding they weren't willing to give their lives for their collection, the Osborns called a meeting of the museum's board of directors following their lunch and announced their decision to liquidate it and put the proceeds earned back into the ministry.

They spent months preparing their collection for auction by Christie's, an event that lasted three days in September 1981. Collectors from Tulsa and elsewhere pored over the collection, its contents ranging in price from $20 to $100,000.

A tag sale on the museum's first floor was opened to everyone and offered knickknacks and smaller items—chopsticks, cow skulls, an elephant's foot, old engine parts, plaster statues—at attractive prices. In the upstairs gallery was what the *Tulsa Tribune* called "an exhibition so classy that the catalog required for admission costs $20," where a painting by Gustave Dore, bronze and marble sculptures, and a bronze Louis XIV clock were auctioned at prices in the tens of thousands.

The auction fetched $2 million and was followed by another a year later with Dean Kruse, famed antique car auctioneer from Dearborn, Indiana—who, in 2010, had his license suspended and his auction house revoked on complaints of fraud—at the helm.

"Auction day begins and strangers come," LaDonna said, "art lovers, people who have no interest in humanity per se, certainly not the work of God ... and to just watch those things that have been gathered over a lifetime be hauled out, piece by piece, piece by piece. That was not easy."

The building was gifted to Victory Christian Center, which housed its Victory Bible Institute there, though the ministry retained a portion of it for storage space.

Daisy Osborn died in 1995. LaDonna acts as vice president and CEO of Osborn Ministries International and is founder and overseer of the International Gospel Fellowship. Her father, at 88, is still active in the ministry, traveling regularly until just last year.

The ministry continues to publish literature in 132 languages and films in 80 languages. T.L., Daisy, and LaDonna "have probably reached and led more unreached souls to Christ in non-Christian lands, and may have witnessed more great healing miracles, that any other family in history," their website claims.

The hallways at Fifth and Memorial are plastered with photographs that document the far reaches of their ministry and its every capacity—except for The World Museum. There are a few remaining pieces of art in the office, but most what the family reserved from the auction—some paintings by Dore, marble sculptures, Oriental art—remains in the Osborns' home.

Even the building that once housed the place has been covered up by concrete and steel. Nearly all that remains of the Osborns' World Museum are the Christie's auction program, a couple of newspaper clippings and the memories of Tulsa kids—vast student bodies of them—who recall visiting the place and gazing in amazement at its treasures—including three tiny, hollow heads with sewn-up eyes and mouths.

"It's a little gross, but we never were ashamed to show what really is humanity," LaDonna said. "We live in a culture that protects us from anything ugly, anything oozy, anything crazy, anything that's vile. We're protected from it ...

"We've never tried to shelter particularly the Christian community from those things because they need to be reminded: This is what people do who are lost, who are hopeless. They're trying to make appeasement for whatever's going on in their lives—the evil, the hatred, the cruelty people will do to one another."

Originally published
November 2012

by Jennifer Westbrook

HERDING SHEEP

A tale of wool and worship

We picked up Robert last because he lived closest to the highway, my friend following a white car to the small house at the end of the cul-de-sac, the one with a few toys left in the driveway. Robert's mother was already outside on the lawn, and when she saw us, she waved. She was the only mother to do this of the six boys we collected on Saturday. When Robert got in the car, my friend introduced me, said I would be helping out for the day, and I asked if he was excited to go to a sheep farm because it seemed it could not be possible. He said, "Yes," and he seemed earnest enough.

When we pulled over for directions and breakfast, the other boys went inside to get donuts, but Robert said he had not had an appetite for a week. When we were alone, he wanted to know things: how long I had been in Tulsa and how old I was. He said he was in 10th grade and didn't really have a good time at school, and I told him that 10th grade was my least favorite year also. "It is the age you have the most secrets," I said, and he only nodded. I asked him how long he had been a part of this group of boys and what exactly the group was. The best I could make out was that these boys were probably somewhat troubled and were being mentored by a friend of a friend, a young man who spent his spare time trying to teach the boys about holy things or tending to one garden or another. I heard the boys referred to as "disciples," and I smiled because these young men live on the north side of Tulsa and wear earrings and are very concerned with the way their hair looks, and I could not imagine one of them saying anything like, "Lord, teach us to pray." Except for Robert: I could almost imagine something like that coming from him.

When we arrived at Shepherd's Cross there was a sign that said, "Blessed coming in," and I joked that the other side of the sign would say, "Blessed going out," and it did. For all its quirkiness, the farm was beautiful and idyllic enough. Past the wooden fence were green hills and a small pond with sheep roaming freely. The tall grass and the trees beyond made the place seem more a picture of a Scottish highland than anything one would see in Oklahoma, though one is quickly reminded you are here based on the Christian ideology spread quite heavily on every inch of the place. Next to a red barn and the pasture was a white farmhouse with a biblical garden and a

peacock walking proudly in the picnic area. There was also a llama grazing, and for a place so full of purpose I was never told why.

We were there to see sheep being shorn, and a woman in front of the barn told us that we had better hurry because the line for the shearing room was filling up quickly. Instead we went upstairs where we could see demonstrations of the various ways a sheep's wool can be useful. We also taste-tested lamb. The boys liked the taste, said it was the same as beef, although and one of the youngest boys, LaTrelle, complained that it was still with him about an hour later. A woman sitting at a spinning wheel watched us closely. Robert always seemed to be out of view, always alone, looking at something odd in a corner somewhere or in another room entirely.

In the waiting area the boys looked out one window and seemed unnecessarily nervous as though we were the next group in line to ride a rollercoaster. A little girl started crying because she assumed the sheep were being hurt on the other side of the door. Her father assured her that this was not the case, that they were being shaved because it was summer and they were hot, and I held up my toothpick from the taste test and made an obvious joke to one of the boys next to me. I was on little sleep, and waiting to watch a sheep get shorn with a group of young, black disciples felt like it belonged to a dream I might have rather than something I would actually choose to do.

The woman at the front of the room spoke about the farm on a microphone, explaining that it was her farm, that she had started it 20 years ago. She referred to herself as a "shepherdess" many times, often explaining that we must be quiet in the shearing room because sheep only know their shepherd's voice. The Christian understanding of this was not lost on her, she made this very clear.

"We are His sheep, and a voice of a stranger we will not follow," she said.

In the shearing room, we sat facing the back pasture. The grown sheep were on one side of the room and their young calves on the other, bleating helplessly and scaring the children. A recording of the shepherdess's voice began, and we watched as one young man caught a sheep by the neck with a staff-hook and brought it to the middle of the room, center stage.

"Sheep are the only animal to sit willingly for the shepherd," the recording explained.

The man took the sheep, which was obviously nervous and trying to free herself, and sat her upright, swaying her body until she went completely limp. There was something trancelike about this. The sheep let him move her limbs about, rolling her over on her sides and shaving her, and somehow this magic worked on me as well, for I fell asleep twice. When I woke fully, people were clapping because the sheep was rid of her coat and would now survive the summer.

I asked Robert as we walked to the garden if the experience was everything he had dreamed it would be. He said, "Yes," and I could feel my sarcasm being lost on him. He asked if I liked it, and I said yes, only I was very tired. He seemed anxious that I should have enjoyed myself, and one of the other boys remarked that he thought he might like to work on a farm someday. An airplane flew overhead, and Robert said it was one thing he wanted to do in life, "ride in a plane."

The garden at Shepherd's Cross was well-kept and simple. One boy sat on a porch swing that hung from a tree, and the rest of us roamed, somewhat disorderly, about the place. I went to the back fence and tried to imagine what it would be like to live there, to walk on the pasture and into the woods for maybe hours a day. The boys walked to the vegetable garden and the small strawberry patch, and their mentor asked them questions about what they had learned. He asked about how to hear the voice of God, and the boys kept pointing out a large strawberry on the ground or making jokes about having one of the boys get his head shorn also. Robert was on the other side of the yard petting a cat.

On the drive home Robert asked if we could listen to one of the songs I'd played for them earlier. "Her voice is very persuasive to me," he said. If I had been his teacher, he would have been my favorite student. I imagine that he would never speak in class but would always be listening, maybe while drawing strange, sad pictures of birds. He would probably even linger in the classroom when the other students left just to get noticed. He told us about a nightmare he had the night before, how he was lost in the woods and ended up on a boat with his mentor. "It wasn't really a nightmare," he said, "only I was scared a little or about to be scared."

When he was asked how to know if you are hearing God's voice or the voice of a stranger, he thought for a few seconds and simply stated, "I guess I would just ask Him if it was His," and looked down at his hands. I followed his eyes and commented on how perfect his nails were, and he smiled and said that he had never heard that before.

Robert was the last to be dropped off, and when we asked what his plans were for the rest of the day, he said that he was going to go to his father's house. As he stepped out of the car, I couldn't help but tell him that I would see him soon though we both knew I probably wouldn't. He walked inside quickly, waving from the doorway but not really looking at anyone.

Negative No.
58
130
430
135
54
85

Originally published
January 2015

by Mike Mariani

TONGUES OF FIRE IN KANSAS

The birth of the Pentecostal movement

Pentecostalism, a branch of Christianity that grew out of Protestantism in the early 20th century, has 280 million adherents worldwide. The movement is twice the size of the Baptists; three times the size of Lutheranism; and six times larger than Presbyterianism.[1]

It's almost unfathomable that the Pentecostals—often referred to as the "third force" in Christianity behind Protestantism and Catholicism, which trace their roots back to the Reformation and the life of Christ, respectively—have been around for little more than a century. Their distinguishing feature, the raison d'être that has made them spread through Christendom like flames licking through a bone-dry forest, is their belief in "baptism with the Holy Spirit." For Christians the world over, baptism with the Holy Spirit is a way to experience God under your skin, to have him rip through your viscera like an electric current and make your religious conviction dynamically manifest. This subjective miracle of contact, a private thirst for God that is suddenly slaked, is the heart of the Pentecostal movement.

In the summer of 1898, Charles Fox Parham, a promising 25-year-old evangelist, moved his family from Ottawa to Topeka, Kansas. By then the fiery young preacher had already been leading religious services for over a decade, since he was 15. He had risen rapidly in the Methodist Episcopal Church, taking an appointment as supply pastor in Eudora, Kansas, in 1893, at the age of 20. Two years later he somewhat abruptly left the Methodist Church, choosing instead to align himself with the growing Holiness movement and its more radical gospel. When he left in 1895, Parham founded his own ministry, one that would, over time, come to emphasize divine healing.

It was in Ottawa that Parham would first gain renown for the healing powers of his services. His wife, Sarah, recalled the miraculous healing of Ella Cook, afflicted with dropsy[2]:

1 That figure—280 million—which counts among its flock congregations in Brazil, Mozambique, Myanmar, and South Korea, does not even include mainline churches swept up by the charismatic movement, which gained traction in the 1960s and draws largely from the style and practices of Pentecostalism.

2 Dropsy is an antiquated term for edema, or an accumulation of fluid in body tissue, often resulting in severe swelling.

> In a few moments she opened her eyes, smiled, and we assisted her to her feet. She not only walked down the stairs alone, but walked for over a mile to her home, shouting and praising the Lord; people along the way followed to see what would take place. Neighbors came running in and until three o'clock in the morning people were getting to God and others were wonderfully healed.

The infectious fervor surrounding Parham's mission grew rapidly, as members of his congregation claimed themselves cured of heart disease and consumption.

To meet the growing demand for his services, which incorporated not only faith-based healing but also the evangelist style and doctrines of the then-vogue Holiness movement, Parham moved his wife and young son to the Kansas capital. In Topeka, he set up the Bethel Healing Home, which was to be the centerpiece of his fledgling ministry for the next two years. In addition to the Bethel Home, Parham established a Bible institute, an orphanage, and the *Apostolic Faith* magazine. Parham hoped subscription fees for the magazine would offset the cost of running the Bethel Healing Home, which charged no rent to its convalescing residents. *Apostolic Faith* also served as a platform to run testimonials from Bethel residents who had experienced extraordinary recoveries. While the healing home may not have been financially profitable, it helped to build Parham's reputation as a powerful, charismatic force in nondenominational Christianity and the Holiness movement.

But the placid healing home alone could not contain Parham's ambitions. The preacher wasn't merely interested in maintaining a small, faith-based sanitarium in downtown Topeka. He had always been a passionate theologian at heart, relentlessly analyzing Christian doctrine and evolving his own views on sanctification, immortality, and baptismal immersion.[3] After all, it was his radical interpretation of Christian rituals, including a prolonged renunciation of water baptism, that contributed to his departure from the Methodist Church in 1895. So in June 1900, after feeling a sense of disenchantment with his ministry and its firmly established financial limitations, Parham left the Bethel Healing Home in order to "know more fully the latest truths restored by latter day movements." It was during this three-month sabbatical that Parham visited Frank Sandford's ministry in Durham, Maine, galvanizing what would become his most important theological views and setting the stage for a new, more visceral wave of the Christian Restoration Movement.

• • •

Like Parham, Frank Sandford left his denomination, the Baptist Church, to start his own evangelist ministry. Claiming that God spoke to him and told him to build a Bible school on a sandy hill, Sandford began construction on the massive compound known as Shiloh with three cents in his pocket. By the time Parham arrived in the summer of 1900, it had a seven-story chapel, a school, a healing home, and a 500-room dormitory. But it wasn't just the scope of Sandford's ministry that had an intoxicating effect on Parham. The original name of Sandford's movement was The Holy Ghost and Us, and it operated as if on call for divine inspiration: classes were frequently surrendered without warning to long prayer sessions; there was no faculty save Sandford; no curriculum save the Bible; and schedules were always at the mercy of what students called "the Holy Ghost's latest."

At Shiloh, Sandford claimed that the Holy Ghost spoke directly through him, making the school and its pupils subject to his every holy whim. Parham wasn't exclusively interested in Sandford's autocratic rule, though; it was the passion and fervor of the students and the Shiloh community that inspired him. At Shiloh, worship services were long, unpredictable, and featured a near-feral zealotry: worshippers testified at great length; "fought" off the devil, exorcising themselves through violent spasms; and prayed at all hours. The January 6, 1900, edition of *The Lewiston Evening Journal* even claimed that during Shiloh's New Year's Eve prayer services "the gift of tongues... descended." One observer described the school thusly: "This is the Holy Ghost's work. This is real teaching. This is supernatural." Parham was captivated. He left the Methodist Church so that he could escape its rigid structure and dispassionate formalism. Here was the complete antithesis to that frigid propriety: an assembly of followers who writhed with direct inspiration from God and the Holy Spirit; men and women who met each day not with pious decorum, but pious abandon, rapt and breathlessly awaiting the "Holy Ghost's latest." Parham returned to Topeka determined to found his own school and ministry in the fashion of Shiloh.

---

3 Parham had, at different times, practiced both single and triple immersion baptism. Triple immersion is a threefold baptism in which the person is baptized in the name of the Father, the Son, and the Holy Spirit. It cites Jesus' command in Matthew 28:19 as evidence. Single immersion prescribes baptism "into the name of Christ" or "into the death of Christ" only. It's biblical support can be found in Acts 8:16 and through John the Baptist, who likely administered single immersion.

Upon his return to the Bethel Healing Home, Parham found the ministers he had left it with unwilling, or at least highly resistant, to turning it back over to him. Although he would later denounce the ministers for stealing his mission, his focus at the time was elsewhere. After a period of intense prayer in which Parham sought guidance from God for his next step, he took advantage of an opportunity to rent an old mansion known as Stone's Folly from the American Bible Society of Philadelphia. Built around 1887 by Erastus Stone but never finished, it was constructed in the style of an English castle. The three-story, 18-room building featured parapets on multiple floors, ornate towers topped by gilded spires, and decorative white columns framing the third-story windows. It was as bizarre as it was beautiful, a conspicuous hybrid of plantation country houses and 18th century Gothic castles. Here, in October 1900, Parham founded the Bethel Bible College.

One of the attendees at the building's dedication to the school that fall was Captain L.H. Tuttle, a friend of Parham's who would later write the preface to his book *A Voice Crying in the Wilderness*. Looking out from one of the steeples during the dedication, Tuttle reported seeing "a vast lake of fresh water about to overflow, containing enough to satisfy every thirsty soul." Tuttle's vision synchronized perfectly with Parham's own conviction that, despite the surge in evangelism throughout the country and popularity of the Holiness movement at the time, there was something much greater to come. The vision would later be seen as a prophecy of the coming of the Pentecostal Church.

Classes began at Bethel on October 15, with some 40 students in attendance. According to *A Voice Crying in the Wilderness*, Parham's central aim for his school was "utter abandonment in obedience to the commandments of Jesus, however unconventional and impractical this might seem." In this way, he was clearly taking after Sandford, who emphasized the Bible as sole text and claiming to be a medium for the Holy Spirit. The room of Tuttle's precognition became known as the "Prayer Tower," and in it students created a 24-hour prayer chain, each taking turns completing three-hour shifts. The Prayer Tower became a powerful symbol of Bethel's unceasing relationship with God. Although the congregation remained small and money tight, the students were ferociously dedicated, living and worshipping together on a seemingly continuous loop.

Even while teaching his students and claiming himself an instrument for the Holy Ghost, Parham's theological beliefs remained in flux. When he was still with the Methodist Church, Parham rejected the water baptism, viewing it as an empty ritual emblematic of the Church's complacent formalities. Instead, he sought out a "true baptism" that emphasized divine inspiration and a more direct relationship with God. He found it in the gospel preached by the Holiness movement, which introduced "baptism with the Holy Spirit" as a religious phenomenon distinct from the initiation sacraments of baptism, confirmation, and Eucharist.

But there were other thorny theological concerns. Developed by John Wesley, co-founder of Methodism, Christian perfection (also known as entire sanctification and the second blessing) is the idea that the born-again Christian may achieve not only freedom from overtly committed sins but also be released from the state of original sin handed down by Adam. The absolution from original sin was the "second blessing" that cleansed the human vessel and allowed an inpouring of the Holy Spirit. In other words, this second blessing and completion of entire sanctification *was* the baptism of the Holy Spirit.

This didn't sit well with Parham, who became obsessed with finding evidence of the Holy Spirit baptism as a religious experience independent of Wesley's Christian perfection. His convictions were buoyed by the teachings of an outsider preacher from Lincoln, Nebraska, by the name of Benjamin Hardin Irwin. A onetime Baptist minister with his own unorthodox views, Irwin believed in a third blessing which he called "baptism with the Holy Ghost and fire." When he bestowed this third gift on followers during his evangelist services, the results were rapturous. According to *Fields White Unto Harvest*, "seekers receiving the third Christian experience exhibited an emotional release and, flooded with religious joy, they would shout, scream, and experience the 'jerks.'" Even for the charisma-inflected Holiness movement, this was heresy, an explicit flouting of their sanctification tenets. But the Fire Baptism, as it was often called, encouraged Parham to continue on his obscure path toward a more direct experience with God.

• • •

It was December 1900 and classes were coming to an end. Parham was to give his students exams on repentance, consecration, sanctification, and the second coming. But, as he put it, "We had reached in our studies a problem." Parham's infatuation with how the Holy Spirit might reveal itself had not abated, and he decided to recruit his students to aid him in the inquiry.

Around Christmas, before leaving for a trip to Kansas City, Parham gave them a special assignment: find biblical evidence of the baptism of the Holy Spirit. Parham's sister-in-law Lillian Thistlewaite recalled what he told them before leaving:

Processions of choirs at a Pentecostal church, 1941
Photos by Russell Lee, courtesy Library of Congress

> Students, as I have studied the teachings of the various Bible schools and full gospel movements, conviction, conversion, healing, and sanctification are taught virtually the same, but on the baptism there is a difference among them. Some accept Stephen Merrit's teaching of baptism at sanctification, while others say this is only the anointing, and there is a baptism received through the "laying on of hands" or the gift of the Holy Ghost. Yet they agree on no definite evidence. Some claim this fulfillment of promise "by faith" without any special witness, while others have wonderful blessings or demonstrations, such as shouting or jumping. Though I honor the Holy Ghost in anointing power both in conversion and in sanctification, yet I believe there is a greater revelation of His power. The gifts are in the Holy Spirit and with the baptism of the Holy Spirit the gifts, as well as the graces, should be manifested. Now students, while I am gone, see if there is not some evidence given of the baptism so there may be no doubt on the subject.

What happened immediately upon Parham's return to Topeka remains largely in dispute. According to the 27-year-old minister, when he returned and asked his students what they'd found, their response was unanimous: every instance of baptism of the Holy Spirit in the Bible was accompanied by speaking in tongues. Parham was obviously satisfied with their conclusion, as he'd arguably nudged them toward it by suggesting that they focus on the second chapter of the Book of Acts. Regardless, the matter was settled: Baptism by the Holy Spirit was conferred through speaking in tongues.

This revelation had a powerful effect on one particular student, 30-year-old Agnes Ozman. Ozman was an itinerant believer, wandering from one Bible school to the next without ever settling down. Having joined and left multiple ministries throughout her 20s, she was clearly in pursuit of *something*—though what, specifically, she probably didn't know. Ozman later confessed that "when I learned that the Holy Ghost was yet to be poured out in greater fullness, my heart became hungry for the promised comforter and I began to cry out for an enduement with power from on high." On the night of January 1, 1901, on the first day of the 20th century, she would get her enduement "from on high."

On January 1, 1901, Charles Parham and his 40 students held a 10:30 PM prayer service at Stone's Folly. About 75 people attended from outside Bethel, bringing a total of 115 people to the "watch night" service. At around 11 PM, Agnes Ozman asked Parham to lay his hands upon her so that she might receive the gift of the Holy Ghost. He refused at first, having not yet himself received the Holy Ghost, but eventually laid his hands on her head and began reciting from Hebrews 13:20: "Now the God of peace, that brought again from the dead our Lord Jesus, that great shepherd of the sheep, through the blood of the everlasting covenant, make you perfect in every good work to do his will..." Suddenly a halo appeared to surround her face and head, and Ozman began speaking in tongues. Parham and the other students later reported that Ozman spoke in Chinese. In recalling that night, Ozman herself asserted that the "Holy Spirit fell upon me and I began to speak in tongues, glorifying God. I talked several languages, and it was clearly manifest when a new dialect was spoken." The sudden burst of alleged xenoglossia was only the beginning of an extraordinary paroxysm of faith and the supernatural at Stone's Folly.

Parham reported that, following the initial incident, Ozman could only speak in Chinese for three days. When she tried to write, all that came out were Chinese characters. This was disputed by a local newspaper, which contended that Ozman's writings were not symbols at all but rather crude, indecipherable scrawl. Nonetheless, over the course of the next few days, at least a dozen other students at Bethel Bible College began speaking in tongues. As if to overpower any doubters, Parham claimed that his students were speaking many languages, including Japanese, Hungarian, Syrian, and Hindi. At one point Parham recounted the paranormal story of returning to Stone's Folly and finding a room on the second floor filled with white light, in which 12 ministers were simultaneously speaking in tongues as "cloven tongues of fire" hung over their heads. Blurred lines between fact and fabrication notwithstanding, Ozman's New Year's Day outburst seemed just the beginning, merely the struck match for a much greater fire baptism of the Holy Ghost that swept through Parham's congregation.

Before long, Bethel Bible College began attracting attention from the press in Topeka and other major cities. Newspapers like the *Topeka Capitol* and *Kansas City World* reported "Strange Acts... Believers Speak in Strange Languages," dubbed Bethel "The School of Tongues," and wrote that the congregation had "a faith almost incomprehensible at this day."

Despite Parham's quixotic accounts of his students speaking in foreign languages they had never learned, most newspapers reported witnessing glossolalia rather than xenoglossia.[4] For example, the *Topeka State Journal* wrote of an encounter with Lillian Thistlewaite: "She at first answered that the Lord had not inspired her to say anything but soon began to utter strange words which sounded like this: 'Euossa, Euossa, use rela sema calah mala kanah leulla ssage nalan. Ligle loge lazie logle. Ene mine mo, sah rah el me san rah me.'" Whatever the intelligibility of the words spoken, the religious frenzy had Kansas transfixed. In late January when Parham and his students visited Galena, Kansas, the experience left the town rapt and mystified. In addition to the steady influx of reporters, language professors and even government interpreters descended on Stone's Folly to get a read on the thrilling religious phenomenon.

But just as quickly as the fever had struck, it was silenced. After failing to secure enough support or funding, Bethel Bible School was forced to close in July 1901, just over a year after it was founded. The reverberations of that January gust of supernatural faith, cult contagion, or simply The Topeka Outpouring, as it has since been called, would not be felt for some time.

Five years later, in 1906, a scarred, one-eyed black preacher named William J. Seymour would hold his first services at 214 Bonnie Brae Street in Los Angeles. On April 9 of that year, after weeks of praying to receive baptism by the Holy Spirit, parishioner Edward S. Lee spoke in tongues. Seymour was ecstatic. After all, he was one of Parham's original students at Bethel Bible College; he had been committed to this new form of baptism, this physical manifestation of the Holy Spirit for years now. A few days after the first incident of tongues, Seymour moved the congregation to a derelict old building on 312 Azusa Street. In the years that followed, thousands of people would report speaking in tongues at the Azusa Street Revival. The cloven tongues had finally broken out of the Gothic belfries and cupolas of Stone's Folly. The spiritual gift cited in the Book of Acts spread like wildfire through cities, churches, denominations. The Pentecost had arrived.

Originally published
December 2014

by Jamie Birdwell-Branson

ICEE DATES, EVANGELICAL GAMES, AND MISSIONAL POSITIONS

Inside Falls Creek, Oklahoma's most popular Christian summer camp

I remember the crying. Girls with mascara smeared across their faces, racing down the aisles of the tabernacle toward the preacher. Some went in pairs, clutching each other and whispering. The boys typically walked alone, proud and sure of themselves as they went down to inform a Falls Creek counselor of their decisions, whether it be to accept Jesus Christ as their Lord and savior, or to answer a call to missions. Or perhaps they felt like they had fallen off the bandwagon and taken up smoking or drinking, and they wanted to publicly declare that they were going to live their lives for Jesus once again. Campers and youth ministers applauded their decisions.

There I stood, 14 years old, watching hundreds of my peers have life-changing religious experiences, but all I could do was wonder why my eyes were completely dry and why God wasn't speaking to me. If God was going to talk to anyone, it should have been me. I was the Baptist golden child: My grandfather on my father's side is a Baptist minister and my late grandfather on my mother's side was a Baptist music minister, who often sang at church revivals, with my grandmother accompanying him at the piano. My parents were raised in the church, going every time the doors were open and often staying after everyone else had left. My parents made it a priority to do the same when they started their own family. Summer camp at the Falls Creek Baptist Conference Center was a family tradition.

If you ask someone in Oklahoma to tell you about their time at Falls Creek, you'll get a variety of responses. They might tell you about how they got saved at an altar call, how they got stung by a bee in evening tabernacle, or how they heard someone at their high school getting pregnant at the camp. Or how, like me, they felt more alienated and confused than euphoric. Whether Falls Creek was an annual event, a friend dragged you there, or you just knew someone who attended, most Oklahomans have heard of and have an opinion about the place affectionately referred to as "The Creek."

Though Falls Creek is famous inside the state of Oklahoma, until recently it was doubtful that anyone outside the state knew of it. This all changed in 2009, when James Lankford, Falls Creek camp director, decided to run for Mary Fallin's open seat in the U.S. House of Representatives after she announced she was running for governor. He took a chance by quitting his position at Falls Creek, one he'd held for 13 years, to run his campaign. Lankford had no prior political experience and was not from a political dynasty. He has said repeatedly in interviews that he took the chance to run simply because he felt called by God.

After a runoff in the primaries, Lankford was elected to run against Democrat Billy Coyle in 2010. Lankford, a political outsider, easily won with 62 percent of the votes for the 5th District. The victory put Falls Creek on the political radar.

SAVED AT SUMMER CAMP

Unless you're looking for it, you'll drive right past Falls Creek. Amidst the Arbuckle Mountains and the thicket of trees that pepper the side of I-35 near Davis, Oklahoma, are acres of land that house the largest Christian youth encampment in the country.

Past the winding road and the entrance gate is a miniature civilization comprised of Oklahoma youths—around 50,000 of them—each summer.

Two men, William Durant (W.D.) Moorer and James Burley (J.B.) Rounds, established Falls Creek in 1917. Moorer and Rounds wanted to train leaders for the Baptist churches in Oklahoma through the Baptist Young Peoples Union (BYPU), a missionary association. As early as 1906, the BYPU appointed Moorer and Rounds to find a good location for the future camp. The men were looking for a location that was central to the state and one that would provide a serene, isolated area for the campers to worship.

"Rounds and Moorer first viewed the Falls Creek property in a photograph on a barbershop wall in Davis, Oklahoma. They were immediately attracted to the 160-acre parcel and agreed it was the place for the annual summer meetings of the Baptist Young People's Union," the Falls Creek website informs.

After getting their proposal approved at the BYPU Convention of 1916, Rounds and Moorer purchased the property for $1,200 from the Aetna Building and Loan Association of Topeka, Kansas.

The first official camp week was August 16–26, 1917, and the registration fee was just $1. Campers could either rent a tent and cot or bring their own. Campers accessed the camp by car, driving south from Oklahoma City, or took the train on the Santa Fe Railroad to Rayford and then paid a 10-cent fee to ferry across the Washita River. An estimated 273 campers went to Falls Creek that first year.

Though Rounds and Moorer were hoping for just one salvation that first camp meeting, 13 people made a decision that first summer. Within two decades, Falls Creek became one of the largest Baptist encampments in the world. Attendance grew rapidly every summer until 1943, when camp was canceled due to an infantile paralysis outbreak in the state. Camp was also canceled in 1944 and 1945 due to World War II.

After the war, attendance at Falls Creek surged once again, and a second week of camp was added in 1952 to accommodate the amount of campers. The camp then increased to three weeks in 1957, four weeks in 1967, and five weeks in 1976. In 1999 and 2000, James Lankford added the sixth and seventh weeks. Currently, there are eight weeks in the summer program.

THE EVANGELISM GAME

Lankford started working with the Baptist General Convention of Oklahoma in student evangelism, working with churches and youth ministries in 1995. In 1996, the executive director asked him to direct Falls Creek. During Lankford's tenure at Falls Creek, attendance numbers soared to more than 50,000 per summer. Also during his tenure, the Board of Directors for the BGCO approved a plan by the Falls Creek Strategic Planning Committee to build a 7,200-seat indoor conference center to replace the decades-old outdoor Moorer-Rounds Tabernacle, which seated 7,000. They presented the plan at the annual BGCO meeting and it was overwhelmingly approved.

The original Moorer-Rounds Tabernacle had undergone several transformations since it was built in 1929. The original steel-girded tabernacle cost $4,359.21 and was paid off in November 1929 using an unusual fundraising technique. According to the *Baptist Messenger*:

> Thad Farmer, Sunday School secretary for Oklahoma Baptists, had the idea to use posters showing a train. Those who contributed nothing rode as hoboes; if you gave a small amount, you rode on the 'Jim Crow' car, and if you gave up around $25, you were entitled to Pullman privileges.

The Raymond A. Young tabernacle project, which was completed in 2007, cost about $30 million and the BGCO received thousands of donations from churches, individuals, corporations, and foundations.

Though the new tabernacle provides a physical snapshot of the change that occurred during Lankford's time at Falls Creek, much of his time was spent getting teens interested in missions. Lankford was given the responsibility of recruiting missionaries to speak at Falls Creek in 1998. Missionaries had been speaking to campers since 1946, but it was originally the responsibility of the Women's Missionary Union to recruit them. Once the job was Lankford's, he decided to use a different strategy.

Traditionally, missionaries who were retired or those who were temporarily in the area were the ones who spoke to the teens, but Lankford started bringing in younger, active, and short-term missionaries to inspire campers. Sermons and lessons were geared toward sharing the gospel at school, at home with your family, and anywhere else you might go.

Lankford tried in every way possible to get campers involved in proselytizing, including something he called "The Evangelism Game." According to a dissertation entitled *The Evangelistic Contributions of Falls Creek Baptist Assembly of the Baptist General Convention of Oklahoma* by Shane Scott Spannagel, Lankford introduced the game during the 2001 Friday morning service in place of a concert.

The idea was simple. No one in the room was "saved" except for 12 missionaries. These 12 missionaries would then share their faith with the rest of the congregation during the game.

"Every 90 seconds a 'disaster' would strike," Spannagel writes. "For example, all people wearing yellow 'died.' If a person died and was fortunate enough to hear the gospel from one of the original missionaries or new converts, they went up to the choir loft or 'Heaven.' If a person had not heard the gospel, they went to 'Hell' at the back of the tabernacle."

After 13 summers working as camp director of Falls Creek, Lankford decided to step down to make a run for office.

"I was always interested in issues. My mom was a librarian. We grew up around ideas, study, and research," Lankford said in an interview. "I was in speech and debate in the fourth grade. I never ran for an office. I just wasn't interested in the politics. I was interested in the idea side of things."

Though he claims that Falls Creek wasn't a preparation for his political career, it did hone his ability to work with people, he said.

Falls Creek also earned him name recognition. According to a report by the *Daily Oklahoman*, 41 percent of GOP primary voters have a connection to Falls Creek, as found in polling by Oklahoma City's CMA Strategies.

"I don't think I'm changing Falls Creek's influence. I still don't think Falls Creek is political," Lankford said. "Eight to 10 percent of all teenagers in the state go to Falls Creek every summer. Adults go as sponsors. The impact comes with the quantity."

Though Lankford is no longer associated with the BGCO or Falls Creek, his Christian beliefs are still a forefront of his politics.

"We cannot get so consumed with the task of legislating," Lankford said, describing his chats with other religious legislators in a 2012 podcast interview with the *Baptist Messenger*. "We miss the mission of why we're specifically here. It's missional."

Lankford has said he won't compromise his morals or ethics for the sake of politics.

"[My beliefs] don't interfere. They accelerate my responsibilities," Lankford said. "I have every responsibility to stay who I am. The great frustration that the American people have is that politicians change when they go to Washington. I am a Christian. It deals with my ethics. It deals with my moral choices."

A MOUNTAIN TOP EXPERIENCE

Today, Falls Creek is more popular than ever before. The camp has its own post office, water tower, and a couple of small stores that sell groceries and snacks to campers and staffers. It has become its own little city, an isolated teenage paradise away from the responsibilities of home.

Campers participate in group sports, swimming, hiking, kayaking, and other outdoor activities, but prayer, worship, and study are the main events at Falls Creek.

There is a lot of free time at Falls Creek in the afternoons, much of which becomes occupied with flings between campers and dates after tabernacle. The most famous Falls Creek courtship is the "Icee date." The tradition goes that if you see someone cute, you ask him or her to meet you at the Icee stand after evening tabernacle. The practice of asking someone on an Icee date has become so commonplace that Falls Creek issued a "Jesus is my Icee date" parody t-shirt.

Growing up, I heard many Oklahomans refer to Falls Creek as "The Baptist Breeding Ground." Some say it's a joke about young girls getting pregnant at camp, but others say they're referring to the heavy concentration of flirting that happens in the Arbuckle Mountains. At Falls Creek, sex still happens.

"After we met we went to tabernacle that night and the next couple of days. Thursday and Friday we started hooking up," Matt Clifton, a former camper said about one of his camp encounters. "We went to a big forest that no one really walked through."

The large area of Falls Creek and the hours of free time guaranteed time alone, which led to Clifton losing his virginity.

"Everyone has these raging hormones. They preached 'don't have sex before marriage,' but [teenagers are] going to do it. There's not enough supervision, and it's a giant place. We outnumbered the sponsors," he said. "There were way too many places to hide."

Clifton said that not all Falls Creek campers had the same experience as he did, but it was there if you looked.

When asked why the camp is so successful, Dr. Anthony L. Jordan, executive director and treasurer for the BGCO responded, "The answer as to why Falls Creek continues to be successful year after year is simply prayer. God has blessed us because of His goodness and the prayers of His people."

Rosa

Originally published
June 2015

by Sarah Morice Brubaker

HEAVEN IS A PLACE FOR SALE

It's easier than ever to visit Heaven, write a book, and get famous

Roberts Liardon loves talking about the sofa he sat on in Heaven.

"It was alive," he tells the congregation at Kensington Temple church in London. His voice is gravelly and confident, a bit Lewis Black's but less grouchy and more Southern. "It was alive with comfort. When you sat on that sofa, comfort reached up and cuddled you while you were sitting there."

This may seem like an odd detail to remember from a vision of Heaven, let alone to recount much later in a 2010 sermon. Liardon is a Pentecostal Christian minister, but nothing in the Bible suggests that there are sofas in Heaven. (Aside from the fact that biblical authors were vague on the heavenly details, sofas were not invented until the 17th century.)

As Liardon points out, though, he was no biblical scholar at the time. He was an eight-year-old child, who moments earlier had been reading the Bible in his family's home in Tulsa in 1974. All at once, according to Liardon, a "supernatural pull came out of Heaven and swallowed me," whisking him away to the gates of Heaven. There, he was met by Jesus and given a day pass of sorts—a chance to tour the place without having to commit.

Heaven, as experienced by the eight-year-old Liardon, resembled an American suburb, or perhaps a Disney World resort. There were golden curbs adorned with humming flowers. The streets were clean and made of something like crystal. The single-family homes were well tended and furnished. Everyone was very, very polite. As he meandered around the heavenly streets and cul-de-sacs, residents would cordially wish him a good day and tell him how much they hoped he enjoyed his tour.

Young Liardon was particularly impressed that the residents of Heaven addressed him by his proper name: "Roberts," with an "s." Named in honor of Oral Roberts—whose fledgling university his mother had moved to Tulsa to attend in 1965—Liardon had often corrected those who shortened his first name to the more typical "Robert." Not so in Heaven, where everyone recognized exactly who he was and why he was there.

The citizens of Liardon's Heaven were also beautiful. "The way you look here on Earth, you're gonna look in Heaven," Liardon assures his London audience, "but you're gonna look perfect and not fat." Li-

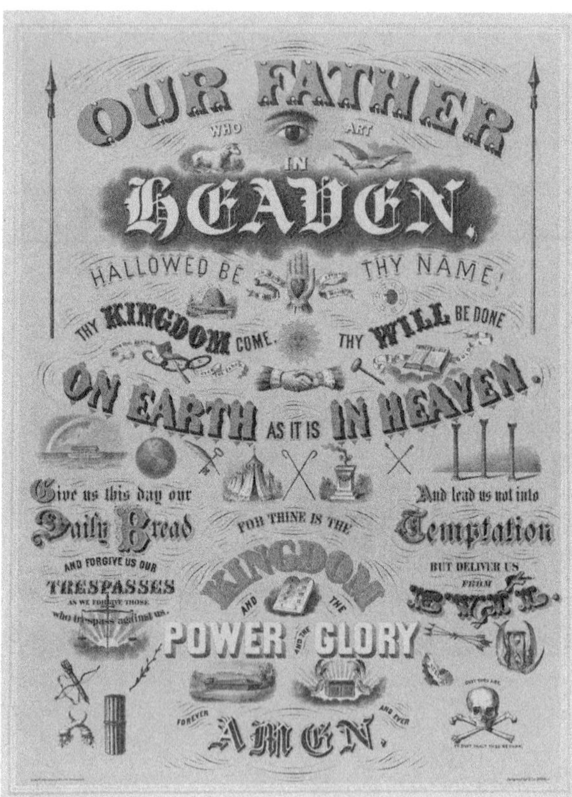

"Our Father Who Art in Heaven" designed by W.A. Welsher

ardon found Jesus particularly handsome. His messiah stood at a cool six feet tall, with hair down to his shoulders. (New Testament scholar John Dominic Crossan surmises that Jesus of Nazareth was around five feet tall and 110 pounds, the average for a Palestinian male in Jesus' day. So presumably Heaven can correct weight in either direction.) And Jesus had biceps and a big belly laugh. Of this, Liardon is sure. "I remember the biceps, and I remember the laugh."

• • •

Liardon's first book, *I Saw Heaven,* was published in 1983 when he was 17. It has done well, selling 1.5 million copies since its publication. More to the point, it helped launch Liardon's career as a celebrity Pentecostal minister, complete with a large church and school in California. (And, later, a scandal. In 2002, Liardon temporarily stepped away from ministry after admitting to an affair with his church's male youth minister.)

In hindsight, it's easy to admire the nerve of Liardon, just as it's easy to see the poignancy of his description of Heaven. Depictions of Heaven's bliss have tended to reflect the longings of a particular group. Starving medieval peasants imagined a place of feasting, while Gilded Age bourgeoisie imagined a Heaven where their favorite earthly activities could continue, and alienated post-modern Westerners imagine a place of belonging and acceptance. One can appreciate why a teenage Liardon—whose father had left when he was a toddler—might have imagined Heaven as a tidy, polite, comfortable place where everyone welcomed him (including his six-foot-tall muscly tour guide).

It's also impressive that a teenager should happen upon a pattern of success that would soon become so well established: visit Heaven, write a book, get famous.

Compare Liardon to another Tulsa Pentecostal, Kenneth Hagin. Hagin's own hereafter story, *I Went To Hell,* had come out the year before Liardon's *I Saw Heaven.* In it, Hagin recounts an experience he had had when he was 15 and bedridden with a serious illness. He felt himself pulled into Hell several times before he finally prayed the sinner's prayer and was released. Four months later, he experienced "the glory cloud": not Heaven, not exactly, but a divine visitation that filled his sick room with a glowing cloud of God's presence. Hagin had not been transported "up," but God's splendor had come "down"—a religious law of physics that would shape the rest of his career. Hagin later earned fame as the grandfather of the "prosperity gospel" movement; its adherents believe that the truly faithful can expect to be showered with material blessings, including money, in this life.

But all that had happened in 1933, nearly 50 years before *I Went to Hell* was published. In the interim, Hagin had to become famous the hard way: by preaching on the radio, then appearing on television, then starting a magazine, and then founding Rhema Bible Training College and its associate programs.

Not Liardon. He wrote the book first, and then the fame came. The American reading public of the early 1980s was primed for heavenly visions. By then, parapsychologist Raymond Moody's best-selling *Life After Life* had introduced the idea of near-death experiences into the popular imagination—thereby affording legitimacy to first-person accounts of Heaven, like Liardon's, that involved no brush with death. Meanwhile, 1960s counterculture had sparked widespread interest in altered states of consciousness. The phrase "out-of-body experience" entered everyday conversation. Intrepid readers bought books like Robert A. Monroe's *Far Journeys* and tried to have their own.

Charismatic Christianity was also gaining wider acceptance. In the early 20th century, when the first Pentecostals had preached "baptism of the Holy Ghost," other North American Christians tended to view charismatics with suspicion. But by the early 1980s, Oral Roberts' organization was pulling in $120 million a year. The charismatic movement had gotten a foothold in non-Pentecostal denominations, with worshipers in formerly buttoned-up congregations—Episcopalians, Lutherans, Presbyterians, Catholics—becoming holy rollers. They spoke in tongues, received miraculous healings, and prophesied. And the influence ran the other way, too: by the early '80s, Oral Roberts had joined Boston Avenue United Methodist Church. The Pentecostals, he felt, cramped his style too much for television. Curious about the otherworldly, yet concerned to be respectable: this is the world to which the teenage Liardon proclaimed his good news of a clean, polite, attractive, neighborly Heaven.

• • •

The past 30 years have not been the best for American Christianity's membership numbers. They have, however, been fantastic for selling there-and-back stories about visiting Heaven. A sampling from the past decade or so includes such titles as: *The Day I Died, My Time in Heaven, My Journey to Heaven, To Heaven and Back, A Glimpse of Heaven, Heaven Is for Real, A Vision from Heaven, Waking Up in Heaven,* and *Face to Face with Jesus*, among others. (There is also *23 Minutes in Hell,* in which author Bill Wiese recounts the time God sent him to Hell so that he could come back and warn others of its ghastly heat, cramped cells, and flesh-devouring beasts. Unlike Dante, Wiese is not treated to a tour led by the poet Virgil. Perhaps Hell's event planners figured that Wiese, then a real estate broker, would be able to manage a solo tour.)

Like many lucrative gigs, "Heaven tourism" may have attracted a few double-dealers. A recent *Esquire* piece by Luke Dittrich uncovers glaring inconsistencies in *Proof of Heaven,* the 2012 near-death memoir by Harvard-trained neurosurgeon Eben Alexander. Key elements of his account—like his claim that he had no brain activity during his vision of Heaven—do not square with evidence or other eyewitness accounts. Still, Alexander stands by his story. Kevin Malarkey, the boy behind *The Boy Who Came Back from Heaven,* has entirely retracted his.

"I said I went to Heaven because I thought it would get me attention," he wrote on his blog. "I did not die. I did not go to Heaven." According to a piece in *The Guardian* by Michelle Dean, Kevin's mother, Beth, had been trying to get the book pulled for two years, with no luck. The book was selling so well, she claims, no one in the evangelical publishing industry wanted to recall it.

The scandals, coupled with criticisms from more biblically minded Christians, have recently prompted LifeWay Christian Stores to pull the entire genre from its shelves. That purge could be a real blow to prospective celestial memoirists. LifeWay, affiliated with the Southern Baptist Convention, is one of the largest Christian retailers. They operate more than 1,200 retail stores and conduct a robust online business. But perhaps such a purge was inevitable, given that LifeWay is a Southern Baptist organization. For a church whose faith stands on the unchanging words of the B-I-B-L-E, such fanciful descriptions of Heaven can be hard to swing. Why go to all the trouble of asserting the primacy of scripture if, at the end of the day, you're inviting people to be edified by a four-year-old's story about Jesus riding a rainbow-colored horse? (That image comes courtesy of Colton Burpo, and is recounted in *Heaven Is for Real.*)

The ones buying the books (and the movies and the associated merchandise) do not seem to be much bothered, though. Sales are still strong, with more titles planned for the coming year. Given American consumers' love of novelty, the next heavenly memoirs may well offer even more fanciful descriptions, out of the mouths of even more guileless visionaries. Hagin's cloud of glory and Liardon's comfortable sofa might seem unbearably quaint now, but give them credit. They saw Heaven before it was cool.

Originally published
July 2011

by Thomas Conner

WOODY GUTHRIE & UNIONS, AMEN!

Behold, in the day of your fast
You seek your own pleasure and oppress all your workers.

— Isaiah 58: 3

Our song is our meeting and our music is our union.
Yes. It is so. It is true.

— Woody Guthrie

On February 24, amid weeks of protest in and around Wisconsin's state capitol over Gov. Scott Walker's bill stripping unions of their right to collective bargaining—their most basic reason for existing—members of several unions joined a conference call with regional religious leaders, urging support from people of faith for the workers' struggle. "The future of the common good is at stake," warned one union president, according to a report in The Progressive Christian magazine. An Ohio pastor agreed: "There's always a danger that workers will be oppressed if there aren't safeguards in place to assure they have a place at the table. It is crucial in 2011 for people of faith to stand with labor, because if we don't, some fundamental rights and values will be under assault. Our faith traditions stand for human dignity, and so do unions."

Can I get an amen?

Fairness, equal opportunity, charity, justice—these are more than mere matters of government policy, they are indeed "fundamental rights and values." Labor rights are supported by the doctrines of every major American denomination, from the Presbyterians' "Principles of Vocation and Work" to the "Workplace Fairness Resolution" from the Central Conference of American Rabbis. Catholics have a lengthy tradition in the workplace; as recently as May 2010 the Catholic Scholars for Worker Justice published a position paper titled "Union Busting Is a Mortal Sin," which says, "Since the right to form labor unions is rooted in the Divine Law, no created law may be invoked to deny, or frustrate, or impede that right."

Why don't we hear the left wielding language like that on cable news? We're facing a long haul through difficult economic times—and the wealthiest 1 percent no doubt will continue employing its shock doctrine to further degrade the power of labor in the name of prudence and frugality—but American unions have lost the skill or the will to frame their argument in the debate as a moral mandate with the same religious fervor of the right.

But there's precedent on our side. Try this on for size: "Every single human being is looking for a better way ... when there shall be no want among you ... when the Rich will give their goods into [sic] the poor. I believe in this Way. I just can't believe in any other Way. This is the Christian Way and it is already on a big part of the earth and it will come. To own everything in Common. That's what the bible says. Common means all of us. This is pure old Commonism."

That's from Woody Guthrie—an unofficial leftist saint, a man who saw no fundamental distinction between the writings of Marx and the teachings of Jesus, a writer and folk singer who thought of social programs and caring for "the least among you" as not only basic common sense but as the same sharing of resources called for in the Bible. In his many essays and songs, he gave rich people hell, chastising them for being Christian hypocrites as millions of poor suffered and wandered. It's a world view that's very Woody and—once upon a time, anyway—utterly Oklahoman.

JESUS WAS A MAN

"They say they are 'religious,' say they're 'Christians,' say they're 'good'," Woody wrote in an essay inside the songbook *Hard Hitting Songs for Hard-Hit People* (compiled in 1940 but not published until 1962). "These big greedy Rich Men ain't no more Christians than the Man in the Moon." He wraps it up, saying, "For God's sake, man, get on the side of the Poor Folks."

Woody—yes, that nefarious atheist commie Woody Guthrie—idealized Jesus Christ and frequently utilized his story as inspiration for working people. The essence of Christ's moral code, Woody believed, was the basis of what we today call socialism. In his autobiographical novel *Bound for Glory*, he tried to explain:

> That's what "social" means, me and you and you working on something together and owning it together. What the hell's wrong with this, anybody—speak up! If Jesus Christ was sitting right here, right now, he'd say this very same damn thing. You just ask Jesus how the hell come a couple of thousand of us living out here in this jungle camp like a bunch of wild animals. You just ask Jesus how many millions of other folks are living the same way? Sharecroppers down South, big city people that work in factories and live like rats in the

> dirty slums. You know what Jesus'll say back to you? He'll tell you we all just mortally got to work together, build things together, fix up old things together, clean out old filth together, put up new buildings, schools and churches, banks and factories together, and own everything together. Sure, they'll call it a bad ism. Jesus don't care if you call it socialism or communism, or just me and you.

During his Depression-era wanderings, Woody met displaced people who were denied basic services. He witnessed a lack of charity that ran contrary to one of Jesus' principle teachings—"Whatever you did not do for one of the last of these, you did not do for me" (Matthew 25: 41-45)—and one day, he recalls in an autobiographical essay, "About Woody," he experienced it himself while begging for food and shelter in Tucson, Ariz. A priest responded to him: "Sorry, Son, but we're livin' on charity our selves, there's nothing here for you. I looked up at the cathedral, every single rock in it cost ten dollars to lay and ten to chop out, and I thought, Boy, you're right—there's nothing here for me."

Woody thereafter abandoned organized religion as just another arena for class conflict, but he held on to Jesus as an icon for the company he kept—the meek that allegedly were to inherit the earth. By early 1940, Woody had relocated to New York City, where he flopped in a midtown flophouse and wrote two of his best songs—the two that most eloquently sum up his Christian philosophy.

The first was an exercise in exorcism. Woody wrote "God Blessed America," later changing the title to "This Land Was Made for You and Me," as a response to Irving Berlin's hit celebration of reward and passivity, "God Bless America." As Joe Klein wrote in his biography *Woody Guthrie: A Life*, "No piece of music had bothered him so much since 'This World Is Not My Home,' although Bing Crosby's narcotic, lay-down-and-die version of 'Wrap Your Troubles in Dreams, and Dream Your Troubles Away' had come close. 'God Bless America,' indeed—it was just another of those songs that told people not to worry, that God was in the driver's seat." God had already blessed America, Woody believed—made it for you and me—and argued that it's our duty as working people to maintain that blessing.

The other song written in that room gets more to his point: "Jesus Christ Was a Man." Decades before Pier Paolo Pasolini's film *The Gospel According to St. Matthew* or Nikos Kazantzakis' novel *The Last Temptation of Christ*, Woody addresses Jesus less as a deity and more as a man, specifically a worker ("a carpenter true and brave") who championed the rights of the common people and was betrayed by the political elite:

> *When Jesus come to town, all the working folks around*
> *believed what he did say*
> *But the bankers and the preachers, they nailed Him on the cross*
> *and they laid Jesus Christ in his grave.*

COME ON PEOPLE NOW

The concept driving Woody's idea of Jesus' love was togetherness, community, cooperation—union. His union was a broad ideal, a brotherhood of men that stretched far beyond mere wages and workplace benefits. Woody explained this as common sense, a foregone conclusion in his introduction to the *Hard Hitting Songs* chapter titled "One Big Union": "Most Folks believe in Union. They believe in One Big Union. Preachers preach it, screechers screech it, Talkers talk it, Singers sing it. One Big Union has got to come. You believe in it. I know you do. You believe in it because the bible says You'll all be One in the Father. That is as High as Religion goes."

A book that most effectively illuminated for me Woody and his loftier ideas is one that never mentions him: Jim Bissett's *Agrarian Socialism in America: Marx, Jefferson and Jesus in the Oklahoma Countryside, 1904-1920*. Bissett's thorough study—I can't recommend it highly enough, still available from the University of Oklahoma Press—plumbs the origins and consequences of basic facts likely known to *This Land* readers: that the state briefly boasted the nation's largest number of registered socialist voters. Bissett also deftly illustrates how Oklahomans put a unique spin on socialism, infusing it with religion. "Jesus was celebrated as a great socialist hero," Bisset writes, quoting prayers ("Permeate our souls with divine discontent and righteous rebellion") and poems ("I think he is a fellow working man / A carpenter they say, from Galilee") published in Oklahoma newspapers in the first decade of the 20th century. Only through socialism, one editorial insisted, is it "possible for a man to do unto others as he would have them do unto him, as taught by the Carpenter." Another editor, shortly after Woody was born, insisted "the ethics of Socialism and the ethics of Christianity are identical." "Here," Bissett says of Oklahoma, "the theology of fundamentalism meshed seamlessly with the politics of Marxism."

No doubt Woody tuned into some of this as he grew up in Okemah—a warble and a whisper from Seminole, the origin of the Green Corn Rebellion—then he began his exploration of universalist religion after moving to the Texas panhandle after high school. It began as killing time in the Pampa library, voraciously reading everything from psychology textbooks (he actually wrote his own; the library even shelved and catalogued it but later threw it out) and faith-healing guides to Omar Khayyam and repeatedly Kahlil Gibran's *The Prophet* ("All work is empty save when there is love; and when you work with love you bind yourself to yourself, and to one another, and to God"). He meditated, practiced yoga. He began signing letters as "The Soul Doctor" and even saw patients as a faith healer, printing up business cards for himself advertising "Divine Healing and Consultation." In Okemah his family sometimes had attended the First Methodist Church; in Pampa, Woody visited tent revivals and eventually was baptized in the Church of Christ (oddly, a denomination that frowned on musical instruments). Biographer Ed Cray mentions that "a youthful Guthrie had once toyed with the idea of converting to Catholicism and even taking orders."

We shouldn't make too much of these particulars—Woody was drawn to ideas, not organizations, though he did once cite his library auto didacticism as credentials ("I studied religion 6 years")—but we can draw a fairly clear line between these early explorations and his eventual concept, shared more pragmatically by the Industrial Workers of the World, of "one big union." By the mid-'30s, about the same time he finally recorded "This Land" and "Jesus Christ," Woody scribbled in his notebook, "The best religion I ever felt or ever seen is world union. The highest step in any religion is your joining up with the union of every mind and hand in the world."

Later, as he focused his thoughts during long hours at sea during WWII, he tried out one verse of his own hymn, "Union's My Religion":

I just now heard a salty seaman
On this deep and dangerous sea;
Talking to some Army chaplain
That had preached to set him free:
"When I seen my union vision
Then I made my quick decision;
Yes, that union's my religion;
That I know."
(And that I know)

TOGETHER IN SONG

Protest songs still reverberate inside the Wisconsin state capitol. That's not just me being dramatic. The rallies and sit-ins occurred in February and into early March, yet despite the bill's passage (and mid-June approval in the Wisconsin Supreme Court) angry Wisconsin workers are still meeting every weekday at noon in the capitol's rotunda. They organize via the Solidarity Sing-Along page on Facebook. They stand in a circle, on the marble floor and in front of massive marble pillars, and they sing.

The songs they sing—mostly from the Solidarity Sing-Along Songbook compiled by the Wisconsin Network for Peace and Justice—are rousing unions songs, many of which are reupholstered hymns and religious songs—"We Shall Not Be Moved" was written as "I Shall Not Be Moved," a spiritual, as was "Ain't Gonna Let Nobody Turn Me 'Round" (originally "Don't Let Nobody Turn You 'Round"). "Solidarity Forever" is just new words on an old tune, the same tune as "The Battle Hymn of the Republic"— *"Glory, glory, hallelujah!"*

The songbook includes Woody, too: "I'm Stickin' to the Union" (aka "Union Maid," written in Oklahoma City) and the requisite "This Land." The Solidarity Sing-Along version of the latter Woody tune tweaks the words to be more inspiring to cheeseheads: *"From Lake Geneva to Madeline Island / from the rolling prairies to our lovely dairies / Wisconsin was made for you and me!"*

Woody would *love* that. (Watch the Raging Grannies sing it on YouTube!) He'd love the punks, too, many of whom—Tom Morello from the band Rage Against the Machine, Wayne Kramer from the MC5, Tim McIlrath from Rise Against and others—gathered in the frigid cold on Feb. 21 to inspire Madison's marchers with fiery songs of discontent, including Neil Young's "Ohio" and Billy Bragg's "There Is Power in a Union." They closed, of course, with "This Land." The crowd held hands, singing it like a hymn. Later, when I spoke with McIlrath, he told me something else Woody would love—and union reps should strive for: "Everybody was singing and somehow all together. It was like a religious experience."

Originally published November 2012

by Lee Roy Chapman and Michael Mason

THE STRANGE LOVE OF DR. BILLY JAMES HARGIS

How a Tulsa preacher and an Army general created America's religious right

Billy James Hargis in Tulsa, 1970
Photo by Gaylord Oscar Herron

When the radio evangelist Billy James Hargis forged a friendship with an extremist Army general, Edwin "Ted" Walker, a new brand of politics emerged from the middle of America, establishing Oklahoma as the birthplace of the religious right. Both men weren't just politically minded, however. Recently revealed documents indicate that the FBI regarded them as national threats.

Little Rock was shell-shocked. It was July 1960, and in the past year, five bombings had terrorized the city's public school system. The state legislature of Arkansas attempted to thwart desegregation by shutting down Little Rock's public high schools, but the bombings sent a far more violent message to the city's pioneering civil rights community. Similar incidents throughout the South grabbed the country's attention, forcing the federal government to intervene. In Arkansas, the government put a zealous Army general in command of the military district to ensure safety and integration.

Federal Bureau of Investigation agents combed Arkansas for suspects in the bombings, and they were looking for one man in particular: a high-profile segregationist preacher from Oklahoma named Billy James Hargis. According to FBI Special Agent Joe Casper, Hargis was planning to bomb the Philander Smith College in Little Rock soon. The preacher had recently met with two other bombing suspects at a Memphis restaurant.

"We ought to get a permissive search warrant from him [Hargis] to search his home, car, and any outbuildings at his residence," Casper suggested. "We have evidence that these people we have arrested in Little Rock have been in contact with him."

The FBI had cause to be concerned. Hargis' tirades mirrored those from any number of early 20th century Ku Klux Klan pamphlets. He was anticommunist, anti-union, pro-segregation, and he preached those values on a 15-minute daily radio show that aired on stations throughout North America. Based in Tulsa, the Christian Crusade was the public name of Hargis' media empire, one that included a magazine, the daily radio program, Christian Crusade Publications, and a pioneering direct mail operation that expertly distributed Hargis' propaganda throughout the world. By 1960, Hargis had the

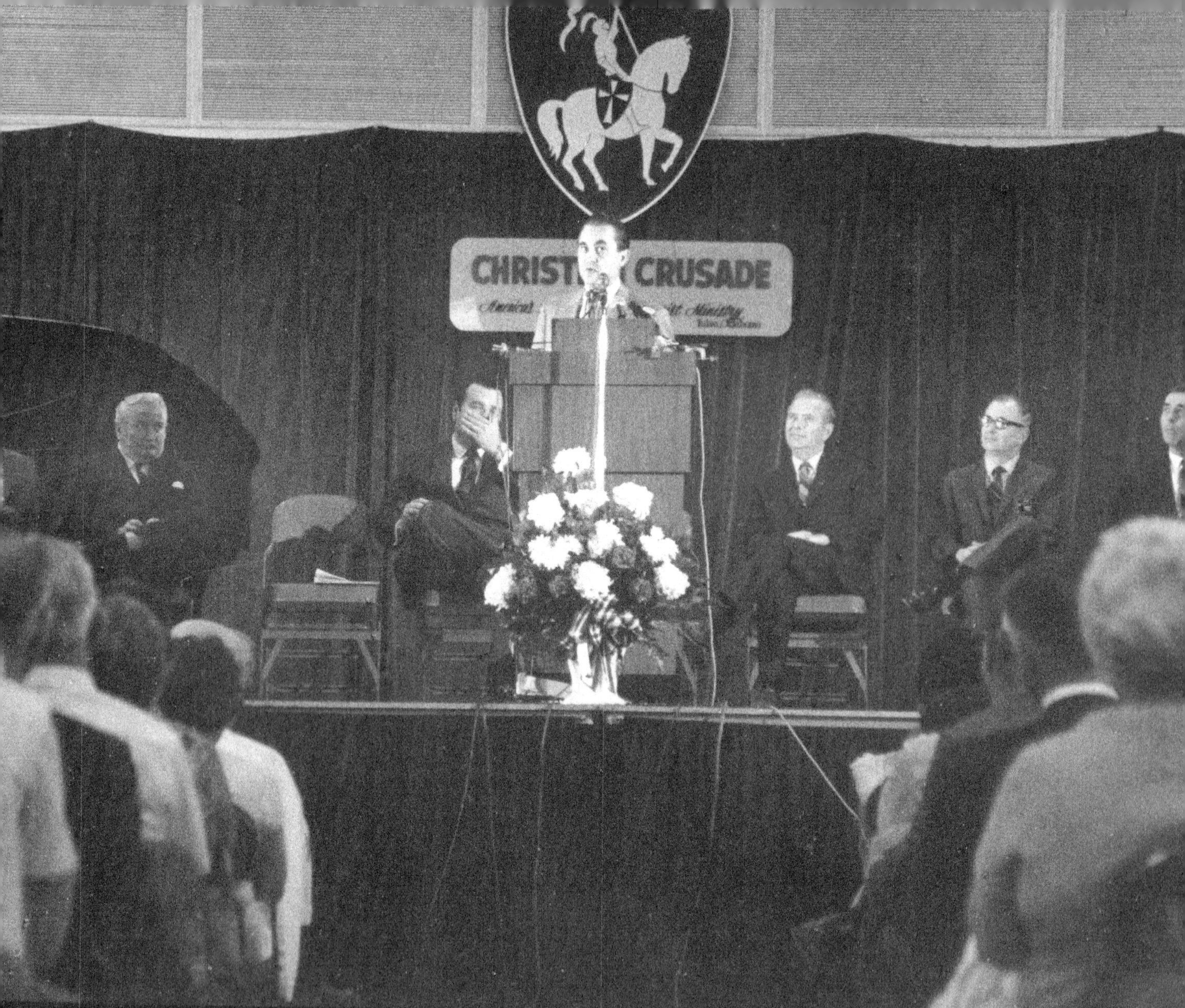

George Wallace addressing the Christian Crusade in Tulsa, Oklahoma. Hargis is pictured to the left and Walker to the far right. Photo by Gaylord Oscar Herron

ability to martial sizable crowds and stir them with his incendiary speeches. In the eyes of the FBI, he was a serious threat; in the minds of many Cold War Americans, though, Hargis was a new kind of patriot.

Crusading for Purity and Essence

Before anyone heard Rush Limbaugh infiltrating AM radio, before televangelists like Pat Robertson and James Dobson organized the Christian Right, before Tea Party favorites Rand Paul and Paul Ryan began their campaigns, there was Billy James Hargis. Born in Texarkana, Texas, in 1925, Hargis was raised in poverty during the Great Depression and at an early age decided to commit his life to Christianity. Clean-cut, chubby, and baby-faced, he looked like a Kip's Big Boy statue come to life. By the age of 22, Hargis had become a religious renegade. After a brief stint as a pastor in Sapulpa, Oklahoma, he married a woman named Betty Jane and in 1948 started his own religious non-profit, Christian Echoes Ministry, where he began preaching against communism.

Anti-communism wasn't a new message in Oklahoma; as early as 1917, with the start of the Bolshevik Revolution, civic organizations like the Tulsa Councils of Defense,[1] in conjunction with local publications like the *Tulsa World* and *Tulsa Tribune*, contributed to an atmosphere of repression and paranoia, now known as the Red Scare. But it was the strong presence of the Invisible Knights of the Ku Klux Klan in Oklahoma that made anti-communism an integral part of the Protestant faith—the Klan opposed Catholicism and Judaism as much as it railed against communism.[2]

The KKK took their symbolic cues from the Christian crusades of medieval Europe—knights, white robes, and fiery crosses—and they borrowed the terminology of the period. They called themselves the Invisible Empire, Knights, Dragons, and Wizards. By the time Hargis was a young man in the late 1940s, the Klan was in its decline in Oklahoma—but its potent mix of segregationist ideology, Evangelical Protestantism, and anti-communism found a champion in the gifted young evangelist.

During the early part of the 1950s, Hargis traveled the country, lecturing on the many conspiracies facing Americans, like communist infiltration and fluoridated water. Hargis' Christian Crusade floundered at first, until Hargis came up with a flamboyant plan in 1953: He would take Bible verses, tie them to tens of thousands of hydrogen-filled balloons, and launch them from Chalms, Germany, with hopes that the balloons would land over the Iron Curtain. His idea managed to attract the support of the International Council of Christian Churches,[3] which helped fund and realize the project. The ICCC's support of Hargis brought him onto the world stage of an emerging post-war phenomenon, right-wing evangelism. Hargis was now poised to become the spokesman for a new movement that fused American politics with fundamentalist Christianity.

No Fighting in the War Room

Hargis' crusade found many allies, but it was his collaboration with one man that proved to be a catalyst for the formation of America's religious right. A West Point graduate, Major General Edwin "Ted" Walker was a WWII Army hero and leader in the Korean War. In 1957, Walker found himself in command of the Arkansas Military District in Little Rock, just as the city's civil rights tensions were escalating.

As President Eisenhower prepared to use federal troops to enforce the desegregation of Little Rock's public schools, Walker was protesting the matter directly to Eisenhower; he opposed racial integration. Nevertheless, Walker followed Ike's orders and ended up receiving national praise for helping to integrate Little Rock; a 1957 cover of *Time* magazine portrayed him as a hero. Walker would later state that he led forces for the wrong side in Little Rock—he believed black students had no business attending white schools.

Before the integration of Little Rock, Walker was a garden-variety anti-communist, but when the incident at Little Rock propelled him into the political spotlight, he became radicalized. The same year, both Billy James Hargis and Texas oil tycoon H.L. Hunt were bombarding Arkansas radio waves with their rightist sermons—programs that aligned completely with the position of Senator Joseph McCarthy, who believed communists had infiltrated the U.S. government.[4] Hargis, however, advanced McCarthy's views even further, and preached that the civil rights movement was itself a godless communist plot.

In 1959, when Walker was still in command in Little Rock, he met with a conservative publisher named Robert Welch, who had recently founded the John Birch Society on the premise that Eisenhower was in reality a communist.[5] Walker, primed for years by Hargis' radio rants, joined the society and turned against the government. He attempted to resign from the Army, citing concerns over communist encroachment in the U.S.—but Eisenhower refused Walker's resignation and instead promoted him to the position of Commanding General of the 24th Infantry Division.

Convinced that his commander-in-chief was a dreaded communist, Walker nevertheless agreed to accept Eisenhower's offer. In October 1959, Walker took command of 10,000 troops in Augsburg, Germany. Now at the height of his military career, Walker devised a plan to propagate his views to U.S. service-

1. In 1917, the National Council of Defense organized a national propaganda system in each state. In Oklahoma, the councils functioned primarily to identify anyone who did not approve of America and its presence in the war. The Tulsa County Council of Defense was organized through the Tulsa Chamber of Commerce and was a particularly enthusiastic participant in extralegal vigilante activities.

2. Following the Tulsa Race Riot of 1921, the Ku Klux Klan in Tulsa owned a large temple or "klavern" called Beno Hall: "The Tulsa Benevolent Association [KKK] sold the storied building to the Temple Baptist Church in 1930. During the Depression, the building housed a speak-easy, then a skating rink, then a lumberyard, and finally a dance hall before radio evangelist Steve Pringle turned it into the Evangelistic Temple of the First Pentecostal Church. In his first revival meeting, Pringle introduced a little-known Enid preacher by the name of Oral Roberts, who worked his animated, faith-healing magic on the bare lot next door. Roberts impressed in the tent atmosphere and preached with his cohort inside the vast auditorium." Excerpted from "Beno Hall: Tulsa's Den of Terror," by Steve Gerkin, published in *This Land* Volume 2, Issue 11, September 15, 2011.

3. The International Council of Christian Churches was founded by Carl McIntire, a fundamentalist radio broadcaster from Durant, Oklahoma.

4. Hargis claimed that he had ghostwritten a number of speeches for Senator McCarthy.

5. The John Birch Society is a conservative political advocacy organization. One of its founders was Fred Koch, who also founded Koch Industries. Koch advised JBS President Robert Welch on numerous issues. He believed many U.S. companies had been infiltrated by communism, as evidenced by the presence of labor unions. Today, two of Koch's sons, David and Charles, are one of the largest contributors to conservative political campaigns and causes in America.

men who trusted his leadership—views that came directly from the teachings of the John Birch Society and the Christian Crusade.

While Walker was commanding his troops in Europe, the political landscape in America was changing drastically. John F. Kennedy was the embodiment of everything Walker hated and feared: he was Catholic, he was liberal, and he was sympathetic to the United Nations. Camelot—as Kennedy's presidency came to be known—was, in Walker's eyes, evidence that the U.S. government had succumbed to communism. Kennedy was sworn into the office of the presidency on January 20, 1961, just as Walker was establishing the guidelines for the strict regime that would govern his troops.

"Within my authority and within the requirements of training necessity, I devised an anti-communist training program second to none—called 'Pro-Blue,'" Walker wrote in a memoir. "Equally important—I organized a Psychological Warfare section with the Division to extend the Pro-Blue program through six echelons, to include every officer and soldier—chaplain, medic and rifleman."

Established as an official U.S. Army project in January 1961, the Pro-Blue program was the result of Walker's fear and paranoia about communism; the official plan was turgid with reprogramming techniques. Under the Pro-Blue program, troops of the 24th Division were required to participate in a series of indoctrination methods that included publications from the John Birch Society that were supplied by Hargis. Service members and their families were required to participate in 11 different special activities, including a six-hour training session involving "communist techniques," the Freedom vs. Communism program, the Freedom Speaks program, which offered lectures from Pro-Blue writings, and the Ladies Club and NCO Wives Club, which were discussion groups featuring guest lectures on anti-communism.

In 1961, the threat of communism came within 90 miles of America. Publicly, the Cuban revolutionary Fidel Castro insisted that he was not a communist, but Cubans themselves began revolting against his socialist reforms. That spring, communist countries came to Cuba's aid and squelched a U.S.-backed attempt to overthrow Castro's regime. The incident, known as the Bay of Pigs, cemented America's fear of Soviet encroachment, and that fear was promulgated through the upper echelons of the Department of Defense. Walker's Pro-Blue program confronted the threat of communism directly and aimed to "produce tough, aggressive, disciplined and spiritually motivated fighters for freedom."

The Pentagon admired Walker's program and planned to promote him to Lieutenant General in command of the 8th Corp in Texas.

"Dear Ted," wrote the Pentagon's Major General William Quinn, "One of our basic philosophies is that Commanders should tailor their troop information to their own ideas and needs. That is why we have followed the progress of your Pro-Blue with interest and with pleasure."

The intended promotion, however, never arrived. In April 1961, military-themed magazine *The Overseas Weekly* published an investigative report that detailed Walker's distribution of John Birch Society literature to the troops—readings that contained inflammatory material questioning the presidency and U.S. government policies.

A media controversy ensued.[6] Some outlets criticized Walker for his extreme views and suggested that military commanders had no business plying their troops with political propaganda; conservative outlets balked that politicians were muzzling the military. Finally, President John F. Kennedy himself weighed in on the matter:

> The discordant voices of extremism are heard once again in the land—men who are unwilling to face up to the danger from without are convinced that the real danger comes from within. They look suspiciously at their neighbors and their leaders. They call for a "man on horseback" because they do not trust the people.[7] They find treason in our finest churches, in our highest court, and even in the treatment of our water.[8] They equate the Democratic Party with the welfare state, the welfare state with socialism, and socialism with communism. They object quite rightly to politics intruding on the military—but they are anxious for the military to engage in politics.

6. Hargis would later claim that a plot to smear Walker was hatched by the Kremlin because they feared what might happen if Walker gained more power in the military.

7. The Texas Minutemen were an extreme right-wing paramilitary group that supplied weapons to Cuban exile groups in Dallas and New Orleans. Walker has been often cited as its leader, though he denied being involved before the Warren Commission.

8. General Jack Ripper in the film *Dr. Strangelove* cites the fluoridation of America's water supply as evidence that communists had infiltrated the highest powers of government and were trying to destroy America's "precious bodily fluids." The character Ripper was based on General Curtis LeMay and Major General Edwin Walker. On November 22, 1963, *Dr. Strangelove* was set for its first screening. When news of President Kennedy's assassination reached Kubrick in California, he canceled the screenings and rescheduled the screenings for the following January. While waiting for the shock of the assassination to pass, Kubrick edited out a reference to "Dallas" in the film and changed it to "Vegas."

The John Birch Society opposed the fluoridation of water, arguing that it was part of a communist plot to poison Americans. By 1960, about 50 million Americans were drinking fluoridated water, resulting in an estimate reduction of tooth cavities by 40 percent. Today, about 66 percent of the U.S. population drinks received fluoridated water through their public water system. Hargis kept a file on fluoridation.

The Pentagon responded to political pressure by relieving Walker of his command and transferring him to Germany. It would not be the last time a Kennedy angered General Walker.

"When the administrators of federal government serve a higher world government or a doctrine not provided by the people and the Congress, there is no Constitutional President," Walker later reflected in a small booklet. "With no President, there is no Commander in Chief of the U.S. Armed Forces. I resigned."[9]

Walker left the Army on November 4, 1961. Instead of seeing it as the end of his career, he sensed America was ripe for a political insurgency, and that he could help bring about a revolution of his own, one that did not include communists or atheists. While in the military, Walker enjoyed the support of countless personnel to help disseminate his ideas. Now, with political aspirations in mind, he sought the support of an organization that aligned with his sense of Americanism and anti-communism. He needed the Christian Crusade.

The Christian Crusade Gets on the Hump

In 1951, the *Harvard Business Review* published a quiet yet peculiar essay by a business executive for James Grey Incorporated. In "Direct Mail Advertising," Edward Mayer outlined a persuasive argument for bombarding the American public with mail solicitations—a predecessor of email spam techniques. It was an early day manifesto that would eventually become a cornerstone of the Billy James Hargis empire. Using direct mail marketing, Hargis began asking for small donations to be sent to his ministry in Tulsa.

Throughout 1950s and early '60s, Hargis' Christian Crusade built momentum. During that period, Hargis hired a promising young Texan named Richard Viguerie. Armed with a keen understanding of databases, Viguerie devised mass mailings targeting donors who were likely to be fundamentalist separatists—the kind of people who would respond to antics like Hargis' balloon drops. With Viguerie's genius, Hargis reached a widening audience, but the Christian Crusade still needed an overall strategy that would propel it toward success. It was around this same time that Hargis met a publicist named Pete White, who had once helped the televangelist Oral Roberts build a successful ministry through the manipulation of mass media. By using the same strategies used by Roberts, combined with Viguerie's direct mail ingenuity, Hargis' Christian Crusade rocketed from a small operation to a ministry that had "billings from $400 to $500K a year in 1963."[10] During this time period, Christian Echoes Ministry mailed an average of 2,000 letters every day—many of those letters returning with a dollar or two stuffed in the envelope.

"Ours is purely an educational program," Hargis told the *Tulsa Tribune* from his Boston Avenue office decorated with gold-sprayed Joan of Arc statues. "We have the most extensive files anywhere on this matter of communism and we are trying to get that word to the people."

Hargis became more adept in rightist political rhetoric, which began earning him a national reputation as a conservative leader. In 1959, a Chicago-based organization called We, the People, designated Billy James Hargis as its president. Founded by Henry T. Everingham to support conservative politicians, We, the People produced pamphlets promoting anti-communism and criticizing integration. In 1962, the organization held its first "T-Party" rally which aimed to end the "taxes, treason, and tyranny" of the political left. At that time, Hargis stepped down as president, ceding the position to Mormon leader Ezra Taft Benson, who referred to America's South as a "Negro Soviet Republic." Benson later served as president of The Church of Jesus Christ of Latter-day Saints.[11] Today, We, the People stands as one of the earliest collusions in conservative politics between Christians and Mormons.

As the Christian Crusade ministry increasingly reached into mailboxes and across airwaves, its message became more threatening to the civil rights movement. The FBI questioned Hargis over his involvement in the Arkansas school bombing plot and continued to monitor his activities. Hargis told his followers that the National Association for the Advancement of Colored People (NAACP) was a

9. Since Walker resigned instead of retired from the military, he relinquished his pension and military benefits. In 1982, President Ronald Reagan returned Walker to an active role status in the Army, allowing Walker to enjoy full benefits.

10. Hendershot, Heather. *What's Fair on the Air: Cold War Right Wing Broadcasting and the Public Interest.* Pg 183.

11. Marion Romney, a cousin to the father of politician Mitt Romney, was supposed to succeed Benson as president of the Church of Latter-day Saints, but his health prevented him from doing so.

communist plot; he published a book called *The Negro Question: Communist Civil War Policy*, in which the author warned that "communists are deliberately maneuvering among the American Negroes to create a situation for the outbreak of racial violence"; he believed segregation was "one of God's natural laws"; he called Martin Luther King Jr. a communist-educated traitor and an "Uncle Tom for special interests." Despite the patronizing attitudes that Hargis held against African Americans, he publicly asserted he was not a racist. It wasn't until Hargis joined forces with former Major General Edwin Walker, however, that racial bigotry became a common characteristic of the religious right.

Operation Midnight Ride: Too Important to Be Left to the Generals

Shortly after his resignation from the military, Edwin Walker began forging a friendship with fellow John Birch Society member Billy James Hargis. They agreed to go on a speaking tour of the U.S. together; Hargis would sermonize on the perils of communism at the national level and Walker would expound on the international threat. Walker parlayed these early lectures into political gain. He soon decided to run for governor of Texas and enjoyed the support of Dallas oilman H.L. Hunt. Walker ran under the Southern Democratic (Dixiecrat) ticket, though, and ended up in last place in the Democratic primary of February 1962.

Later that year, in September, Walker caught wind that the federal government planned to force the integration of an African American man, James Meredith, into the University of Mississippi. This was Walker's chance to retaliate against the government that had forced him to integrate Little Rock back in 1957. Walker took to the airwaves to instigate an insurrection against governmental control.

"I call for a national protest against the conspiracy from within," Walker declared. "Rally to the cause of freedom in righteous indignation, violent vocal protest, and bitter silence under the flag of Mississippi at the use of federal troops."

The next day, September 30, 1962, riots broke out on the university campus, resulting in hundreds being injured and two dead. Six federal marshals had been shot. Walker was immediately arrested and charged with sedition and insurrection against the United States.

Behind the closed doors of the FBI, however, government officials worried about Walker's mental health. Informants whispered that he appeared irrational during his public talks. The rumors were enough to compel U.S. Attorney General Robert F. Kennedy to order Walker placed under a 90-day psychiatric evaluation at a forensic center in Springfield, Missouri. Both the American Civil Liberties Union and prominent psychiatrist Thomas Szasz protested the hospitalization. Walker's attorney in Oklahoma City, Clyde Watts, fought the order of detention and was able to get Walker freed after only five days.

The detention radicalized Walker even further, but by siding with the racists during the Ole Miss riot, he began to cause concern amongst his allies.

"Walker has also been listening to advice from another source and refusing to pay attention to those who have tried to caution him," wrote Robert Welch, founder of the John Birch Society, adding that Walker could cause "very serious embarrassment to conservatives and the conservative cause in general."

In November 1962, Walker stood before a grand jury regarding his role in the Ole Miss riot. His mental health was called into question and his role in the riot scrutinized, yet one of the most important black witnesses, Reverend Duncan Grey Jr., was never called to testify. The all-white Mississippi grand jury chose not to indict Walker.

Energized by the perceived escape from governmental injustice, Walker teamed up once again with Billy James Hargis. This time, they planned a 12-week, 29-city speaking tour starting in Memphis, Tennessee, in late February 1963. They called their series "Operation Midnight Ride," and planned to use the talks to create a larger support base. At this point, Hargis' Christian Crusade had grown to a monthly budget of $75,000—but that money wasn't necessarily representative of a large audience. Hargis told the *New York Times* that most of his funding came from oil companies.[12]

While Hargis and Walker were trying to push the general population to the right, they were also galvanizing the extreme fringes of conservatism with their neo-confederate message. According to Walker's FBI files, the Ku Klux Klan sponsored Operation Midnight Ride in both South Carolina and Arkansas.[13] Throughout America, Hargis and Walker preached against the evils of communism and invited popular right-wing speakers like Benjamin Gitlow, former Army chief of intelligence General Charles Willoughby, and Congressman John Rousselot to join them. The FBI reported that in Washington, D.C., there were about 100 attendees of Operation Midnight Ride and all of

12. It should be noted that at the Washington, D.C., stop for Operation Midnight Ride, Hargis stated that he had never received a penny from Texas oilman H.L. Hunt.

13. Walker's ties to the Klan ran deep. In 1964, he was the main speaker for Americans for the Preservation of the White Race in Brookhaven, Mississippi. A year later, in 1965, the Imperial Wizard of the United Klans of America offered Walker the position of Grand Dragon of the UKA of Texas. Walker turned the offer down.

Hargis in the recording studio

them were white.[14] While many inflammatory statements were made at the meetings, the FBI seemed most alarmed by Walker's rhetoric. In their files, the FBI deemed Walker a presidential threat probably due to Walker's proclivity to charge presidents as communist leaders and deny them allegiance; there may have been more serious reasons.[15]

More than 4,000 people attended the last stop of Operation Midnight Ride in Los Angeles in early April 1963.[16] Members of the John Birch Society, which had taken over the Young Republicans Organization, welcomed the speakers. They presented Walker with a plaque calling him the "greatest living American," and they listened patiently while Hargis delivered an almost two-hour long talk. The entire operation was a smashing success, or in the recent words of conservative talk show host Bill O'Reilly, "a Paul Revere-like barnstorming tour."

As Hargis and Walker fomented fears of communism, they could not have anticipated their agitation of one particularly troubled man in Dallas. Lee Harvey Oswald, a former Marine, had recently purchased

14. According to Hargis' recollection 30 years later, 2,000 people attended the first evening of Operation Midnight Ride in Washington, D.C. He also stated that he and Walker had toured 100 cities and that their rallies were attended by over 100,000 people.

15. The FBI kept Walker under regular surveillance following his resignation from the Army. Please refer to footnotes 17 and 20 for additional motives the FBI had to monitor Walker's activities.

16. One week prior to the finale of Operation Midnight Ride in Los Angeles, a bombing destroyed the offices of the American Association for the United Nations in nearby Encino. The executive director blamed the bombing on the incitement of UN fearmongering by extremists; it was no secret that Walker and Hargis vehemently opposed the UN.

a 6.5mm Mannlicker Carcano Model 91/38 rifle by mail order. Oswald had been following Walker closely enough to formulate an opinion that Walker was a fascist. He had also cased Walker's Dallas residence at 4011 East Turtle Creek Boulevard and took photos of the house. According to the FBI's questioning of Oswald's wife Marina, Oswald took a bus to Walker's house on April 10, 1963, just days after the first leg of Operation Midnight Ride ended. Hidden in bushes about a hundred feet away, Oswald waited until the moment was right and fired a shot through Walker's window, barely missing his head. Walker glanced around, thinking at first that a firecracker had been tossed into the room. Oswald claimed to Marina that he fled the scene on foot and took a bus home, but other records suggest that he may have acted with two other accomplices.[17, 18]

"Nothing in my 50-year career of standing up for Christ and fighting Satanic communism equals the success of that undertaking," Hargis would later reminisce about the tour.

With Operation Midnight Ride behind them, Walker and Hargis turned their aspirations to the national political races, making it clear that their choice for president was the libertarian senator Barry Goldwater. In August 1963, Martin Luther King Jr. delivered his momentous "I Have a Dream" speech in Washington, D.C.; its hopeful message of peace and unity was in direct opposition to Walker and Hargis' aggressive calls for civil uprising. Two months later, in October 1963, Walker attended a conference in Dallas in which he once again bashed President Kennedy and his policies. He was probably unaware that Lee Harvey Oswald was in the audience listening.

Hargis and Walker reunited for another tour of Operation Midnight Ride, this time throughout Texas during the month of November. On November 17th in Dallas, they were joined by Alabama's segregationist governor, George Wallace, who opposed Kennedy's plan to run on a Democratic ticket. It was well known to many that Kennedy would soon be in Texas campaigning for the '64 election.

"There were concerns among people close to Kennedy about his traveling to Dallas," says historian Robert Dallek. "Because the city had a reputation for being the bastion of the right wing."

With the bulk of their energies devoted to vitriolic political speeches and publications, both Hargis and Walker fostered an environment where an assassination could occur.

According to Warren Commission reports, Walker was involved in two controversial printings criticizing Kennedy in November 1963: an advertisement in *Dallas Morning News,* which stated, "Welcome Mr. Kennedy" and accused Kennedy of communist sympathies, and "Wanted for Treason," a handbill that mimicked FBI wanted posters, with front and profile views of Kennedy. Prior to Kennedy's arrival in Dallas, Walker made the extravagant gesture of flying three flags upside down in front of his house—the international distress signal.

On November 22, 1963, Kennedy was assassinated at 12:30 PM.[19] Following 10 months of investigation, the Warren Commission concluded that Lee Harvey Oswald, acting alone, shot and killed the president.[20]

"Our hearts, as a Christian people, go out to Mrs. Kennedy and her family, as well as to our new president," Hargis wrote in December of '63. "We stand as one man in disbelief that an enemy of our country could be so brazen in our midst."

Soon after Kennedy's assassination, Walker flew his flags right side up and at full mast, in defiance of the traditional half-mast position declared during times of national mourning.

Before All the Facts Are In

Throughout the '60s, Hargis' Christian Crusade enjoyed tremendous success, but not without its challenges. The Internal Revenue Service began its battle with Hargis, alleging that the Christian Crusade overstepped the political boundaries of a religious organization.[21] Undeterred, Hargis continued building his empire and publishing tracts, pamphlets, and books. He started a foundation for missionaries, and created an anti-abortion organization.

In 1971, Hargis founded American Christian College and changed the mission of the Christian Cru-

17. Walker's conflicting testimonies, actions, and activities surrounding the Kennedy assassination have created a number of challenges for researchers and historians. Here's what we do know: according to FBI records, Walker was informed shortly after his assassination attempt that the shooter was Lee Harvey Oswald, and that Oswald was likely not alone—yet before the Warren Commission, Walker denied knowing any of this prior to the Kennedy assassination. Not long after the attempt on his life, Walker hired two detectives from Oklahoma City to pose as men seeking to kill Walker. The detectives attempted to entrap a man named William Duff, a former live-in friend of Walker's (there were several). Duff accepted the hit, but then turned around and called the FBI. Duff also passed a polygraph test denying that he tried to shoot Walker, and the case against Duff was dropped.

18. Hargis believed that Fidel Castro ordered Lee Harvey Oswald to shoot Walker.

19. At the exact time of Kennedy's assassination, both Hargis and Walker were passengers in different airplanes. Hargis was en route from Los Angeles to San Diego; Walker was between New Orleans and Shreveport.

20. In 1962, a former Castro sympathizer turned CIA informant named Harry Dean infiltrated the John Birch Society. He claimed that society members Walker and John Rousselot hired two gunmen to kill John F. Kennedy, and that they planned to frame Lee Harvey Oswald. Dean, however, could not produce any evidence to substantiate his claim.

In this triptych: Hargis at the mic (center) and at a Christian Crusade mortgage burning ceremony (bottom)

Photos by Howard Hopkins, courtesy the Dewey Bartlett Collection

sade. No longer would it focus on external problems (anti-communism) but instead "internal moral problems" like drug use, the sexual revolution, and "Satan worship." He remained incredibly productive and financially successful, and rightfully referred to Tulsa as the Christian "Fundamentalist Capital of the World."

That world met its doomsday when, in 1974, *Time* magazine accused Hargis of sexual misconduct with several of his Bible college students, both female and male. The incident forced Hargis' resignation from the college.

"It was a really challenging time for our family," recalls Hargis' daughter, Becky Frank, who now serves as the president of the Tulsa Chamber of Commerce. "I think Mom and Dad did a really beautiful job working through all of those things." As an owner of a Tulsa-based public relations firm, Frank helps religious organizations manage crises through their faith-based consulting services. Among the firm's more conservative clients are Oral Roberts University, which faced a major financial scandal, and Victory Christian Center, a Tulsa megachurch currently embroiled in a child rape investigation.

"Several of our team members have first-hand experience in working for faith-based universities and organizations, both inside and as a consultant," boasts the firm's website. "The team understands the culture and knows the challenges. Not only do they understand where you are—chances are, they've been in your shoes."

Not long after Hargis' scandal, General Walker fondled an undercover policeman in the restroom of a public park in Dallas and was arrested for public lewdness. Twice. Walker pleaded no contest and paid a fine; Hargis denied the allegations of sexual misconduct yet told a reporter that he was "guilty of a sin but not the sin I was accused of."[22]

The American Christian College closed its doors in 1977.

The allegations of Walker's attempted assassination by Oswald remains one of the most fascinating and obfuscated subplots related to the Kennedy assassination. That connection haunted Walker his entire life; his personal papers are replete with Freedom of Information Act requests that petition for the release of government files surrounding the assassination. Walker died of lung cancer on Halloween day, 1993.

"My heart is sad today. I lost one of my best friends Sunday," Hargis said in a televised tribute, adding, "I never had a greater friend than General Edwin A. Walker; I never knew a greater patriot."

The many political and religious figures who associated with Hargis continue to shape America's conservative landscape today. Hargis's mail-order apprentice Richard Viguerie helped establish the Young Americans for Freedom, a conservative activism program for youth. Viguerie later became a pioneer of direct mail politics and one of the GOP's most successful fundraisers.[23] Conservative talk radio hosts like Rush Limbaugh, Bill O'Reilly, Sean Hannity, and Glenn Beck all borrow—knowingly or not—from Hargis' pioneering speaking style and Old South ideology. Former American Christian College President David Noebel, a fellow "Bircher," authored numerous books that argued against perceived evils such as rock music, homosexuality, and, most recently, communism.

Hargis continued his ministry until his death from complications related to Alzheimer's disease in 2004. His son, Billy James Hargis II, continues the Christian Crusade online, though publications are somewhat irregular.

Note: Research for this article was conducted with the help of Special Collections at the University of Arkansas Libraries in Fayetteville, the Dolph Briscoe Center for American History, University of Texas at Austin, and the Eagle Forum Archives and Library in Saint Louis, Missouri. Special thanks to independent researchers Ernie Lazar and Paul Trejo for their assistance.

21. The Tenth Circuit Court of Appeals eventually upheld a ruling in 1972 that caused Hargis' Christian Crusade to lose its tax-exempt status. Other churches have since lost their tax-exempt status for participating in political campaigns.

22. During much of the Red Scare, homosexuality was often conflated with communism. David K. Johnson, author of *The Lavender Scare: The Cold War Persecution of Gays and Lesbians in the Federal Government*, says ,"The politicians behind the Lavender Scare asserted that homosexuals were susceptible to blackmail by enemy agents and so could be coerced into revealing government secrets. In other words, the official rationale wasn't that homosexuals were communists but that they could be used by communists."

23. In 2004, Viguerie commented to the *New York Times* that Karl Rove was one of his direct mail marketing competitors in Austin. Rove employed the same strategies that Viguerie pioneered in order to help mobilize the religious right in George W. Bush's favor.

JESUS SAVES

Originally published
April 2012

by Lee Roy Chapman
and Joshua Kline

WHO'S AFRAID OF ELOHIM CITY?

A journey into the mysterious community at the center of several Oklahoma City bombing conspiracies

Bad men are drawn to the City of God. The Southern Poverty Law Center calls it the meeting ground for America's most sinister extremists. Many Oklahomans regard it as the most dangerous and mysterious place in the state.

For 30-plus years, a small, isolated community in northeast Oklahoma has been the subject of endless scrutiny. Law enforcement agencies and conspiracy theorists insist that Elohim City is a breeding ground for neo-Nazis and anti-government militias hell-bent on overthrowing the "Zionist Occupied Government" (ZOG) of the United States. The most damning accusation suggests Elohim City played a central role in the planning and execution of the Oklahoma City bombing.

When asked if she'd ever had the chance to visit Elohim, a woman with the *Stilwell Democrat Journal* deadpanned, "No, we like to breathe."

• • •

"I find them to be quite upstanding citizens of my community," says Adair County Sheriff Austin Young.

A sharp, stern man with a military presence, Young has the towering, no-bullshit persona of a Clint Eastwood character. His white hair is neatly cropped, his eyes maintain contact and rarely blink.

"What I read in the papers, I never experienced that with them," he says.

Young says that, as game warden of Sequoyah County (just south of Adair) in the early '80s, he once received a report of poaching that ultimately led him to Elohim City, where the suspect resided. As he approached the entrance of the community, he was met by Elohim City founder Robert Millar and several armed guards. Young politely told Millar that the weapons made him a little nervous.

"Robert said to me, 'Well, you have a firearm, don't you think that makes us nervous,'" the sheriff remembers. "So I unholstered my weapon and placed it in my vehicle. And then he sent the armed guards away."

This encounter began a 30-year rapport between Young and Elohim City. Young ran for sheriff in the mid-90s, when neo-Nazis, a German Nationalist, the Midwest bank robbers, and Timothy McVeigh were supposedly frequenting the compound.

"I campaigned in all parts of the county, including Elohim, and as far as I know, they supported me," Young says.

Shortly after the Oklahoma City bombing, a rumor spread that members of Elohim were planning a terrorist attack in Stilwell during the town's annual strawberry festival. Young called and asked him point-blank if the rumor was true. Millar answered, "Of course not. We would never do that." The strawberry festival went off without incident.

After offering his opinions ("they're not violent, not resistant, not how the media paints them"), Young suggests we go straight to the horse's mouth.

He dials up John Millar, pastor and de facto leader of Elohim, and son of the community's late founder. When Millar picks up, he explains that he has a couple of journalists from Tulsa who wish to visit Elohim. But instead of waiting for Millar to respond, Young offers the receiver to us.

"You're not interested in repeating all those lies that were told about us?" Millar asks. And then he invites us for a visit.

• • •

Stephen Jones is a towering figure in Oklahoma's legal community. Over his 46-year career as a defense attorney, the Enid native has represented a slew of high-profile pariahs and controversial characters, including anarchist Abbie Hoffman, serial killer Bobby Wayne Collins, suspected SLA radical Harawese Moore[1] and, most recently, indicted Tulsa Police Officer Jeff Henderson. But it was his work as Timothy McVeigh's court-appointed defender for which he's best remembered.

"When the Oklahoma City bombing happened, it didn't surprise me at all," Jones tells us one Saturday afternoon in his Enid office. "I was shocked that it was Oklahoma City. But that somebody would blow up a building and kill a lot of federal employees? That wasn't a surprise at all. I had sensed for some period of time that there was a significant alienation of people in the Great Plains. There was a genuine hatred of the federal government, a hatred of the Clintons. I had not seen anything like it since I worked for the Republican State Committee in Texas when the Kennedys were in office in the early '60s."

Jones believes that this anti-government sentiment reached a tipping point on April 19, 1993, when ATF and FBI agents assaulted another eccentric religious community: the Branch-Davidian compound in Waco, Texas. When the siege was over, 81 men, women, and children were dead.

"You have the primitive evangelical community," Jones says. "And the defining moment for a lot of those people—and this narrows down to Elohim City—was the assault on the Branch-Davidians ... Tim McVeigh told me that he sat in a Bradley tank; he knew what those tanks could do. And those images of that tank punching holes in that building, for several million people, probably more than 10 million people, that was a niblical prophecy come true."

McVeigh watched closely, first on television and then in person, as the nightmare at Waco unfolded. This proved to be his breaking point. Disturbed by what he witnessed, McVeigh began to plot his own revenge on behalf of the Branch-Davidians. Two years later, his vengeance became a reality when 168 people, including 19 children, died in the Oklahoma City bombing.

It's well documented that Jones did not buy the government's conclusion (re-enforced by McVeigh himself) that McVeigh conceived and executed the bombing almost entirely alone, with only the most minimal assistance from Terry Nichols and Michael Fortier. Jones believes the government was desperate for swift, quantifiable justice and chose to focus only on developing an airtight case against McVeigh and Nichols rather than fog the issue of their guilt by fully exploring the possibility of a broader conspiracy. Jones does not believe the evidence against Elohim City provides a sufficient answer.

"There is no smoking gun that shows involvement of any of the people in Elohim City," he says. "There is certainly, in two or three instances, against the backdrop of this, a pretty convincing case that some people in Elohim City may have been involved."

For the man who spent years studying every tiny pebble of the mountainous evidence, Elohim City is just another "what if?" scenario, doomed to float in the ether, a question mark whose answer is forever unknowable.

He agrees, though, that Adair County is a poetic fit for the community.

"Throughout the history of (eastern Oklahoma), there has been more chicanery, isolationism, parochialism, xenophobic attitudes, distrust of outsiders, 'We settle things our way,'" he explains. "So Elohim City, yes, is comfortably located. Very comfortably. Historically, it blends in."

1 Coincidentally, like Jones's most famous client, Moore was also accused of bombing the Murrah building. In 1998's controversial tome on the OKC bombing, *The Oklahoma City Bombing and the Politics of Terror,* author David Hoffman writes, "In the mid-1970s, Oklahoma resident Harawese Moore was convicted of planting an incendiary explosive device outside both the federal courthouse and the Alfred P. Murrah Building."

John Millar, pastor and de facto leader of Elohim City

• • •

You won't find Elohim City on any map. The FBI has dedicated an incredible amount of time, money, and manpower to investigating and monitoring the town's activities. Yet, this idyllic hamlet (known to its residents as "God's City," the Hebrew translation of *Elohim*) remains well hidden, impossible to find without the assistance of one of the few people in the world who've actually been there. Some reports reference Fort Smith as the nearest town, others Sallisaw, Muldrow, or Stilwell. They're all more or less right, but also dead wrong: Elohim City is not "near" any town; its 400 acres are situated as far as possible from nearby civilization.

The western edge of the Ozarks begins here in Adair County, a sparsely populated spread of bucolic communities with a mere 22,000 residents (43 percent of whom claim Native-American blood) over 577 square miles. The pastoral beauty of the majestic, unpredictable terrain stands in stark contrast to the rural poverty that plagues much of its population. Roadsides are often littered with garbage—discarded, empty cans of Busch beer, cast-off plastic grocery bags, cigarette butts—and road signs are peppered with bullet holes. Gutted shotgun shacks and ramshackle houses with landfill front yards rest precariously next to forests of resilient pines and dead, twisted post oaks. Multitudes of modest white churches adorned with hand-painted signage offer a point of communion for residents to congregate and socialize.

Underneath the surface malaise and natural wonder of Adair lies an explosive history, one that informs Elohim's existence. This is the heart of the Cherokee Nation, the last stop on the Trail of Tears where 11,000 Cherokee Indians were forcibly relocated. The area's history is America's history, fraught with instances of revolt and rebellion, of fierce individualism repeatedly clashing with a government status quo. This is the territory where Cherokee general Stand Waite held out against Union troops, making him the last Confederate general to surrender at the end of the Civil War, thus ending the South's campaign for secession. It's the home of Ned Christie, a Keetowah Cherokee traditionalist falsely accused of killing a federal marshal. When he wouldn't surrender, a posse of hired guns from Fort Smith pushed a burning wagon into Christie's fortified home.

The James Gang hid out here, as did Belle Starr and her bunch, the Dalton Boys, and Charles "Pretty Boy" Floyd. In 1977, Gene Leroy Hart, a Cherokee, was accused of the brutal rape and murder of three Girl Scouts in Mayes County. Hart was a violent local fugitive who'd previously been convicted of raping two Tulsa women. Despite the public outcry, a Mayes County jury acquitted Hart.

Today, the Cherokee Nation is humble home to small-town Oklahomans, many of whom are largely untouched by 21st century development. The landscape is wild and primitive, and self-governance is necessary for day-to-day survival. And the area's legacy of isolationism and individualism continues, carried on in large part by Elohim City.

• • •

For five miles, a dirt path snakes alongside a mountain. Then suddenly you see it: a poster featuring the Ten Commandments tacked to the silver gate of a barbwire fence. Nearby, a mangled, abandoned mailbox limply hangs, begging to be put out of its misery. Several hundred yards later, the incline abruptly levels as the trail penetrates the outskirts of Elohim City.

Serenity permeates the village. The day is bright and sunny, and the view of the Ozarks is breathtaking. For all the violence and racism assigned by outsiders, the town feels more like a spiritual oasis than a terrorist compound. There are no armed guards waiting. A small terrier roams free while children play in the road. A quirky collection of huts, trailers, and cottages spread across the property intermingled with several hulking, alien-like stone structures whose bubbled, dome roofs betray the off-kilter eccentricity of their builders and inhabitants.

A modest cottage rests on the side of the town's only artery, its Main Street. A tattered, faded American flag waves in the front yard not far from a child's jungle gym.

The portly, white-haired man on the porch is John Millar.

"Y'all get lost?" he asks, smiling, in a country drawl. His tone is relaxed and friendly and he invites us in.

Millar's home could be a model showroom for Pottery Barn—simple, clean, and elegant, with hardwood floors and a modern kitchen furnished with contemporary appliances. The décor is exact and unobtrusive. On one wall hangs a large digital clock, on another a faux-rustic bronze piece etched with the phrase "The Destination is the Journey." Framed photographs of family on coffee and end tables are given ample room to breathe. You could mistake the locale for middle-class suburbia.

Millar settles into his chair.

"So, what do y'all wanna know?"

• • •

In 1973, an ex-Mennonite pastor from Canada named Robert Millar, acting on what he believed was a vision from God, moved his family from rural Maryland to a large patch of land nestled high in the Ozarks, a mere stone's throw from the Oklahoma-Arkansas border. Elohim City was conceived as a spiritual city of refuge for followers of an obscure offshoot of Protestantism called Christian Identity, which teaches a racialist, Eurocentric take on Old Testament fire-and-brimstone piety. Though the elder Millar's vision that prompted the move could be called "apocalyptic"—he claimed to see future wars, natural disasters and civil unrest—John Millar maintains that Elohim was not created to be a spiritual bomb shelter.

"We didn't come out here to escape like some people do," Millar tells us. "They think the world's going to explode or fly away or something, and that's their right to believe that. But that's not our vision. Armageddon is not our vision. We came out here to express what we feel the Holy One, or God, is wanting to express through us. And so our hearts are turned towards the heavenly spiritual realm."

The pastor insists that his community is focused on heaven alone. Not the government, not a race war, just peaceful communion with the Creator. He cited factoids—"None of us have ever been convicted of a felony"—and repeatedly renounced the idea that they're a hate group. "People think that because we believe in Christian Identity that we hate other races. We don't teach hate. We don't put up with that."

Millar is polite, generous, and accommodating throughout the interview, never once taking the hardline on any issue. The idea of a "white separatist compound" conjures images of a completely autonomous community forbidden from interacting with mainstream society; this is not Elohim City. When Millar speaks of politics and morality, his ideas have a surprisingly Libertarian, live-and-let-live bent to them.

Many of Elohim's residents, for instance, hold jobs in town. The children are homeschooled in communal fashion—most of the parents take an active role in the education of not just their own kids, but in their neighbors' as well; it's Hillary Clinton's "It takes a village" concept realized in the most literal sense. Weekly trips to town to eat at local restaurants, visit the library, or see a movie are not uncommon. The homes even have Wi-Fi. There's little difference in living conditions between Elohim and your typical Edmond or Moore outliers.

Millar does acknowledge that Christian Identity's racially charged theology is at odds with modern notions of equality and color blindness.

"We teach that the scripture is against intermarriage with other races," he confesses. According to the Oklahoma Department of Commerce, 26.3 percent of marriages occurring between 2008 and 2010 were between two people of different races, ranking Oklahoma second in the nation for interracial couples. "[Intermarriage] is a big issue; most of your churches want to promote that. We think that's totally unscriptural. That doesn't mean we hate them, not at all. We think you destroy both races when you marry in."

The core philosophy of Christian Identity is an uncomfortable mixture of traditional Judeo-Christian mythology and a passive form of modern white supremacy. Elohim residents observe the Sabbath on Saturday, and many adhere to the ancient dietary restrictions of the Old Testament, though Millar is careful to point out that it's not a requirement. According to Identity, when ancient Israel fragmented, the tribe of Judah, "God's chosen people," migrated to northern Europe and eventually the U.S. In other words, the true Jews, according to Millar and Identity followers, are Caucasians.[2]

"That might sound really strange to you," says Millar. "But we believe that your Scandinavian, your Germanic, your Anglo-Saxon, your Celtic people, are different waves of immigration that came through. They're really all cousins and they're part of the same people from ancient Israel."

• • •

Since the OKC bombing, three things fueled suspicion about Elohim's complicity: the company Elohim founder Robert Millar chose to keep, the testimony of a government informant named Carol Howe who infiltrated the community, and circumstantial evidence suggesting that Timothy McVeigh may have been in contact with Elohim residents in the months leading up to the bombing.

"For over a year we were scrutinized by the FBI," Millar tells us. "We didn't like it, but we thought it was the duty of the federal government to chase down whoever did that. So we were scrutinized sideways, every which way you could think."

Millar maintains that the residents of Elohim never held a violent agenda against the government, nor any desire to participate in some apocalyptic religious battle. But according to Mark Hamm, a professor of criminology at Indiana University, in the early '80s,

2 References to the Christian Identity belief can be traced as far back as the Declaration of Arbroath on April 6, 1320, in which 37 Scottish Chieftains wrote the Pope asking for assistance in Scotland's battle against England.

the peaceful residents and elders of Elohim became radicalized as they developed a rapport with a similar white Separatist group from the northern Ozarks called "The Covenant, the Sword, and the Arm of the Lord" (CSA). Unlike the benign Elohim City, the members of CSA didn't just passively distrust the U.S. government—they were stockpiling weapons and conducting rigorous military training in order to overthrow it. Furthermore, CSA had close ties to the Order of the Silent Brotherhood, a shadowy organization of bloodthirsty neo-Nazis who fashioned themselves as Aryan Warriors in the tradition of the Phineas Priesthood.[3]

From Hamm's 2001 book *In Bad Company: America's Terrorist Underground:*

> Originally a pacifist community, Elohim City began a long, slow tilt toward militancy following Millar's 1982 address before another far-right group's gathering—the Covenant, the Sword, and the Arm of the Lord's national convocation at CSA headquarters in nearby Bull Shoals Lake, Arkansas. It was there that Millar met CSA founder James Ellison, a militant neo-Nazi who would later join forces with Robert Mathews's Order in what was to become what is called the War of '84—a campaign of terror against ZOG including a series of assassinations, fire-bombings, and robberies. "Millar taught CSA about God, and they taught Millar about guns," said a former CSA member to a reporter.

The FBI considered the CSA to be the "best trained civilian paramilitary group in America," and was closely monitoring its activity.

On April 19, 1985, exactly 10 years prior to the Oklahoma City bombing, the FBI surrounded CSA and demanded the surrender of Ellison, who was wanted for conspiring to acquire automatic weapons. For four days, a tense cold war ensued as Ellison refused to surrender. Robert Millar traveled to the compound under the guise of negotiator, but according to Ellison's righ- hand man Kerry Noble (who ultimately renounced the CSA and now writes and speaks on the dangers of right-wing extremism) Millar was actually there as a witness in the event that the government drew first blood. Later, the newly militant Millar bemoaned the fact that Ellison ultimately surrendered peacefully.

"Jim was wrong to surrender," Millar told Noble while visiting him in prison. "He should've shot it out with the feds."

Millar also served as spiritual adviser to Richard Wayne Snell, one of CSA's most violent members, who was put to death for the murders of a black state trooper and a pawn shop owner whom he believed to be Jewish.[4] During the trial, Millar testified as a character witness on Snell's behalf. Snell was executed on April 19, 1995, in Fort Smith Arkansas, 12 hours after the Oklahoma City bombing and 10 years to the day after the FBI's siege of CSA. Millar and his son John later retrieved Snell's remains from the state and ultimately buried him in Elohim City.

When asked about his father's relationship with Snell, Millar's tone becomes sharp.

"Snell's body is here," he says. "I went to pick it up with my dad, his remains, at the request of his wife, okay?"

By forging a relationship with Ellison, Snell, and the CSA, Elohim City effectively laid the foundation for the scrutiny, suspicion, and rumors that would plague the community in the years to come, reaching a fever pitch in the mid-90s.

• • •

"We didn't know Timothy McVeigh," Millar insists. "Never heard of him until the bombing. No connection whatsoever."

In the grand jury indictment of McVeigh, the government alleged that the plotting of the bombing began in early September of 1994, while McVeigh was staying at a motel in Vian, Oklahoma, less than an hour away from Elohim City.

"It is true that Tim McVeigh was there that day, that's what the hotel registration shows, and it is true that that's off the beaten path for him," Jones acknowledges. "Tim McVeigh almost never went to eastern Oklahoma via western Oklahoma."

It's believed that during this time, McVeigh was in contact with members of the Aryan Republican Army

3 In the book of Numbers, upon discovering an Israelite man and a Midianite woman copulating, the Jewish warrior Phinehas bludgeoned the couple with a spear as punishment for the interracial relationship (race-mixing was expressly forbidden by God). For the execution, Phinehas was rewarded by God with "an everlasting priesthood." Many militant white supremacists believe that they are called by God to carry on this legacy and it's been speculated that historical figures such as John Wilkes Booth and Jesse James considered themselves to be Phineas Priests. Robert Mathews and his organization the Order of the Silent Brotherhood are among the most violent recent examples of men committing heinous acts of murder and mayhem under the banner of the Phineas Priesthood.

4 In 1983, Snell, Ellison, and Noble traveled to Oklahoma City to case the Murrah Federal Building as the potential target of a CSA attack. However, during preparations, the men interpreted a weapons malfunction as a sign from God and the plan for attack was canceled. There's been some conjecture that the Murrah building may have been chosen as the target of the April 19, 1995, attack as a tribute to Snell, who was scheduled for execution the same day.

(ARA), a ragtag group of white supremacists who executed a series of bank robberies in order to fund anti-government activities (earning the media nickname "the Midwest bank bandits"). Evidence suggests the ARA was in Elohim City at the same time McVeigh was in Vian. The exact nature of McVeigh's relationship with these men (Pete Langan,[5] Richard Guthrie, Scott Stedeford, Kevin McCarthy, and Michael Brescia) and, by proxy, Elohim City, is foggy. People like Mark Hamm hypothesize that the ARA helped to fund the bombing with their loot and used Elohim as a sort of safe house, an idea known as the "theory of multiple John Does." In Hamm's book, ARA leader Pete Langan, who is currently serving a life sentence plus 35 years for his role in the robberies, is interviewed extensively and appears to be honest and forthcoming about his criminal activities. But he denies any connection to the bombing, and he minimizes Elohim's significance as anything other than a spiritual refuge. McVeigh denied the existence of accomplices to his dying breath. It's argued that there are a multitude of potential reasons for both men to lie, but the fact remains that nothing has been proven.

• • •

In March of 1995, the government had planned to raid Elohim City based on ATF informant Carol Howe's allegations.

Howe, a 24-year-old Tulsa debutante-turned-skinhead trophy queen, was brought to Elohim City by her boyfriend, white supremacist and would-be celebrity of the militia movement, Dennis Mahon. A former Imperial Dragon of the KKK, Mahon was now leader of the White Aryan Resistance (WAR) in Tulsa.[6]

Jones calls Mahon a "freakshow," a "burlesque figure of comedy," a man prone to "making extreme statements and engaging in extreme acts of self-promotion." John Millar calls him a friend.

"I don't know what he's done in his life," Millar demurs, when asked about Elohim's relationship with Mahon. "He seemed like a decent man to me. I agree with some of his thoughts. Not all of them, not by a long shot, but I do agree with some of his thoughts."

Mahon had plucked Howe from her privileged existence and taken her as a lover and protégé. He delivered her to his friends at Elohim for spiritual indoctrination, but she'd already been contacted by the ATF and turned into an informant. Upon her arrival, she began reporting her findings. She claimed Millar and company were stockpiling weapons, preaching increasingly aggressive anti-government rhetoric, and, most importantly, discussing plans for an attack of some sort. This seemed to confirm the government's worst fears: Elohim City was a powder keg of anti-government rage, a place where, in Hamm's words, "every resident down to the smallest child was armed and dangerous" and "underground bunkers held vast stores of ammunition, grenades, and explosives, even chemical and biological weapons."

Howe's was one of the more sensational puzzle pieces of the bombing case. When investigative reporter J.D. Cash broke her story in the *McCurtain Daily Gazette* during the Terry Nichols trial, a national media feeding frenzy ensued. She was profiled in numerous magazines and newspapers, interviewed by Diane Sawyer, frequently referred to by reporters as "glamorous" and "beautiful."

In linking Elohim to Oklahoma City, many conspiracy theorists point to Howe's testimony in the Nichols trial, in which she claims to have witnessed Timothy McVeigh's presence at the compound. From the court transcript:

Q. Now, are you familiar with what Timothy McVeigh looks like, Ms. Howe?

A. Yes, sir.

Q. Have you seen photographs of Timothy McVeigh?

A. Yes, I have.

Q. Did you ever see Timothy McVeigh at the Elohim City compound?

A. I believe I did.

Q. All right. When did you see him?

A. It was in July of 1994.

5 Langan was the ARA's unofficial leader and a self-proclaimed member of the Phineas Priesthood. Upon Langan's arrest in 1996, authorities discovered that his toenails were painted pink and his entire body was devoid of hair. It later came out that Langan was a pre-op transsexual who, when not robbing banks, cross-dressed and lived as a woman named Donna.

6 In February 2012, Mahon was convicted in federal court of a 2004 bombing in Scottsdale, Arizona, that injured Donald Logan, a black city official. Mahon's sentencing hearing is May 22; he could face up to 100 years in prison. Evidence against Mahon was produced in large part through information provided by Rebecca Willams, a government informant who met Mahon and his twin brother Daniel (who was also tried but acquitted) at a Catoosa, Oklahoma, trailer park in 2005.

Q. Okay. And where did you see him?

A. He was at a section of the compound walking across a lawn near the church building.

But Howe was problematic. She had a history of lying. Her stories were inconsistent and contradictory, and with more attention each story grew more elaborate.

"Like many former Soviet spies that come to the United States, Howe's story tended to get better over a period of time," Jones says now. "And then there's always new revelations as [informants] think they've been abandoned or forgotten or they want to increase their stipend or whatever. They remember something new." Jones says he discounted everything Carol Howe said after she acquired an attorney and was thrust into the spotlight.

The FBI's March 1995 planned raid against Elohim never materialized due to growing doubt on the government's part over Howe's credibility. Furthermore, Howe was ultimately deemed unreliable and her testimony in the Nichols trial was thrown out, making it unavailable for consideration to the jury. Mention her name to Millar, and you can almost see the blood boiling beneath his skin.

"They wouldn't even use her testimony," he says with incredulity. "She's so unstable *they wouldn't even use her testimony*. That's one of the things we don't appreciate about our government. They use people who are unstable, give them money and finance them to do unethical things. And that's what they found—she was so unethical they wouldn't even use her as a witness, okay?"

• • •

Another difficult question regarding Elohim's connection to the bombing centers around Timothy McVeigh's relationship with a German Nationalist named Andreas Strassmeier. Strassmeier wore fatigues and a swastika, was obsessed with firearms, and lived in Elohim City. McVeigh met Strassmeier at a Tulsa gun show in 1993.

"There was a lot of speculation on how they made contact," Millar says. "We don't know. We have a little over a hundred residents, and if they go to a gun show or a movie or a restaurant, I don't know. I don't want to know. I'm not interested. But I don't want them doing anything illegal, okay? And we make that very clear."

In Kingman, Arizona, shortly after he'd rented the Ryder truck he would eventually convert into a weapon of mass destruction, McVeigh used a calling card to dial Elohim City. McVeigh asked the woman who answered if he could speak with "Andi the German."

According to Howe, Strassmeier was the community's head of security, though Millar vehemently denies this.

"Never—he was here, but he wasn't head of Elohim City security," says Millar. "He liked playing with guns, so maybe he thought he was head of security and wanted to walk around with that. We let people think what they want, we believe in freedom. But we never gave him that position of authority."

The question of plausible deniability looms large over Elohim. The racialist ideology of Christian Identity and the geographic seclusion of Millar's community no doubt attracted men with agendas, but are the community's elders responsible for the behavior of every guest that passes through? For his part, Robert Millar quickly expelled Andreas Strassmeier from Elohim City soon after he became aware that the FBI was looking at Strassmeier for possible ties to McVeigh and the bombing. Strassmeier ultimately fled to Germany and was never prosecuted.

• • •

"I have a niece who's going to a local college," Millar tells us. "She wants to be a lawyer. Her criminal justice professor was talking about terrorists and the Arabs and the Muslims, and then he said, 'Well, we have [terrorists] right up our hill from here, and if you go up there, they hate other races and they're liable to just shoot you for anything.' And my niece raised her hand and said, 'I live up there! That doesn't happen!' "

Millar is clearly vexed by this judgment. He points out that in the 38 years of Elohim's existence, nobody's ever been shot on its property, unlike the surrounding communities. "But because of the stigma and because of us not being politically correct in the eyes of the media, we have a professor in the criminal justice class who throws us in with the terrorists. I don't appreciate that, and he will hear from me. That just happened two weeks ago, okay?"

He pauses, then adds: "You can write that: 'We've never had anyone killed here.' "

Before we depart, Millar gives us a tour of Elohim's new sanctuary, still under construction. The reverend leads us into the beautiful, cavernous chapel, built with the hands of the residents. He apologetically explains that he would normally show us their current church, but the community has no doubt already congregated, and reporters aren't allowed to sit in on their services. Outsiders still make the community uncomfortable.

After the tour, we say our goodbyes and Millar leaves us to find our own way out. With its residents all gathered for service, Elohim City is a ghost town. The air is still and peaceful. The warmth of the sun, the soothing hum of the natural ambience, the majestic view of the Arkansas wilderness—in this moment, it's obvious why these people are here. On the way out, we notice a primitive, white sign mounted on the side of the road, adorned with a bright red spray-painted phrase: "Jesus Saves."

• • •

After decades of scrutiny and mountains of circumstantial evidence, the government has still found no cause to take action against Elohim City. A second Grand Jury investigation of the bombing, convened by State Representative Charles Key to examine loose ends Key and others believed the government did not address to satisfaction in its initial investigation, came up empty-handed on the community.

"We have made every effort to try to identify any plausible connection between [Elohim City] and the bombing," it concluded. "In spite of a possible telephone call from Timothy McVeigh to Elohim City in April 1995, we have been unable to find such a connection."

Does God's City deserve to be granted peace? The questions raised by its proximity to violent right-wing extremism will likely continue to haunt the town for the span of its existence. Image rehabilitation is hardly an option, considering the endless documentation devoted to impeaching the community's collective character. It doesn't help that Millar's own sympathies to violent men ensure that Elohim City will continue to attract them. Then again, Millar and his community aren't seeking social acceptance; they want the right to exist peacefully, outside the parameters of mainstream society. Whether or not society allows that is another matter.

Originally published
March 2011

by Lindsey Neal Kuykendall

THE GOSPEL OF JOHN

Searching for John Lennon's lost letter to Oral Roberts

In the early 1970s, Oral Roberts' evangelical TV program was at a peak, with an estimated 37 million viewers. After each show, the ministry commonly received upwards of 500,000 letters. One of those letters in particular has since caught the world's attention.

On Friday, January 26, 1973, Roberts stood behind the podium at the Mabee Center and held up a sheet of paper to an audience comprised of his university students and faculty. Nobody could have expected the claim Roberts was about to make.

"I hold in my hand probably one of the most unique letters or documents that I've ever shared with anybody in the world," Roberts said. "It happens to be from one of the Beatles, John Lennon, who was probably the most gifted song writer of the group. And he wrote it by hand."

Sitting in the audience that day was Scott Aycock, who remembers the chapel service vividly.

"The majority of students at that time were converted hippies. We called ourselves Jesus Freaks," recalls Aycock. "When John Lennon writes to Oral Roberts, you can believe it had a huge impact. There was hardly a dry eye in the place."

The most commonly cited source for the letter is David Edwin Harrell's 1985 biography *Oral Roberts: An American Life*. It appears to offer the full text of Lennon's letter and cites an audiotaped transcript as its source. The actual transcript, however, is different. Harrell Jr.'s book contains some telling omissions—omissions that add new intrigue and dimension to one of the most trying phases in Lennon's life.

In the version below, Lennon admits to his disenchantment with being a Beatle. Although he claims to be under the influence of pills while writing the letter, Lennon openly discloses his police record involving drug use and check forgery, and he confesses to prompting the break-up of The Beatles. Additionally, we learn that Lennon's marriage to Yoko Ono created a major barrier in his relationship with his son Julian, and that Ono is "going crazy" over the disappearance of her daughter.

In this reprinted transcript of the audiotaped sermon, Oral Roberts' asides appear in italics and any underlined text indicates phrases that were omitted from Harrell Jr.'s biography.

This is what Oral Roberts said that day:

Rev. Roberts, this is ex-Beatle, John Lennon.

Aside: And it's a little hard for me to read, so I had it typed. I don't mean that in a bad way, don't misunderstand me. I just don't always get every word, as people don't always get every word I write by hand, too. Are you ready? This is quite a letter.

Rev. Roberts, this is ex-Beatle, John Lennon. I've been wanting to write you but I guess I didn't really want to face reality. I never do this, this is why I take drugs. Reality frightens me and paranoids me. True, I have a lot of money, being a Beatle, been all around the world, but basically I'm afraid to face the problems of life. Let me begin to say, I regret that I said the Beatles were more popular than Jesus. I don't even like myself anymore, guilt. My cousin, Marilyn McCabe has tried to help me. She told me you were praying for me.

Here's my life.

Aside: In his letter he said it like so many do over there, here's 'me' life.

Here's me life.

Born in Liverpool, my mom died when I was little. My father left me at three. It was rough because just my aunt raised me. I never really liked her. I had an unhappy childhood, depressed a lot. Always missing my mom. Maybe if I'd had a father like you, I would have been a better person. My own father I hate with a passion because he left my mom and me, came to me after we found *A Hard Day's Night* and asked for some money. It made me so mad, Paul had to hold me down. I was going to kill him. I was under the influence of pills at that time.

Married Cynthia, had a son John. I had to marry her, I really never loved her. She always embarrassed me walking around pregnant, not married, so I married her. Only one regret, John has had to suffer a lot because recently she's been married again. He and me never get to see each other because she refuses because I'm married to Yoko.

Aside: I hope I'm pronouncing the name right, Yoko.

So life as a Beatle hasn't been all that great.[1]

I came out and told them I wanted a divorce[2] because Paul and me never got along anymore and that's how the four ended. Since 1967 I've had a police record for dope and forging 12 checks to America. My wife Yoko and I have searched all over for her daughter, we can find.[3] Her ex-husband took her away, Yoko is going crazy.

As the song we wrote is that we wrote, Paul and me, "Money Can't Buy Me Love," it's true.

The point is this, I want happiness. I don't want to keep up with drugs. Paul told me once, "You made fun of me for not taking drugs, but you will regret it in the end."

Aside: He doesn't mean me personally.

Explain to me what Christianity can do for me? Is it phoney? Can He love me? I want out of hell.

P.S. This address staying at the cousin's house. Rev. Roberts, also, I did watch your show until Channel 6 took if off the air. Please try to get it back on. A lot of people I know loved your show. I especially like the World Action Singers, your son Richard is a real good singer. George told me he met you and them when he was at the studio.

Aside: This was George Harrison, isn't it? I didn't get to meet George, but the singers did at NBC.

Sincerely, John

P.S. I am, I hate to say, under the influence of pills now. I can't stop. I only wish I could thank you for caring.

After reading the letter, Roberts said, "This handwritten letter of his was three pages and I wrote him four or five back. Would you like to hear a little of what I'm saying to him? The second time, I'm writing to him again because the urge just wouldn't leave me."

Roberts went on to read the students a letter he had addressed to both John and Yoko. He said there may have been "some truth" in Lennon's infamous "more popular than Jesus" statement at the time, but that "Jesus is the only reality." He then asks John to keep writing him and expresses his hope that God will save his soul.

"I never dreamed that someone like John Lennon would have been watching the television program," Roberts said later in the chapel sermon. "Is that the way you feel? It never would have entered your mind and we never know what we are doing for the Lord."

In addition to writing back to Lennon personally, Roberts also orchestrated a return message from the students of Oral Roberts University.

"Oral asked all of the students to come to the cafeteria where they had a huge roll of butcher paper," recalls Aycock. "They rolled it out on several tables and asked all of the students that wished to, to write a note to John Lennon, in response to his letter. Of course, being young and a fan, I participated in writing a note to John."

Lennon's letter received a tremendous amount of fanfare, both at the time of the reading and since then. It has been mentioned in several books, numerous blog posts, a *Christianity Today* article, and was even referenced in Roberts' obituary in the *New York Times*. However, every reference to the letter cites the incomplete version in the Harrell Jr. biography. And all of these references may actually be wrong. Why?

"We have looked for the original for years, but it is nowhere to be found," explains Roger Rydin, curator of the Oral Roberts University (ORU) archive. "We have done a good job over the years of keeping up with these kind of items, but this one got away. We had a researcher here in 1985, and it was 'lost' then, and has not been found since."

Without the original letter, it's impossible to verify whether it was actually Lennon who wrote it. When Roberts read the letter at the chapel, he was reading a typed version of the letter, and when he read it out loud, he frequently interrupted the letter and altered the words. The most accurate record of the letter is Roberts' audiotaped sermon, but representatives from ORU are oddly skittish about allowing access to the audiotape; their public relations director ignored repeated requests for permission to hear the tape.

While we may never know for certain if Lennon actually penned the letter, there's an interesting allusion Lennon left for us to consider—and we have audio of John Lennon singing it.

On November 14, 1980, less than a month from his murder, Lennon recorded a song he had written to Yoko called "You Saved My Soul." It exists only as a rough demo of the very last recording he ever sang on, passed around as a bootleg copy.

The lyrics read:

> When I was lonely and scared, I nearly fell for a TV preacher in a hotel room in Tokyo. Remember the time I went to jump right out the apartment window on the west side of town of old New York. You saved me from that suicide and ... I wanna thank you, thank you, thank you for saving my soul with your true love.

It appears that Lennon had found the savior he was seeking.

"I know personally, my heart went out to him, and I thought of him often after that and wondered if he was happier later in life," says Aycock, speaking of Lennon.

"It certainly seemed he was happier in the few years leading up to his death."

1 From the transcript, it is uncertain whether this line is an aside from Roberts or a portion of Lennon's letter.

2 In 2009, a lost interview with John Lennon surfaced, indicating that indeed Lennon had asked Paul McCartney for a "divorce." Prior to 2009, it was widely believed that McCartney was responsible for The Beatles disbanding. "At the meeting Paul just kept mithering on about what we were going to do," says Lennon. "So in the end I just said, 'I think you're daft. I want a divorce.' "

3 Possible transcription error; the sentence may more accurately state "We can't find." Ono was reunited with her daughter Kyoko Cox in 1994.

Originally published
May 2010

by Randy Roberts Potts

SOMETHING GOOD IS GOING TO HAPPEN TO YOU

Growing up gay in the Oral Roberts' family

I was 12 years old when it happened, in the seventh grade, attending Victory Christian School on 71st Street in South Tulsa. My grandfather, Oral Roberts, climbed up into a tower and began telling the world on national television that God had commanded him to bring in eight million dollars to further his work on Earth. If he didn't come up with the cash, the Lord, my grandfather said, would take him home.

I was 12 years old and, in the world I was living in, this wasn't as unusual as you might expect. There was a rhyme and reason to everything in God's world—if you had a question, the Bible always had the answer. So when my grandfather climbed into that tower, I randomly opened the Bible for guidance and my fingers landed on this passage from the book of Isaiah:

> Behold, I have given him for a witness to the people, a leader and commander to the people. Behold, thou shalt call a nation that thou knowest not, and nations that knew not thee shall run unto thee because of the Lord thy God, and for the Holy One of Israel; for he hath glorified thee.

I was 12 years old, and this tower business didn't really make sense, but then again, there was that passage from Isaiah, with God seeming to speak directly to me.

At night I had dreams that the eight million dollars in donations wouldn't come in, and my grandfather would be taken up to Heaven in a fiery chariot like Ezekiel, another Old Testament favorite of mine. Once at school I overheard two teachers talking about how Oral was a Cherokee Indian, and how it was a longstanding tradition among Indian chiefs to declare the day of their death as a way to get the tribe to do something drastic it didn't want to do, and the teachers said that if the tribe didn't cooperate, the chief literally fell over and died on the promised day. Turns out there is no such tradition, but even so, I imagined my grandfather, who at 70 years of age, with his long-hanging ears and bulbous, impressive nose really did look the part of an Indian chief, sitting up there in the Prayer Tower one day and suddenly expiring on his prayer rug. I imagined a lot of things, all far-fetched seeming now, but at the time completely in line with the culture I lived in, a culture in many ways shaped by the teachings of my grandfather.

Oral began "preaching the Word" in the late 1930s as a 19-year-old during the Great Depression—my grandmother Evelyn told me that food was often scarce, and Oral would sometimes go out and shoot "swamp rabbits" which she would then dutifully clean and bring downtown where you could rent communal freezer space. Oral's ministry grew slowly, reaching its prime in the '60s and '70s when he built Oral Roberts University and pioneered the "electric church," becoming the first television evangelist. His television programs came out of studios in Burbank, California, and his message was simple, and contrary, to what priests and preachers had been telling us for thousands of years: God, according to Oral, wasn't very interested in punishing us. In fact, God was just dying to heal us. All we needed to do was stretch out our hands in faith and believe, and God would bring healing. Healing to our bodies, healing to our marriages, healing to our loved ones and, yup, healing to our pocketbooks. It was a revolutionary message and one that hadn't really been heard before in quite the same way.

"God is a GOOD God," Oral intoned on national television. "Something GOOD is GOING to HAPPEN to YOU!"

By January of 1987, when Oral climbed into that tower, donations had been falling off for years. The fall of Jim Bakker, the fall of Jimmy Swaggart, and the failure of the City of Faith, Oral's 60-story hospital complex (much of it still sits empty today, 23 years later) were all part of the reason for the decline in revenue, as well as an ebb in popularity for the brand of televangelism Oral helped create. His efforts to bring in the money to keep his empire afloat became more and more ridiculous, but he continued using that feel-good phrase, "Something GOOD is GOING to HAPPEN to YOU!"

Even now, as a 35-year-old gay man whose church and family has rejected him, I can see the appeal in those words. "Hope is the thing with feathers," Emily Dickinson once wrote, "that perches in the soul, and sings the tune—without the words, and never stops at all." These days selling hope is a well-worn path, and Barack Obama, for whom my grandfather voted, inspired the nation by blanketing walls and subway stations and billboards with this one powerful word. It's surprising, I'm sure, that Oral voted for Obama, but given a choice between a man selling fear—fear of nuclear weapons, fear of the black man, fear of change, fear of Muslims, fear of a bright, sunny future—and a man who simply said, "Yes, We Can," it must have been an easy choice for Granville Oral Roberts, who grew up in a shotgun shack in an impoverished corner of Oklahoma. He ended up building a 500-acre kingdom on the banks of the Arkansas River, a kingdom funded by faith, and faith alone. "Something GOOD is GOING to HAPPEN to YOU!"

But I digress. I'm not 35, an out-of-the-closet gay writer happily raising his kids in Dallas, Texas; nope, I'm just 12 years old, and my grandfather just climbed into a 200-foot-tall tower, and the whole city of Tulsa, Oklahoma, and the evangelical reaches of the entire world (which numbers, perhaps, in the hundreds of millions) were holding their collective breath awaiting the outcome. And me? I wasn't so worried about Oral. I figured either he would get the money and come down, or he wouldn't and God would take him to Heaven—either way, if you believed the hype, it was a win-win situation. When you're 12, you buy just about everything your family tells you, so I really didn't worry much at all. About Oral, that is.

What I did worry about, and continued to worry about for at least the next 15 years, was the condition of my soul. While everybody else was worrying about Oral, I was worried that Jesus would come down, perched on a cloud in the sky, and whisk all the Christians up to Heaven in "the twinkling of an eye," as the Bible says. Like the title of the popular evangelical novel blares loudly from its cover, I was worried about being *Left Behind*.

Why choose 1987 to start worrying about the rapture? It wasn't, after all, until 1989 that Oral first said Jesus was coming back and the world was going to end, when I was in ninth grade attending Jenks High School. The year 1987 made sense because Oral was up in that tower, and that tower, for me, was a symbol of the Second Coming of Christ, and this is exactly how Oral planned it. The Prayer Tower was built, along with most of the other buildings on the Oral Roberts University campus, in the late 1960s as a symbol of hope. At that time, on college campuses across the nation, students were sitting in groups by the thousands, smoking pot, drinking, swearing, having sex, wearing their hair long, and spending a lot of time saying "No!" to The Man.

Parents were scared, and Oral had an idea: why not build an evangelical university, where the students keep their hair short, their faces shaved, and their skirts long, and rather than saying "No!" are instead taught to say "Yes!" to the calling of God on their hearts? And in the middle of this campus, why not build a tower, constructed in such a way that, from any angle, it represents the image of the cross? In this tower he installed two things: a phone bank manned by faithful, little old ladies who would answer your call, day or night, and pray with you on

Christmas 1992, outside of Oral's home in Newport Beach, California

From left — Oral, Randy's wife Robyn, Randy (author), Marcia, and John (Marcia was Rebecca Roberts' daughter, Oral's second child)

Fall 1999
from left: Evelyn Roberts, Randy, Randy's daughter Lucy, Roberta Roberts Potts, Oral

a toll-free number; and a gas flame, installed on the top of the tower, manned at all times by a born-again Christian whose heart was "right with God."

This tower became the focus of my fear of the rapture. In 1987 I had a dog, a scruffy, old, monstrously-huge Irish Wolfhound, the kind of dog you see in movies about medieval England sitting calmly at the foot of the king in his castle. His name was Samson, and because he was such a big dog, I had to take him on a long walk every day or he would go stir-crazy and eat the cushions off our couch. We were living on the Oral Roberts compound off of 75th Street, in South Tulsa, just north of Lewis Avenue, a three-acre piece of land surrounded by an eight-foot stockade fence and a chain-link topped with barbed wire and electrified. I would walk down my 50-yard-long driveway, out the first gate, and out the second gate (always waving to the security guard in his little hut) and across 75th Street to the campus of ORU. There was another gate, and as soon as Samson and I went through, there was the Prayer Tower in the distance, that gas flame shining brightly on the top.

Or, at least, I hoped it was. On bright, sunny days it was almost impossible to tell, and that's where the fear crept in. The whole point of having that gas flame manned by a born-again Christian whose heart was "right with God" was this: if Jesus were to come down, perched on a cloud, and whisk away all the born-again Christians (the Catholics, and probably even the Episcopalians, were not really included in this group), that gas-flame operator would also be whisked away, and the flame would go out. That flame, perched on top of a 200-foot tower at the center of campus was both a promise and a threat—Jesus is coming back, but he's not here yet, so if you've sinned, get your heart right with God, because He might come at any moment.

Well, how do you know if your heart is right with God? Even at 35, I still haven't figured that one out.

So while everyone else was worried about Oral in that tower, I was worried about that gas-flame operator, looking every day to see if the flame was still there. On weekends, the campus could be awfully still and quiet, and if the sun was at just the right angle and I couldn't quite tell if the flame was still lit, chills would go down my spine. In fact, sitting here writing this, they still do. Some things just don't go away. I'm not scared of the rapture anymore, or the boogie man, or going to hell because I'm gay, but some nights when the house is too quiet I almost wish there were a tower across the street to remind me that all is well.

I was 12, my grandfather was in a tower, and I was worried about the rapture, but I was also a seventh-grade gay kid in an evangelical Christian middle school, trying my best to develop crushes on girls. There was one girl I asked out every single day for a month and she said no every time, until it became a sort of joke and I asked her the way I scratched my nose, that is, quickly and sharply. And why did I ask her every day? Because my best friend at the time, a boy I haven't seen since 1988 but still remember his full name and telephone number (918-528-0897), had kissed this girl. I think I was hoping that, if I kissed her too, I would somehow get some of his germs. Or something like that. None of this was conscious, but looking back it's the only way I can make sense of it. Because, looking back, while I romanced the girls I ended up being nothing but a pest, stealing their lunch bags, undoing their bra as a joke, etc.—all I was really interested in were boys.

In seventh grade, I went through a series of crushes on boys, five of them to be exact, each one more painful than the one before. I would fall for them, spend a lot of time around them, and then, realizing eventually that they would never feel for me the way I felt for them, would suddenly stop talking to them. The last of the five, in April of 1987, called me up, mad as a hornet, asking why I wouldn't talk to him anymore. "You just go through boys like Kleenex," he said. "You blow your nose on them and throw them away." Neither of us understood what the hell he was talking about, not literally, but we both knew he was right. I swallowed, hard, and quickly hung up. I swore off boys then and there, and didn't really have close friends (other than girls) for a long, long time.

When I was 18, I met a girl the first week I arrived at the University of Oklahoma, and she reminded me of my grandmother Evelyn—graceful, witty, intelligent, and always free to say exactly what was on her mind. I told her I liked men, but that I didn't want to be with one, which was exactly how I felt about things at the time. Two years later we were married. Six years later we had our first daughter on Father's Day, and five years after that, after having three kids and trying our best to build the perfect little picket-fence family, we were divorced after 11 years of marriage. I cried, for at least a year and a half, at this great, great loss. There was nothing I wanted more on earth than to give my children a loving, happy, stable home comprised of a Mommy and a Daddy and a dog and a garden and the whole nine yards. But like in Toni Morrison's novel *Beloved*, sometimes in a relationship between two people a ghost from the past intervenes, and starts shaking things up, and sometimes in the aftermath there's nothing left but a wrecked marriage and a chance to start all over again.

There were several ghosts that wrecked our marriage, things that happened in the Pentecostal compound I grew up in that came back to haunt me, and one of them was the ghost of a man who shot himself in 1982. That ghost would be the presence, in my mind, of my uncle, Ronald David Roberts, Oral's eldest son, and at one time the man Oral had hoped would inherit his kingdom. "Ronnie" to the family, he was, by all accounts, one of the most brilliant men anyone who came across his path had ever met; at Booker T. Washington High School he taught English as well as Russian and Chinese. Nancy McDonald, who worked with him at the time, told me he was not only one of the brightest teachers she had ever met but also one of the most loved by his students. In his mid-30s, Uncle Ronnie was divorced and committed suicide soon thereafter, six months after coming out to Troy Perry, founder of the first gay-friendly congregation in Los Angeles, and four months after he was arraigned in court on prescription drug charges—leaving his two children, ex-wife, and extended family to bear an unbearable burden.

Growing up, I didn't know any of this about my uncle, but I always wanted to be like him. Every time my mother mentioned him I noted two things: one, that she had loved him more than she had ever loved anybody else; and two, that the memory of his path brought more pain to her than any other memory.

I suppose it makes sense I wanted to be like him. I didn't know, when I was a kid, that the "path" my mother said brought him down consisted of being gay, intellectual, and godless. All I knew was, I wanted my mother's eyes to light up like that when she talked about me. Having ended up on this same "path" (gay, intellectual, godless), her eyes don't light up anymore, and haven't in years—for the last five, at least. And that's a shame, because I really do think that if she got along with Uncle Ronnie she could find a way to get along with me. But we were talking about ghosts. The first time the ghost of my Uncle Ronnie entered my life was in the spring of 2002, at Mayflower United Church of Christ in Oklahoma City, Oklahoma.

My wife and I were in transition—having both rejected our Evangelical past, we were trying to find a way to still be Christian but also true to our intellect, and we found ourselves attending Robin Meyers' church, Mayflower. We were there when Carlton Pearson, founder of Higher Dimensions (at one time one of the largest evangelical churches in the nation), came to speak to our liberal, almost-Unitarian Christian church. My family and I had attended Carlton's church in middle school and high school and, in fact, my parents went to Oral Roberts University with him in the early 1970s. At one time, Oral had publicly referred to Carlton as his son, so you might say he felt like an uncle to me, even though I hadn't seen him in years.

Carlton preached an amazing sermon that day, one that brought me to tears. Hearing him was like hearing my grandfather all over again. Here was a man who, instead of preaching that God was sending gays and communists and Catholics to Hell, said there was no Hell, and no mean, angry God dying to punish us. He might as well have said, "GOD is a GOOD GOD" or "Something GOOD is GOING to HAPPEN to YOU!" I had finally admitted to myself a year before that I was homosexual, but being gay, Christian, and married with children does not give you many good options. During that year I had often wished I would die, but Carlton's message gave me hope.

After the sermon, my wife and I waited in line to get a chance to talk to Carlton. It had been a long time since we'd seen each other—I probably hadn't been to his church since I was 15 or 16, and here I was a full-grown man of 28 with his own children in tow. We waited about 10 minutes as Carlton greeted each person who wanted to tell him how much his sermon moved him, and finally there we were, my wife and I, standing about three feet directly in front of Carlton. I smiled, big, and moved as if to hug him, but his face darkened immediately, and I hung back, and a chill passed through my spine. We might have only stood there for 20 seconds, but it felt like an hour—me looking at Carlton with a silly grin pasted on my face, and him looking back at me like he'd seen a ghost. He clutched his Bible tightly and his face went white, as white, anyway, as a black man's face can go.

"Which one are you?" he finally asked, barely breathing, still looking scared. After another long pause, he said, "You're Ron and Roberta's son, aren't you?" and I nodded, "I'm Randy," I said." He nodded back. "I thought you were Ronnie," he said. And we both stared at each other, and then, finally, hugged. It was a big bear hug, a reunion of sorts, and we were both misty-eyed as we talked that day.

Sometimes, a particular mantle is thrust upon you, whether you like it or not. My grandfather, with all his faults, was at heart a man who wanted to spread a message of hope. While it's likely that many of the decisions he made later in life were motivated by money or at least the desire to keep his ministry afloat, it's not my impression that's what he was thinking when he was 20, 21, 22 years old and standing in healing lines and touching, for hours upon hours, people with tuberculosis and cerebral palsy and cancer. It's not my impression that he started out to make a quick buck. Oral started out as a preacher, in tiny towns in southeastern Oklahoma, convinced that the mantle thrust upon him was to encourage the poor Pentecostals around him that God was a good God, that God did not want them to be poor, that God did not bring on diseases (as some evangelicals have suggested that God brought HIV to kill off gay men). Oral's mantle was one he felt thrust upon him, and his message of hope transformed the evangelical church.

A year ago I took my children to Los Angeles for spring break; for them it was a chance to go to Disneyland, to Universal Studios, and to see movie stars, but for me it was a chance to pay my last respects to a man who had overshadowed almost every memory from my childhood. Oral spent the last 20 years of his life living in a home on a golf course in Newport Beach, California, and while this sounds ostentatious, his home was fairly simple, a 1,000 square-foot condominium, the dining room table covered in water rings, the living room small and cramped, and the 60-year-old home smelling vaguely of mold. I hadn't spent more than five minutes with him in the previous 10 years, and a man changes a lot from 81 to 91. I felt sorry for him. Without my grandmother by his side, he seemed lonely.

Oral never could remember my name when I was growing up; even though I lived just down the hill from him and ran up to see my grandmother several times a week, "boy" and "son" were the only things he ever called me, if he called me at all. But in the spring of 2009 he eagerly played at great-grandfather, showing off that he had done his homework by greeting each of my three children by name, and, because he was no longer the scary grandfather I remembered but, instead, a 91-year-old man barely able to hear and completely unable to leave his chair without assistance, I gladly played along. Although we never spoke of it, Oral knew I was gay, and yet that day, it didn't seem to matter—he signed a copy of his newest book for my children and gave them each a $20 bill, and our hour-long visit passed quickly.

I'm grateful for that afternoon with my grandfather because, frankly, the man I grew up with in the compound was not a kind, warm grandfather. He was a driven man, one who slept four hours a night and the other 20 working. Even while "relaxing" on the golf course, Oral would be processing his next sermon in his mind or networking with business partners who might be able to help keep his ministry alive. There was always another tower to build, or another tower to climb up into; that mantle burdened his soul and there was never any time for children. But this day was different. Oral seemed at peace, happy to sit in his armchair and play great-grandfather.

He looked at me several times during that visit and sighed, and I almost felt that he was looking right through me. Before we left he asked me to come over to his chair; the children were watching a cartoon in the spare bedroom and the living room was quiet as I knelt down beside him and held his hand. Oral had large hands—the 60-foot bronze sculpture of hands clasped in prayer which stands at the entrance to the university are modeled after his—and I noticed that day that they also looked a lot like mine. I was a little shaken up—we both knew this was likely to be our last visit. As I stood up to leave, he held my hand tightly, looked up from his chair with that characteristic twinkle in his eye, and said, "Son, something GOOD is GOING to HAPPEN to YOU!"

Originally published
February 2012

by Randy Roberts Potts

SUNDAY MORNING COMING DOWN

A letter to Ronald Roberts

WEDNESDAY, JUNE 9, 1982.

In the news in Tulsa, Oklahoma:

> "Rotarians change laws to allow black members."
> "She doesn't like going steady rules."
> "Gelatin salads add pizzazz to meal."

This month, *E.T.*, *Poltergeist*, and *Blade Runner* are in the theater; on *Dynasty*, Steven is in the hospital with Alexis and Blake at his side, and Krystle feels left out.

Your horoscope: "Emotions tend to dominate logic. Applies especially in romance department. Young persons, including children, figure prominently. Temptation is to speculate."

It is Wednesday morning and, 1,914 years ago, Nero committed suicide.

And so, incidentally, did you.

• • •

DEAR UNCLE RONNIE,

I haven't written in a few years. I'm sorry. I've been busy. Busy living, busy keeping on, busy loving and raising my kids and working and dreaming.

Maybe you can remember what all that was like? I still miss you. I'm the same age now that you were when you did it. The weather at Will Rogers World Airport, June 9, 1982:

High of 91 degrees, low of 75.
Dewpoint, 69.1F.
Snow depth, N/A.
Observations: Rain/Drizzle.

I was only seven years old, living in Denver, and we were up in the mountains because school was out and we had a home up there. I still remember that my dad and mom and brother and I were taking a walk on the side of Buffalo Mountain and our friends, the Laceys, saw us. Their faces looked worried, and they told us the Roberts family had been trying to reach us, and then my dad sat with me and my brother while my mom went into another room to use the phone, and when she came out you could see she'd been crying.

But that's the thing, Uncle Ronnie. My mother doesn't cry. Not for you, and especially not for me. She just doesn't do that. I was seven and I'd never seen her cry, but there they were, those streaks messing up her makeup. It would be ten years before I'd see those tears again.

I guess I'm still angry with you. I was REALLY angry six years ago, the first time I wrote you. Back then, in December 2005, just before Christmas, I was moving out from the home I'd shared with my wife and *Brokeback Mountain* was playing in the theater and I was crying over the loss of my first boyfriend, the first man I loved. I know. It's backwards, moving out from your soon-to-be-ex-wife and already losing your first boyfriend, but then, I'm a Cancer, not a balanced Libra like you; they say we live life backwards.

Maybe it's true. While I was married, that's when I dated the most men, if you can call arranging hookups a date, and it was after the divorce that I really tried to love a man. First this one, then that one. Finally, just a few weeks ago, I got engaged to my boyfriend.

Have I told you about him? He's really handsome. He helps do the dishes, and he's great with the kids. We're going to get married in May of next year. We'll have a big party here in Dallas and then we'll fly to New York where, well, you'd be shocked to know that it's legal—we can legally get married in New York. Imagine that. Following the ceremony, we're going to Spain for our honeymoon to hike around the Pyrenees. It's legal there too, by the way. No joke.

Did you know that Nero was married, too? To a man? Or, rather, to his *puer delicatus*, which means essentially his younger love slave, a guy, a really handsome one apparently. First Nero had him castrated and then, then he fell in love with him (I'm thinking you don't fall in love and THEN decide to castrate someone, after all). Nero loved Sporus and married him in public, with all the same rites and everything, like everybody else. It was a huge public ceremony, with dances, feasts, the usual.

Maybe you knew that. You might have. You did, after all, know five languages fluently and several more you could "get around" in. You did, or so I hear, get around, didn't you? That's what I've heard. I've talked to a lot of people in the last six years, interviewed your old friends, your minister, your ex-wife. I talked to guys online who say they knew you. From what I gather, you were a lot like me.

It was, after all, 1982. The country was in a dark mood. The *New York Times*, a year after our own recession hit in 2008, said that it was pretty bad but not as bad as 1982. And, come to think of it, those movies playing weren't so hopeful either—ghosts haunting a little girl through a television, a movie where Harrison Ford's best shot at love is with a robot. When the "hopeful" movie is *E.T.*—which suggests that humans are so cruel to cute extraterrestrials that they have to employ gangs of children to rescue them—you know you're hard up. I've often thought gays are like little extra-terrestrials, growing up in human homes, finally realizing there are others out there like us, and, finally, one day, we decide to phone home. Is that what you did on that country road? Is that what that gunshot wound was? A phone call?

"Roberts' body was found early Wednesday in the front seat of his car near old Barnsdall 55 school about five miles northwest of Tulsa in Osage County."

• • •

I read a little pamphlet the other day that my grandmother Munna (Evelyn), your mother, wrote about the day you died. She got the date wrong. I'm sorry, Uncle. Your mother, my mother—they're not exactly attentive to their gay kids. In the pamphlet, "Suicide: A Double Grief," she said it was June 8, a Tuesday, and that Oral and your brother Richard told her around 11:00 am. So she got the date wrong; I can forgive that. I forget my own birthday sometimes. She also wrote something else, though, which is harder for me to forgive: "For years Ronnie had been on drugs. We knew that. We had tried every way we knew to get him off. We had prayed with him and for him. We had sent him to a place where they tried to get him off drugs." But, in fact, they didn't send you anywhere, did they? You asked them to help you, and they sent you away with a $100 bill. They didn't want you in rehab. It would get in the paper. They didn't want scandal. Or that's what I was told anyway, by several family members.

What's the truth? There's no record you were ever in rehab, but there's no record of that $100 bill either. There used to be a record of Munna's pamphlet—it was once a part of the ORU website—you could search the title on Google and it would lead you to a webpage with the full text. And then, after I broke the news that your suicide was much more complicated than merely "drug-related," that webpage disappeared.

I had to get my copy off eBay for $25; some little old lady was going through her attic and selling off stuff like that, and I bought it. Pretty expensive for a 15-page pamphlet, but it's a piece of you, after all, so it was worth it.

"Certainly, no child was ever raised in a stronger atmosphere of moral exhortation and religious preachments than Ronald Roberts." That's what the *Tulsa Tribune* said, on Friday, June 11, the day after your funeral, in the editorial page. Local papers were pretty quiet about the whole thing, even though Munna wrote that "every newspaper from coast to coast carried the story." I love my Munna; she was one of my favorite people on Earth, and I miss her terribly, but you and I both know she had a persecution complex, like much of my family. People were after us; if the news wasn't kind then it was the liberal media savaging us for reasons we couldn't fathom. Anyway, I was in Tulsa last summer and I got out the old microfiche files of the *Tulsa World* and the *Tribune* (that's gone now, by the way, if you haven't heard) and they didn't say much. The *World* had a half-page piece on the 10th, and the *Tribune* waited until you were buried, then ran a four-paragraph editorial on the 11th:

> But these things happen, as one says, "even in the best of families." There will be those who say that the very prominence of the father may have contributed to Ronald Roberts' despair at his self-worth. Perhaps, but prominence is not a crime and there are dark compulsions and motives that amateur psychiatrists little understand.

Indeed. Dark compulsions, you say?

Did you actually know that the date you decided to do it was the same day Nero offed himself? Or was it just coincidence? You were a really bright man, well-read. A teacher, you loved English and linguistics and history. You read about Nero.

The Roman Senate, according to Seutonius, had declared Nero a public enemy, and condemned him to death in the "ancient style." Seutonius continues with the tale:

> Nero asked what "ancient style" meant, and learned that the executioners stripped their victim naked, thrust his head into a wooden fork, and then flogged him to death with sticks. In terror he snatched up the two daggers which he brought along and tried their points; but threw them down again, protesting that the final hour had not yet come. Then he begged Sporus to weep and mourn for him, but also begged one of the other three to set him an example by committing suicide first.

Poor Sporus. Nero eventually had a servant help him stab himself in the throat, and died shortly thereafter, and we hear all about how he was buried, even what clothes he was buried in, but Seutonius didn't seem very interested in Sporus—the story on him remains untold. We know hardly anything about him.

I've talked to several of your lovers, Ronnie, and none of them would even give me their name. One of them agreed to meet me in person at a diner and then, at the last minute, bailed. Then he wouldn't answer his phone. Family members mentioned some guy named Paul, saying he lived with you that last year you were alive, but that was before I was writing about you and now they, too, have clammed up.

Me, I'm gay, and it's 2011, and there's nothing indecent about being a man in love with a man, and polls say, get this, that over 50 percent agree that love between two men or two women is the same as love between a man and a woman. These days, my lovers would probably talk.

Of course, there are still wide clusters of people who don't accept homosexuality. My marriage won't be legal in Texas, where I live with my three children, so it's a sticky situation. My ex-wife has always threatened to sue if I decided to live with my boyfriend or get married ... she started throwing that threat around six years ago, and mentioned it again just a few months ago on the telephone. In Dallas, thank God, family law judges have been dealing with gay couples for decades and you really can't sue to take children away from their father just because he's gay. Or, correction, you can sue, but you won't win, and no lawyer worth their salt will even take the case.

• • •

DEAR UNCLE RONNIE,

Let me start over. First, I want to apologize. When I first started writing you—six years ago, if you can believe that—I was really pissed off. I don't think that I really believed that things would get better. I was getting divorced and coming out because my marriage had fallen apart, and I was gay, and there didn't seem any other honest option, but I wasn't happy or at all optimistic about it.

I was still unable to step outside of that world you and I grew up in, that world where the idea of two men or two women falling in love and raising children and spending a life together not only seems impossible, it seems completely unimaginable. I came out, I was single, and I was determined to be a good father, but the rest, well, let's just say I assumed the worst.

And got a pretty nice surprise. Things finally did take a turn for the better but I guess, as usual, they had to get worse before they got better. In some ways, I had to experience the passing of both your parents, my Andy and Munna, aka Oral and Evelyn Roberts, before I could really let it all go.

My Munna died in 2005. It was spring, I remember well. I cried for about a month. And, after that, well, that's when my wife and I separated. I went to Munna's funeral and there was a tent for the family and an armed security guard refused to let me in. It kind of reminded me of the angel I've heard that bars the gate to paradise, because there I was, teary-eyed, and wanting to sit with my family and close to my Munna's casket, and there was this guard, telling me, "No." That's probably what pushed me over the edge, that's probably why I came out, that's probably why, six months later, in December, I was moving out and starting over.

A few years later, in 2009, Oral died. Yeah, your dad. He died and I went to his funeral and it was pretty miserable. At the graveside service my mother (your sister, Roberta) said that her dad was basically an awful father but that she appreciated the fact that he helped a lot of other people out with his ministry. I can't blame her for that assessment; you probably wouldn't have been as kind. And then Uncle Richard got up and talked about how he had this pair of Oral's boots in his closet and how they didn't fit him, and then his wife Lindsay (did you ever meet her?) said, "Richard, try on those boots!" and, sure enough, they fit. When you were in high school, Oral used to bring you up on stage and tell everybody you were going to be his successor, but then, yeah, you kind of screwed up his plans. Richard wore your boots, until a scandal with the university's finances forced him to step down.

When Oral died, I came up for the funeral. At the public ceremony, in front of 4,000 people, my mom told me I was going to Hell. No wonder you're not around anymore. She always said you were her favorite and I was just like you. I think she has some resentment issues.

The good news is that, about a year after Oral died, this guy named Dan Savage created something called the *It Gets Better* project. I decided to make a video, and I read my first letter to you, out loud, on YouTube (it's kind of like the TV of the future, or pretty close anyway) and I had about a week of panic attacks, I was terrified, putting something like that out there. Since then, gay teenagers across the country have been writing me and Dan Savage and the thousands of other people who've made these videos. There's an *It Gets Better* book now, and I just heard from an 18-year-old at a Catholic college who was given a copy by one of the priests. The *It Gets Better* book is in every big bookstore in America, displayed prominently. I doubt you can really imagine that.

So, yeah, things are getting better. It's slow, and, well, a lot of it might be hard for you to understand. But men like Oral Roberts are just not that big anymore. Jerry Falwell died, too. All the guys who were big in your day, going off about homosexuality, well, they're losing it. Most people laugh at them now.

It's been six years since I came out, and I've been through hell since then, but I've made it. I'm engaged. My kids are doing awesome. My boyfriend (oops, fiancé, I mean) is great, and his whole family loves me, and they've all embraced me as a family member. I'm out at work. I'm out on television, and when I go to my youngest daughter's softball games, sometimes some of the moms come talk to me about my advocacy work.

I love you, Uncle Ronnie. Times are different now, and I wish you could have stuck around, but I'm not angry anymore. I know it was a lot harder for you than it was for me. I'm now the same age you were when you took your last breath, so I've been thinking about you a lot. And, when I do get married, this May, it'll be 30 years since you left us, almost to the day, and on June 9th I might be in New York or Spain, somewhere where my marriage to the best man I've ever met will actually be legal, and then I'll come home and kiss and hug my kiddos and we'll all live happily ever after. Or something like that. If you had a Facebook page I'd show you pictures. You can look over my shoulder anytime you want. You can live vicariously through me, it's OK. I think I always wanted that.

I think I have everything I've ever dreamed of, and I think you're right here beside me. I know it, actually. Thank you for standing by me. It helps.

Your nephew,

Randy

Originally published
September 2014

by Kiera Feldman

THIS IS MY BELOVED SON

How Richard Roberts went from being the chosen heir to his father's empire to a prodigal son ostracized from the kingdom

Two Oral Roberts Ministries employees crouched on a desk on their hands and knees, their heads sticking through a hole in the wall. The voices of the Oral Roberts University Board of Regents on the speakerphone conference call one floor below carried up through the thin ceiling panels. Patriarch Oral Roberts was urging Richard, his successor, not to go on *Larry King Live* that evening.

"I think I should," they heard Richard tell his father. Oral thought Larry King would eat Richard alive.

A week earlier, a lawsuit hit the front pages of the *Tulsa World*, alleging that Richard and Lindsay Roberts, ORU's president and first lady since 1993, treated the university as a personal ATM. The university's finances were inadvertently cracked open by three professors who claimed they'd been fired for questioning Richard's efforts to involve ORU in campaigning for Senator Jim Inhofe's chosen candidate in Tulsa's mayoral election. What's more, the suit claimed Lindsay sent hundreds of text messages to "underage males" between the hours of 1:00 AM and 3:00 AM on cell phones expensed to the university.

ORU's Board of Regents agreed: *Larry King* was a terrible idea. John Hagee, Kenneth Copeland, Benny Hinn, Creflo Dollar—ORU's board was a who's who of televangelists. Oral was the original pioneer of television ministry. He trained up a whole generation of jet-setting mega-church pastors who preached the prosperity gospel: Plant a seed—meaning, send a check—and God will reward you with health, wealth, and happiness.

The eavesdroppers could tell Richard saw the writing on the wall. "There was no exonerating himself at that point," one remembers. "He just thought it would be cool to go on *Larry King*."

Richard had been like a moth to the limelight since childhood, when he began singing in his father's tent crusades. In the 1970s, at the height of Richard's celebrity as a Christian singer, he was starring in prime-time television specials with the likes of Johnny Cash and Robert Goulet, reaching tens of millions of viewers. With his signature streak of white hair and big, telegenic smile, Richard was most in his element when the cameras were rolling. If anyone ever asked if Richard was ready to perform, he'd fire back, "I was born ready."

And so Richard and Lindsay boarded the ORU jet and flew from Tulsa to New York. In the October 9, 2007, broadcast, Larry King listed just a few of the many allegations against the Robertses: remodeling their ORU-owned home 11 times in 14 years at university expense; forcing employees to do their daughters' homework; bestowing over a dozen ORU scholarships upon the children of their wealthy friends; the $39,000 Lindsay expensed in clothing at Chico's in a single year; the stable of horses ORU maintained for the Roberts daughters' exclusive use.

"Does it concern you that your excesses are so obvious that most people don't appear to be shocked to hear of them?" Larry King read aloud from an ORU alum's email. "I have not done anything wrong, Larry," Richard answered.

Off camera, Richard tried to rally the extended Roberts family in his defense. "We're all going to hang," Richard said (according to a niece's deposition). "We can either hang together or we can hang separately."

Meanwhile, the school was $52.5 million in debt. Campus was in shambles. The tiled steps leading up to the library were missing most of their tiles. Even the 200-foot-high Prayer Tower at the center of campus—the very symbol of the university, wrought from steel and tinted glass and resembling a gold-plated Space Needle—was rusting.

Still, hardly anyone knew just how bad things actually were. At this rate, in less than a fortnight the university would have to declare bankruptcy.

Oral, having retired to a condo in Newport Beach, returned to Tulsa for the first time in years. He moved back into "the compound"—the Roberts' six-house, nine-acre gated estate overlooking campus. At a chapel service, the much-beloved 89-year-old patriarch addressed students.

"The devil is not going to steal ORU," Oral promised.

The phone call came for Richard on Thanksgiving. Televangelist and ORU Regent Kenneth Copeland was on the line, according to a source who was present. That morning, another regent, Billy Joe Daugherty—one of Oral's protégés—faxed Copeland the receipts for the ORU jet. There was no denying Richard had been taking his family on lavish vacations and calling them "healing crusades," says the source.

"You're a damn fool. You should've paid the money," Copeland[1] told Richard, according to the source.

"I'm not supporting him," Copeland said to Oral. "Your son's out." (Copeland did not respond to a request for comment.)

Richard hung up the phone. He and his family were to be evicted from the compound—Richard's home of nearly five decades—his ties to ORU severed forever.

These were the terms: Mart Green, heir to the Hobby Lobby franchise of craft stores, would bail out the nearly bankrupt school with a pledge of $70 million—on condition of Richard's ouster. Richard would take with him his inheritance: the name Oral Roberts Ministries, where the checks get sent. In this way, the kingdom was divided.

• • •

"Success without a successor is failure," Oral often said. He dreamed that his brilliant first-born son, Ronnie, would succeed him. Yet, Ronnie refused the mantle, unwilling to play a role in the succession drama into which he'd been born. The eldest child, Rebecca, and the youngest, Roberta, were not considered suitable heirs: Only the sons would carry on the family name. It was Roberta alone among the Roberts children who was enchanted with the mythology of her father, the faith healer, and it was Roberta, a deeply studious child, who so loved the namesake school he built in South Tulsa, near the Arkansas River. But the house that Oral Roberts built had no room for daughters. That left Richard.

"Something Good Is Going to Happen to You" was Oral's slogan on TV. But a life lived on camera takes its toll.

Born in 1918, Oral Roberts was the son of an itinerant preacher in the Pentecostal Holiness Church—"Holycostal Penniless," kids in the church called it. When Oral's father was off preaching from town to town, sometimes the family would run out of money, and Oral and his mother would have to beg food from friends and neighbors. In the first half of the 20th century, Pentecostals were farmers, preachers, janitors, and rural teachers. Indelibly shaped and scarred by poverty, this was the movement that

1 Copeland was one to talk. Earlier that month, at the behest of Senator Charles Grassley, the Senate Finance Committee launched an investigation into the extravagant lifestyles of six prominent televangelists. Private jets, fancy cars, mansions—all paid for by their respective tax-exempt ministries. (Nonprofits are effectively taxpayer subsidized, and so personal enrichment through them is illegal.) Three of the six televangelists under investigation were ORU regents: Kenneth Copeland, Benny Hinn, and Creflo Dollar—the very people who'd been rubberstamping Richard's spending.

birthed the prosperity gospel in the latter half of the century.

In Pentecostalism, Oral is considered the godfather of the charismatic movement, which emphasizes divine miracles and ecstatic experience. Beginning in the late 1940s, Oral held crusades across the country and all over the world, his 10,000-person tent overflowing with those desperate for his touch to heal their suffering bodies and—often—finances. In the decades that followed, Oral turned faith healing into a wildly profitable enterprise. He hired top-notch admen and direct-mail consultants who perfected a method for using targeted mailings to solicit donations. The rate of return was so high that Oral's ministry had to get its own zip code.

Oral longed for middle-class respectability. Being a traveling faith healer and direct-mail mogul would never get him there. But brick and mortar would. When tent crusade audiences began to wane in the early 1960s, Oral switched gears and built a Pentecostal university, the first of its kind. From gold-tinted windows to golden latticework to the Prayer Tower's royal blue stripes and cherry red overhang, the entire campus glittered under the Oklahoma sun. "Nothing second-class for God," Oral liked to say.

Wayne Robinson, a former aide, grew up "Holy-costal Penniless" as well. In his 1976 memoir, *Oral: The Warm, Intimate, Unauthorized Portrait of a Man of God*, Robinson depicts a fundamentally insecure person who spent a lifetime "constructing edifices which, once they are built, must be replaced by new structures—each time larger. Over and over again, these monuments declare, 'I ain't poor no more!' The *nouveau riche* tone of the ORU campus speaks of the poor boy who made it big. The gleaming gold is a reassuring renouncement of empty pockets and an empty stomach."

Oral was an absentee father, always off traveling the world on the tent crusade circuit. The few days a month when he actually was home, anything the family did or said was liable to end up incorporated into a television script. It was all "grist for the mill," remembers Robinson.

Of the four siblings, it was Richard who won his father's attentions, because Richard could be put to use: He could sing and he loved the stage. Plus, he was a jock; Oral needed a golf companion.

Richard never was much of a student. "He's allergic to books," Oral once explained. Richard began getting singing gigs at parties and pizza parlors around Tulsa, much to his parents' dismay. He idolized Frank Sinatra and Pat Boone and dreamed of heading to the nightclubs of Las Vegas or the stages of Broadway.

Richard spent the summer after high school at Interlochen, a prestigious performing arts camp on Lake Michigan. In the Interlochen production of *Annie Get Your Gun*, Richard landed the lead. He didn't talk much about being Oral Roberts' son—although everybody knew it. Once, a kid quoted Oral derisively, recalls Elliott Sirkin, another camper. "But that's not what he said," Richard responded quietly, clearly a little hurt. Otherwise, Richard seemed rather "cynical" about his father's ministry, remembers Allan Janus, another camper. But evidently Richard enjoyed the perks, like Oral's jet. "He would brag about how he could fly wherever," Janus recalls. Handsome, friendly, talented—Richard seemed to live a charmed life.

In the fall of 1966, Richard, dead-set against attending the newly opened ORU, headed for the University of Kansas instead. It was the best rebellion he could muster against his father. Out from under his parents' roof, he could smoke, drink, and chase girls—a tale of wayward youth that he has deployed again and again during his adult life, calling himself "the prodigal son." Home from college one break, father and son went golfing, according to Richard's well-worn account. Oral asked Richard to sing for him in an upcoming crusade.

"Look, Dad, just get off my back and get out of my life," Richard barked. "And don't you ever mention God to me again."

As Richard tells it, one day while taking a nap in his dorm at KU, he heard a voice that he assumed to be his roommate playing a joke on him. "You are in the wrong place," the voice said. Not once, but thrice. Richard checked under the bed, in the closet, everywhere. Nothing. Then he realized it was the Lord. "The Holy Spirit said to me, 'You are supposed to be at Oral Roberts University,'" Richard writes in a 2002 memoir, *Claim Your Inheritance*. "'That's where your destiny is.'"

A former ORU student recalls hearing Richard's mother, Evelyn, tell a slightly different version of that story: She and Oral went up to Kansas and summoned Richard back to the nest, wanting to keep an eye on him.

Richard's college rebellion proved to be short-lived. He flunked out. Singing, however, was different. His voice instructor, Harlan Jennings, remembers him as a highly disciplined and serious student, "one of the best I have taught over a long career."

The summer of 1967, between his freshman year at KU and his sophomore year at ORU, Richard successfully auditioned for a spot on the chorus at the Kansas City Starlight Theatre, an 8,000-seat venue on the regional circuit for Broadway stars. They put on *The Sound of Music* and *My Fair Lady* and *Westside Story* and more—77 shows in all, rehearsing all day and performing all night, seven days a week, with an extra

12:00 AM - 5:00 AM rehearsal early Sunday morning. Richard worked like a dog, just like everyone else.

"I rented an apartment and lived like the devil all summer," Richard writes. It was, he says, "one last fling."

Starlight dancer Kitsey Plavcan was Richard's date to a party where Broadway singer (and later *Partridge Family* star) Shirley Jones made an appearance. Richard drove Plavcan home, and as she tells it, the evening did not end well. "He got drunk, and I was hanging out the door of the car, trying to find the line on the side of the road," she says. Just a few years later, she'd turn on the television, and there was Richard singing about Jesus on the Oral Roberts television show. "I used to sit there and laugh my fool head off at how wholesome he was," Plavcan remembers.

But in 1967, 18-year-old Richard found himself at a crossroads. Late at night, after a good deal of drinking, he'd say things like, "I'm not 100 percent sure about who I am, what I believe, what I believe about my father, is he real, is he all a fraud, is religion itself all a fraud," fellow chorus member Joe Warner recalls. In Christendom, everything would always be handed to Richard. The world beyond his father's kingdom was the great unknown.

Richard seemed resigned to his lot. He'd stay a Preacher's Kid forever—and not just any PK, but the son of Oral Roberts.

"Every PK has their own curse," says Warner. "But I think Richard's was greater than most."

• • •

Oral always conceived of his namesake university in opposition to the counterculture, an institution that would churn out clean-cut men and women in a time of middle-class anxiety over campus rebellion. Arriving on campus in 1965, the inaugural class of ORU students was united by a deep sense of purpose: Their job was to take Oral's vision of a healing God out into the world.

"It wasn't anything like going to college," writes Patti Holcombe. "It was more like founding a country."

Richard arrived at ORU in 1967 without that pioneering spirit. But he was soon drawn to Patti, a poised, feisty co-ed from Oregon with high cheekbones and a strong jaw line. They began to date, taking long walks, according to Patti's memoir, *Ashes to Gold*. "I'd like to sing on Broadway but only if it's God's will for me," he'd tell her. "All my life I've been Oral Roberts' son, but what about me? What about Richard? Why can't I have a life apart from my dad?"

Such a life apart would have to be wrought. "It all had to come to him, or Richard wasn't interested," remembers former ORU Regent Harry McNevin.

To join Oral's ministry, Richard needed a suitable wife. A good Christian girl, Patti fit the mold, although not quite as well as Richard's mother, Evelyn, who was even-tempered, graceful, and endlessly supportive of her husband's ambitions. "Patti has a mind of her own," people said, with varying degrees of admiration.

Shortly after the wedding, Oral called Richard and Patti into his study, sat down in an armchair by the fire, and began to cry. Oral said he'd had a dream: If either of them backslid—the term for leading an unchristian life, especially one outside Oral's domain—they'd be killed in a plane crash.

"It never occurred to us that maybe it wasn't God who had spoken," writes Patti, "but Oral trying to manipulate us to protect the ministry."

On the first night of their honeymoon, Patti wore a frilly lace nightgown, a gift from Evelyn. According to Patti, Richard looked up and said, "You know, you look fatter with your clothes off." They consummated their marriage in a coin-operated bed. Afterward, Patti says Richard put a quarter in the "Magic Fingers" contraption, making the bed vibrate and shake. Richard fell right asleep. The Magic Fingers kept Patti up for hours. They ate Thanksgiving dinner in the hotel. After a few days, they got bored and came home early from their honeymoon. So began their lives as "professional newlyweds," writes Patti.

Back at ORU, plans were soon underway for *Contact*, the first Oral Roberts prime-time television special. Oral was determined to make his telegenic son into a modern Christian celebrity. *Contact* (and its later incarnations in the 1970s) was a wholesome variety show with singing and dancing from the World Action Singers, a group of ORU students led by Richard. The show had flashy sets and costumes, solos by Richard and Patti, and a sermon from Oral. He had admen coin upbeat catchphrases like "Something Good Is Going to Happen to You."

Richard assumed the role of spoiled crown prince. Oral's men were instructed to give Richard small responsibilities to create the illusion of power. "Executive decisions," writes former producer Jerry Sholes in *Give Me That Prime-Time Religion*, "were made by other individuals who knew they were really reporting to Oral." Once, impatient with a television director, Richard turned to Sholes and snapped, "Is he a director or a pussy?" Sholes groaned. Richard didn't seem to care that ORU students—strict Christians—were within earshot. Richard had a golf date he wanted to get off to.

It was a struggle to get Richard to work a full day, say Oral's former aides. Richard was often MIA, and it was anyone's guess whether he was at the Tulsa Country Club or Southern Hills Country Club or elsewhere. "Sometimes we all had assignments to go get him to

come home," remembers Al Bush, a close adviser of Oral's for decades. ("Richard was raised on a country club golf course," Bush once told the *Tulsa Tribune*. "If he's ever been hungry, it's because he overslept.")

According to Richard, he quit school after his junior year to work full-time for his father. According to Wayne Robinson, Oral's aide, the future ORU president flunked out of ORU. Either way, Richard was on the move. In March 1969, gospel singer Mahalia Jackson was the featured guest on the first *Contact* special, and 10 million people tuned in. Pat Boone, Richard's hero, followed as the featured guest on the second prime-time special.

"The golden age, we called it," remembers World Action Singer Larry Wayne Morbitt. They were reaching millions of the unchurched on prime time. ORU was swimming in cash in the 1970s, new campus buildings were going up, and the World Action Singers got to travel the world in luxury. For all his successes, however, Richard could not anticipate that he would face competition for his father's attentions.

A young black Pentecostal named Carlton Pearson, another World Action Singer, became Oral's protégé.

"[Richard] wanted to be perfect. He wanted to impress the people and to please his father," says Pearson. "More than God, I promise you. It wasn't about God," Pearson laughs.

In 1971, Oral brought Pearson into his office, where Richard was seated.

"Twenty-five percent of my income comes consistently from African-Americans," Oral said, according to Pearson. "Richard has the indispensable name of Roberts. He's my biological son. There's nothing you can do about that. But I need a black son. You are my black son."

Soon, Oral hired Pearson as associate evangelist, in large part to help groom Richard to take over the empire, Pearson says.

"I knew what Oral was thinking," says Pearson. "I want my son to succeed me like God's son pleased him. 'This is my beloved son, in whom I'm well pleased.' "

Richard still hadn't graduated college—he didn't get his BA from ORU until 1985, nearly 20 years after he began. But Oral added him to the ORU Board of Regents in 1971, at age 23. When fellow Regent Harry McNevin criticized Richard's plans to use the ORU jet for junkets, Richard declared that he would no longer attend any more meetings with him, according to McNevin. Before long, Oral made Richard vice president of Oral Roberts Evangelistic Association, the ministry.

As the years went on, Patti and others noticed Richard was becoming a clone of his father: how he spoke onstage, how he styled his hair. He recycled Oral's sermons verbatim. Oral had even given the couple their marriage bed.

"We slept in his bed," writes Patti, "and, in many ways, he slept in ours."

Patti readily admits she enjoyed the fruits of seed-faith ministry: glamorous vacations, expensive cars, shopping trips, jet-setting. But, according to her memoir, she grew increasingly uncomfortable with the resemblance seed-faith bore to the selling of indulgences prior to Martin Luther and the Reformation.

At an event in the mid 1970s, Patti happened to meet young Frank Schaeffer, son of the famous Christian philosopher and anti-abortion coalition builder Francis Schaeffer. Talking with Frank, Patti was relieved to find that they "were both angry with the superstar system of American religion," she writes. In her mind, Christian celebrity culture was pure idolatry. Frank heard Patti's concerns about her marriage and then counseled the couple.

Looking back, Frank remembers telling the couple that he eventually planned to make his own life, away from his paternal legacy, and they should too. This life, Frank said, was "poisonous." Richard nodded. "You're right, you're right, this is terrible. We need to get out," Richard said, according to Frank.

Oral's prophecy about Richard and Patti would prove to be slightly misdirected.

In 1977, Rebecca, Oral and Evelyn's eldest child, and her banker husband, Marshall Nash, were killed when, returning from their newly purchased condo in Aspen, their private plane went down over the cornfields of Kansas. Oral took his grief and made it into a television episode.

• • •

At first, Richard and Patti weren't able to conceive, and so they adopted a daughter. But soon Patti became pregnant. When she gave birth, she called Oral from the hospital. She apologized for not having a boy. "That doesn't matter," Oral assured her, according to aide Wayne Robinson. He would be proud of his granddaughter regardless, Oral said. He hung up the phone and turned to Robinson. "But it does matter," Oral confided.

To be on television with his father, Richard had to have it all—the lovely wife, the kids. People had to want to be them, as any adman knows. They were selling their image. It was "a corporate marriage," Patti writes, "designed not to upset the flow of dollars into the prized ministry."

Patti's ambitions began to exceed the family role into which she'd been cast: She wanted to have a singing career of her own. Oral warned Richard that he needed to get her under control, Patti recalls.

"I did not build this university or this ministry for you," Oral once told Patti, she recalls in *Ashes to Gold*.

"I built it for Richard. You will never get to the top. It's not yours; it's Richard's."

Patti had become an unsuitable wife. One day, Richard came back from a fishing trip with his parents and announced they had given their permission to end the marriage. (Oral had a strict policy against employing divorcés, but he bent the rules for Richard.) After the divorce was finalized in early 1979, Patti writes, "Richard came into the bedroom and said, 'I'm so sorry our marriage didn't work out,' and extended his hand for me to shake."

With turmoil erupting in Christendom over the divorce, 30-year-old Richard quickly set about the business of finding another wife. Within a year, he married Linda "Lindsay" Salem, a 23-year-old Christian of Lebanese descent from Florida, who was attending ORU's law school. She had black hair and a heart-shaped face, cute but not regal like Patti.

Lindsay kept having miscarriages. Finally, she carried a baby to term. In 1984, Lindsay gave birth to a male heir. They named him Richard Oral Roberts. So much was riding on that baby. "Oh, how I wanted a son," writes Richard. "Richard Oral was the fulfillment of that dream." Born with a lung defect, the infant lived for just 36 hours.

Oral led the family in prayer before the funeral. They huddled together in the green room of ORU's Christ Chapel, backstage at a funeral.

After Richard Oral, Lindsay gave birth to three daughters.

• • •

Not long after his daughter and son-in-law died in a tragic plane crash, Oral had a vision of a 900-foot Jesus who told him to build a Christian medical center. This led Oral to build the City of Faith, a $250-million medical center that opened in 1981. Three sparkling gold towers arose on the south side of ORU's campus: a 294-bed hospital, a 60-story clinic, and a 20-story research facility.

The problem was that Tulsa already had more than enough hospital beds. Oral predicted—wrongly, it turned out—that believers would flock to Tulsa for a hybrid of modern medicine and faith healing. Instead, City of Faith hemorrhaged cash.

Around the same time, Oral decided that he needed a Beverly Hills home. ("The old idea that religious people should be poor is nonsense," Oral once said in a TV broadcast.) According to Harry McNevin, the former regent, Oral diverted another $7 million from ORU's endowment: $2.4 million to buy the house (as reported by the *Tulsa Tribune*) and the rest on renovations. "The entire ordeal was kept very quiet," remembers Carlton Pearson, who was a regent at the time. McNevin says he couldn't even get any of the other regents to tell him the address of the house. He resigned from the board.

Strapped for cash, in 1986 ORU shuttered both the dentistry and the law school. (Michele Bachmann graduated from ORU's law school the year it closed.) Things reached a new low in 1987. Oral claimed he had raised the dead. Richard backed him up, recalling a boyhood memory of Oral resurrecting an infant who'd died "right in the middle of my dad's sermon."

To great national ridicule, Oral announced that God had told him he'd be "called home" if he didn't raise $8 million for medical school scholarships. "Let's not let this be my dad's last birthday!" Richard wrote in a fundraising letter.

Ultimately, a dog-track owner in Florida cut a check for the last $1.3 million, and Oral was not called home. But, regardless, the medical center closed in 1989. Then, the rest of City of Faith closed in 1991. ORU's unpaid bills were piling higher and higher.

Oral was growing old. He became even more fixated on his problem of succession, worrying whether or not "Richard could carry it," says Pearson. Sure, Oral racked up debts, but he could also bring in the big money. Richard hadn't proved he could raise funds.

Oral turned to his board of regents for reassurance. "What do you think about Richard? How do you think Richard did last night? What do you think about the future? Do you think he can handle this?" Oral asked the mega-pastors. Pearson remembers, "I kept saying we'll be there for him. Billy Joe [Daugherty], myself, Larry Lea—anybody. Kenneth Copeland, all the preachers on the board. Because all those preachers understood they would want their son to succeed them."

There was a time when Oral planned to divvy up responsibilities, Pearson says: Richard would lead the ministry, and Roberta, a graduate of ORU's law school, would lead the university. Oral told Pearson and Billy Joe Daugherty, "I want you to buttress both of them at either end to support them." That idea was quickly scrapped, says Pearson. "Richard wanted everything."

Passing the scepter in 1993, Oral told his son, "You're anointed by God, chosen by the Lord to be the second president." Oral was leaving ORU about $50 million in debt.

"I'm just delighted that the medal is on you and now off of me," Oral said and promptly retired to his condo on a golf course in Newport Beach, California.

• • •

All Souls Unitarian Church is not far from Oral Roberts University. From the pulpit, an All Souls minister once dubbed ORU "Babylon on the Arkansas." According to the Book of Daniel, King Belshazzar of

Babylon declared that his walled city upon the Euphrates would never fall, all the while feasting and drinking from golden goblets plundered by his father.

All Souls was where Ronnie, Oral and Evelyn's eldest son, attended church with his wife and two adopted kids in the 1970s. Ronnie—Oral's would-be successor, the original beloved son—could not have been more different from his brother. Richard conformed; Ronnie rebelled. Marvin Shirley, a close friend from All Souls, remembers Ronnie as a liberal rationalist who read widely, was fluent in five languages, and viewed the Bible as a historical document. This was the ultimate apostasy for a child of Oral Roberts.

Ronnie was loath to participate in the public performance of being a Roberts, remembers All Souls' former minister, Dr. John Wolf. "He really wanted nothing to do with it at all out there [at ORU]," says Wolf. Only Evelyn could talk Ronnie into joining the family on Oral's television specials. Oral would demand that Ronnie shave his beard, for a beard stood for hippies and secularism and everything that the ministry was not; Ronnie would refuse. In the programs Ronnie usually ended up in the background or off to the side of the frame somewhere. "It wasn't just a beard. I mean, it was a *beard*," Wolf says, laughing. "He looked like Rasputin for a while."

One Sunday, the televangelist himself showed up at All Souls, Wolf remembers. Oral and Wolf were friendly antagonists in those days. Seeing Ronnie's father in the Unitarian pews, incredulous, Wolf asked, "Oral, what are you doing here?" Oral replied, "Well, I just want to find out what kind of place my kid was going to."

Ronnie eschewed his royal lineage, seeing it as something of an embarrassment. He left town for college and headed to Stanford, dropped out after a year, and joined the army as a linguist, teaching Mandarin in Vietnam. He had himself removed from the family trust fund. After spending three years in a PhD program at the University of Southern California, it was a job offer that brought Ronnie back to Tulsa. He taught at a local high school and started an antiques business. "He despised what his father did," says Shirley, "the way he bilked the poor." According to Shirley, Ronnie had rejected faith healing since adolescence and thought Oral "was in it for the money."

Toward the end of his life, Ronnie developed an addiction to cold medication. Finally, he reached a breaking point. He pleaded guilty to forging a prescription for Tussionex and was placed on probation. A report filed by probation and parole officers noted Ronnie's "strongest feelings about his childhood were those of alienation and rejection from the family because he chose not to adhere to the religious beliefs of his parents and rest of the family."

On Mother's Day of 1982, Evelyn went to visit her eldest son, writes biographer David Edwin Harrell Jr. Ronnie was considering a job that Oral had recently offered him at the university—a move Oral had made many times, always on condition that he shave his beard and quit smoking. Submit, obey. At the time, Ronnie was estranged from his wife and children, living in an apartment just off Peoria Avenue. He had withdrawn from his friends, most of whom hadn't seen him in months. Ronnie always rejected Oral's job offers. Even though he was at the end of the line—his antiques business had failed, his marriage had failed—this time was no different. Ronnie told his mother that he could never take something simply because he was a Roberts.

Exactly one month later, Ronnie's body was found in his car about five miles outside of Tulsa. He'd shot himself in the heart with a .25-caliber gun.

After hearing word from the police, Richard and one of Oral's aides went to Ronnie's apartment, where they found a note. Ronnie had written that he looked forward to seeing his older sister, Rebecca, again. Richard broke the news to Oral and Evelyn.

The Roberts family arranged to have the funeral at ORU, in Christ's Chapel. Oral's eulogy remembered Ronnie "as a man who was never quite the same after a tour of duty during Vietnam." Evelyn believed the devil was to blame for Ronnie's suicide. Roberta, the youngest Roberts child, traced Ronnie's demise to his undergraduate years at Stanford, where everything "his world rested upon" was challenged.

In the aftermath, Oral and Evelyn pored over their memories, wondering if there was something they could have done differently. Richard assured them there wasn't. "I've had to work hard on my dad and mother," Richard told Harrell, the biographer. "It's natural that they would say, 'If I had just done this or that.' It's not true."

"My son had a will of his own," Oral eventually concluded. "My will cannot cancel out anybody's will."

Lives, especially ones that end in suicide, do not lend themselves to neat lines of causation. Even now, over 30 years later, longtime friend Marvin Shirley is still mystified that Ronnie—a sensitive soul, a flautist—would ever shoot a gun, for any reason.

Upon Oral's death in 2009, Bruce Nickerson, a classmate of Ronnie's at Stanford, wrote a eulogy for father and son:

> Ron was gay—a fact that his father could not accept. However Ron told me his father loved him and had never withdrawn support, either financially or emotionally. He just couldn't get beyond Leviticus...

His family has denied that sexual orientation was a factor [in his suicide]. Remembering his anguish at Stanford, I am certain it was the cause, and that drugs were a futile attempt to mask the pain he must have suffered every day. When I met him he was a terribly troubled youth, struggling with who he was.

It was a time when getting married was the only way to have a normal life, to have a family. "Ronnie was trying very hard to be [part of] the outward couple that Oral wanted," says Wayne Robinson, the former aide.

Oral's youngest child, Roberta, has two adult sons, Randy and Steve. Both are gay. They too were once princelings, living in the royal Roberts compound. In 2005, when Evelyn died, they went together to the funeral. At the grave, they tried to enter the Roberts family tent but were turned away by a guard.

"That's my grandmother inside the coffin," Randy said.

"I know who you are," the guard replied.

The two brothers stood outside the family tent and watched.

• • •

Lindsay changed over the years. By the time she was the first lady of ORU, she had a small village of people she could phone who would do her bidding. Sometimes she was sweet and maternal, sometimes cruel and wrathful. She would throw explosive temper tantrums, according to former employees. (Richard and Lindsay did not respond to several interview requests.)

Richard and Lindsay's eldest daughter began attending ORU in the fall of 2003. (All three eventually enrolled.) Whatever the Roberts daughters wished, they received. They wanted a Pilates class to fulfill their PE requirement, so the school had to invent a Pilates class, recalls a faculty member.

"The girls would do things like check out equipment and basically wreck it," says the faculty member. "They seemed to feel like they could get by with most anything."

Professors got in trouble if the Roberts daughters complained about their teaching, says the faculty member, and Richard and Lindsay routinely asked professors to change their daughters' grades.

A charming figure on campus, Richard was popular with the student body. But the alumni had given up on him long ago. Alums had so little confidence in him that only about six percent were ponying up donations.

"The alumni for years wanted somebody to truthfully tell them, 'Here's where the money goes,'" says then-Provost Mark Lewandowski. "There was a lack of open disclosure and true transparency." That's a nice way to say that alums were tired of donating money, only to have it disappear into thin air. Like the nearly $9 million Richard fundraised to build a new student center that never materialized.

Things came to a head on Wednesday, November 14, 2007, a month after Richard and Lindsay's *Larry King* appearance. Oral summoned the tenured faculty for a three-hour meeting. He said he was there to listen, asking them to speak freely and openly. And yet he'd brought Richard along. One by one, speaking directly to Richard, the professors rattled off their complaints.

"You are my friend and my brother in Christ, but it is time for you to go," Provost Mark Lewandowski told Richard. "I cannot continue to serve under you." It was a major act of defiance, coming from Lewandowski, an ORU loyalist and the son of two ORU professors.

Richard pleaded with them to stay, at least for a few more years. He explained his ministry would be under a cloud if he were to be ousted, remembers the faculty member. Lindsay had resigned from the board of regents and, he promised, would no longer involve herself in university affairs.

"My house has been out of order," Richard confessed, according to the faculty member.

Oral doubled down: If Richard left, he'd walk away with him—arm in arm with his anointed son. Oral called on the faculty to forgive Richard, to take a "fresh start." He was 89-years-old at this point. His hearing was going, and he needed a walker. But ever the benevolent dictator, Oral demanded obedience. He asked everyone who agreed with him to stand—an old power play from his repertoire. One professor stood and bravely ventured, "I don't know what you mean by 'fresh start.' I can forgive Richard. But I am not going to allow him to come back as president."

One by one, Oral started grilling the few professors who remained seated. Suddenly, he stopped.

"No, I shouldn't do this. I'm sorry," he said, dropping his head in his big, wrinkled hands.

• • •

Richard and Roberta, the two youngest Roberts children, are the only surviving siblings of the four. They weren't exactly on speaking terms in 2009 when it came time for Oral's "homecoming," as he called it, but they headed to the hospital together. Approaching his room, Roberta and Richard heard Oral singing from his hospital bed. He was making his way down the list of hits from his old television shows: "God Is a Good God," "Something Good Is Going to Happen to You," "Expect a Miracle." The two siblings joined in.

Richard knew all the words, of course. Those were the tracks off his 1968 debut album, *My Father's Favorite Songs*. Roberta mixed up some of the verses, and Oral, on his deathbed with pneumonia, cut in to correct her—multiple times.

In an interview with KTUL, Richard said that Mart Green, the Hobby Lobby heir who bailed out ORU, "asked me not to come back on campus" after his 2007 ouster. The next time he set foot on ORU's campus was for his father's funeral on December 21, 2009. Richard and Roberta both delivered eulogies. Roberta was terrified of speaking before the crowd in the Mabee Center, the school's main arena. ("I was about to throw up.") Richard—it has to be said—looked a little pleased to be back on stage. He even got to sing a song.

All of the luminaries of the Pentecostal world came to mark the death of the patriarch. Hardly any of them were invited to Oral's graveside service. Richard was meting out punishment for disloyalty—for not standing by him unconditionally as ORU president, says a former regent.

"That was his first chance to be absolutely in charge again," says the regent, "with no one but him calling the shots and commanding the stage since his shameful demotion."

For one day and one day only, Richard ruled supreme.

• • •

Roberta was a lonely child. Left with family friends when Oral and Evelyn were off traveling the world, she found companionship in Jesus and became the strictest Pentecostal in the family. Richard and Oral, meanwhile, were golf buddies.

Roberta and Richard have always been at odds. "When we were little, we'd get our allowance and his would be spent within half an hour," Roberta remembers. She was the kind of careful child who saved and budgeted. Richard would come to her, wanting to borrow her allowance. She'd comply. "You think I ever got paid back? No!" she says, with mock exasperation. "That's the story of his life."

As adults, even when both siblings and their families lived in the compound, the two pretty much only saw one another at holidays, remembers Roberta's son Randy. These days, their contact is even more limited. Roberta sent Richard flowers one Easter; the following December, he dropped a birthday card off at her house, leaving the bright pink envelope for her to find in a flowerpot.

• • •

On the day Roberta shows me around ORU's campus, she seems nervous and has brought a typed list of stories she wants to tell. It is in many ways a list of firsts: the first time her father took the family to see the empty farmland where he planned to build a university; the dorm where she first lived as an ORU student; the first time she saw the man she would marry ("Almost exactly 42 years ago!"). "First kiss" is number nine on the list.

"Isn't that the neatest?" Roberta asks, pointing out each attraction. Her voice is chipper, but she is clearly pained. Her thin, pink lips are drawn tight. She walks much too quickly, which is not an easy thing to do in heels. A slim woman in her 60s with white hair in a pixie cut, Roberta wears a navy ankle-length polka-dot dress with padded shoulders.

"Dad did not really function as a father, at least not toward me—actually until perhaps a year or so before his passing," she writes in her memoir, *My Dad, Oral Roberts*. Before that, she'd been on the outs with Oral for nearly two decades. It was only after the patriarch's death that Roberta became an ORU trustee.

When we enter Christ's Chapel, a soaring sanctuary filled with light, a calm comes over Roberta. She surveys the stage and the roving TV camera boom. She admires the parquet floors, the plush of the seats. Roberta is unabashed in her love, filled with the wonder of her father's creation.

Roberta faces the writing along the back wall. "'Raise up your students to hear my voice. To go where my light is dim,'" she reads aloud. Smiling, she turns her back to the inscription and begins to recite from memory. "Their work will exceed yours, and in this I am well pleased,'" she says. "That's what Dad heard from God."

Later, we wander the halls of the Mabee Center, a rotund, flat-topped building trimmed with gold. An elderly security guard pushes aside his lunch when Roberta asks if he'd mind letting us into the television studios.

"Mrs. Potts," says the guard, "you can get into anything you want."

She laughs. "You shouldn't give me anything I wanted, because I might ask for something I shouldn't."

"I doubt that very seriously. I knew your momma too well," the guard replies. "You had two of the nicest young boys," he adds suddenly. "They always said, 'We're the Potts boys. Can we go into the basketball game? We're Potts children, can we please use the phone?'"

"I trained them well," she says.

We enter the cavernous television studio. The lights are off. We stand in silence, looking into the darkness.

Heading back into the sunshine, Roberta calls out to the guard, "Thank you for your kind comments about my sons. Some day they're going to come back to the Lord." A cure for what she calls their "lifestyle"—that's the miracle she's expecting.

• • •

"How can I say that there were no excesses, when there were?" Roberta writes of Richard's tenure as ORU president. She says she never learned what exactly was true among the allegations against Richard.

"Did you ever learn specifically that any of them were false? Or blown out of proportion?" I ask. "Um, I guess not. I can't think of anything," she stammers. She pushes all that out of her mind.

As it turns out, donors to Oral Roberts Evangelistic Association do, too. In 2010, the ministry's revenue was nearly $13 million, and Richard and Lindsay paid themselves a combined salary of over $800,000, according to tax filings.

In 2010, the ministry also filed an amended tax return for 2006, saying an internal review of "travel and other expenses" found that $100,602 had been incorrectly billed to the ministry—when really it should've been taxed as executive compensation. In other words, it seemed Richard and Lindsay had put their leisure pursuits on the ministry's tab.

"Dear friend," Richard wrote in a recent letter to potential donors. Out of work? In debt? "Perhaps you feel like you can't sow anything anywhere because your financial situation isn't good right now." Yet, Richard continued, "Nothing could be further from the truth."

Meanwhile, ORU had a succession of presidents outside the Roberts family: A protégé of Oral's, Billy Joe Daugherty, stepped in briefly. Daugherty, the founder of a 17,000-person mega-church across the street from ORU, is said to be the son Oral wished he'd had.[2] Then there was Mark Rutland, followed by the current president, William Wilson.

Having bailed out ORU, the Oklahoma City-based Green family mostly stayed out of the spotlight. Soft-spoken, bespectacled Mart Green, successor to Hobby Lobby CEO David Green (net worth: $5.2 billion), served as chairman of ORU's board. The Green's donations to ORU now total over $200 million, according to Roberta Roberts Potts.

ORU is finally out of debt. The professors' wrongful termination lawsuits were settled out of court long ago.[3] It is Hobby Lobby—not ORU—making national headlines these days: In June, the Supreme Court ruled in Hobby Lobby's favor, granting a religious exemption to the Affordable Care Act's employer mandate for covering birth control.

• • •

Richard's toppling from the ORU throne was not the most noble of exits. And yet, afterward, he seemed relieved, like a burden was lifted, says former Oral Roberts Ministries employee Ryan Rhoades. Facial hair was forbidden under the university's strict anti-hippie dress code. But after Richard and his ministry were expelled from campus, the staff relaxed and grew out beards. Even Richard. Settling into their new offices across town, Richard introduced a four-day workweek. He joked around, carefree at last.

Roberta sometimes catches her brother and sister-in-law on *The Place for Miracles*, Richard and Lindsay's daily half-hour television program. Oral looms large on the show—my dad this, and your dad that. Richard sings, as always, although his voice is getting a little flat with age.

In late January 2012, an Oklahoma highway patrolman clocked Richard's black Mercedes going 93 miles per hour along the Creek Turnpike, a tollway just south of ORU. A blast of alcohol fumes greeted the highway patrolman when he leaned into the car. Richard failed the first sobriety test, then a second. Richard's DUI mugshot showed an old man wearing a pink shirt and a black jacket, his face bloated and splotchy, his hair white and thinning. It was shortly after midnight of what would have been Oral's 94th birthday.

Later that year, Richard and Lindsay's house, a cobbled mansion in a gated community a few miles south of ORU, went up for sale for $2.15 million. Soon, there were reports that Richard and Lindsay had decamped for Oral's condo in Newport Beach. In December 2013, the building in Tulsa where Richard taped his TV show went up for sale. The show goes on—but broadcasting, it seems, from California. Richard still travels a bit, speaking and holding "miracle healing services" at churches and hotels around the country and, occasionally, overseas. Sometimes, his daughters join him on stage.

In Richard's absence, ORU finally built the student center he had long promised but failed to deliver. It was ORU's first new building in over 30 years. Designed in a nondescript institutional style, nothing is gold about it. Plans are underway to refurbish the ORU-owned CitiPlex Towers (formerly the City of Faith), swapping the gold-tinted windows for blue. The gilded age is over. The time of Technicolor dreams has given way to more modest aspirations: to be, simply, a normal Christian school.

As this past school year came to a close, Mart Green announced the day had come for him to step down as chairman of ORU's board. He'll stay on as a trustee. The school thanked him with a statue in his honor.

The main entrance to ORU is named Billy Joe Daugherty Drive. It is a stately roundabout, lined with the flags of the world. The iconic bronze, 60-foot-tall Praying Hands sculpture sits in the middle—Oral's healing touch immortalized. There is no Richard Roberts Road, or much of anything else to indicate he was ever there at all.

---

2 In the years leading up to the patriarch's death, Carlton Pearson, Oral's "black son," fell from grace in the Pentecostal world after he stopped believing in hell. Carlton and Oral eventually reconciled—albeit on a personal level, not theologically. Pearson's biopic *Come Sunday* is in the works, and Robert Redford is in talks to play Oral in the film.

3 Much was made of Lindsay's alleged relationships with unnamed "underage males" when the lawsuits hit ORU in 2007. In the years since, Matt Schwoegler, the one-time boyfriend of the youngest Roberts daughter, acknowledged that most of the allegations probably referred to him: the hundreds of late night text messages Lindsay sent teen boys; the nine nights Lindsay and a boy spent in the compound's guest house; the times Lindsay installed a teen boy in her home, leading the Roberts daughters to put deadbolts on their bedroom doors. (Schwoegler has since racked up several criminal convictions, including credit card fraud, forgery, evading arrest, and possession of burglary tools.) Lindsay maintained she "never, ever engaged in any sexual behavior with any man outside of my marriage as the accusations imply." Through the Roberts' attorney, Schwoegler released statements attesting Lindsay had served as a "second mother" and "best friend" to the teen.

"Do I think she slept with him? No, I don't," says a relative. "Do I think he replaced Richard Oral? In many wrong ways for her, yeah." Lindsay couldn't save her own son, long-ago deceased in infancy, but perhaps she found another lost cause and wanted a second chance.

Originally published
July 2015

by Mike Mariani

VIDEO KILLED THE PULPIT STAR

Multimedia multisites like Lifechurch.tv are replacing the old-world magic of the American pastor

A young guy wearing a cobalt blue hoodie and shiny leather jacket has just robbed a woman's purse. Rummaging through his quarry, the thief, all sinister swagger and furtive glances, passes by one of those fortune-telling machines with the wood finish and flashing white lights dancing across a litany of potential fates. He greedily pulls a coin out of the stolen purse and plays the game. The larcenist lands on "Death."

So begins the first episode of LifeChurch.tv's new series, *I Deserve It.* After this cinematic prologue, the video cuts back to Pastor Craig Groeschel at one of LifeChurch.tv's campuses, who proudly declares this to be the church's 19th Easter service. He's using this Easter sermon to launch the *I Deserve It* message series, and soon weaves the hooded thief and the fortune-telling machine into a larger discussion about Christ, the crucifixion, diverging fates at Golgotha, repentance, and humility. On Easter Sunday, the video of Groeschel›s sermon was streamed to all of LifeChurch.tv's 23 satellite "campuses" across the country, in keeping with the church›s highly popular but occasionally maligned multisite model. Publications like *Christianity Today* and countless Christian blogs at times deride multisites for what they perceive as a kind of "selling out"—an act of franchising and branding that runs counter to authentic, immemorial faith and evangelism.

Watching Groeschel's sermon on video, you can more or less see why LifeChurch.tv has used technology to push past the boundaries of traditional services and beam Groeschel into each of its campuses and homes across the country and beyond. He's confident and dynamic, with an athletic build fastidiously preserved from his days on scholarship for tennis at Oklahoma City University; outgoing; articulate without being didactic; and just the right amount of goofy. Two things really give this particular sermon its punch. When Groeschel tells the story of Jesus and the two thieves with whom he shared his pitiless fate, drying out on a cross under a scorching sun and the pecking beaks of scavenging crows, he sprinkles in autobiographical details about his own checkered past. He, too, was a thief, a petty larcenist in his prodigal college days, and sees himself—or his two potential fates—in the two men who died alongside Christ. Groeschel makes the gospel resonant, not through abstract sermonizing, but by laying bare the details of his own life. He also does the one thing all successful, riveting pastors do: he gives the Bible passages immediacy, as if the clouded, abstruse path to personal revelation most of us face while reading the Bible were blasted right open for him; the correspondence perfectly translucent. Groeschel's insight during the Easter Sunday sermon is that each person in his multifarious audience is one of the two thieves suffering next to Jesus: either giving up his repentance or smugly hiding it.

• • •

In 1996, Groeschel began what was then known as Life Covenant Church in the humble setting of many American origin stories: an old garage. Craig and his wife's friends let them use their spacious doublewide, which they had converted into a makeshift auditorium. In an act of shoestring prestidigitation, Craig insisted that they put a massive mirror on the back wall to create the illusion of a larger audience at those early homespun services.

In the next few years, Groeschel's congregation expanded rapidly, leading him to open Life Covenant Church's first facility in Oklahoma City. In 2001, Groeschel was approached by the Edmond-based MetroChurch, which suggested that the two congregations merge. Their name now changed to LifeChurch.tv, Groeschel's garage prayer group was now a "multisite" church—technically just a self-evident description of a congregation that meets at multiple locations, but for some a crossing of the Rubicon that symbolizes a church's unholy relationship with consumerism and corporatization. The online journal *9Marks* has been particularly outspoken in its criticisms, asserting, among other critiques, that multisites have no biblical precedent, violate the tenet of a single assembly, and suffer from the paradoxical misnomer of being one church with multiple congregations.

For a time Groeschel would drive between campuses, delivering his sermons throughout Oklahoma. But in 2001, when his wife was in labor, Groeschel knew he wasn't going to make it to both weekend sermons. So his LifeChurch team decided to videotape his sermon and show it at that Sunday's service. "The response was fairly unremarkable," Pastor and Innovation Leader Bobby Gruenewald told *Metroland* in

2009. Which is to say, it was successful; according to Gruenewald, little, if anything, was lost in digital translation. They had somewhat haphazardly discovered a novel way to harness the charisma of a single pastor within a multisite church. They continued using videotaped sermons by Groeschel at LifeChurch.tv's satellite campuses, and it did nothing to stifle their growth. Even during the early years as a multisite, many of the churchgoers in Oklahoma City and Tulsa never meet Groeschel in person. Their only exposure to the church's head pastor was through his video teachings, and for them that was enough. Groeschel and his team followed up those satellite campuses with church plantings in Stillwater, another in Oklahoma City, and then two in Arizona.

Meanwhile, LifeChurch.tv was burgeoning online in, arguably, even more impressive ways. Thousands were streaming Groeschel's services from all over the world. LifeChurch.tv launched a new "campus" on Second Life, the virtual community of avatars that thrived in the mid-2000s (you can take a virtual tour of LifeChurch's Second Life campus on its YouTube channel). In 2008, LifeChurch.tv had perhaps its most significant technological breakthrough. Gruenewald, the tech-savvy member of Groeschel's leadership circle, debuted YouVersion, Apple's first Bible app. Despite early pushback from Bible publishers over licensing, the app became a phenomenal success. Transcendent, really: as of March 2015, YouVersion has been downloaded nearly 175 million times, in over 700 languages. The app is completely free and is part of a larger host of "digital missions" that includes a second Bible app for kids, free access to online sermons, and resources for other pastors and ministries, or what LifeChurch.tv calls investing in "the capital 'C' Church." The *I Deserve It* series that debuted on Easter Sunday is an example of these online sermons; previous series include *Chasing Light* and *God Never Said That*, the latter of which features Groeschel dispelling comfort maxims mistakenly attributed to God. One apocrypha Groeschel debunks is that "God won't give you more than you can handle," which seems to be a blunter version of a more lyrical aphorism—"If God brings you to it, he'll bring you through it"—splashed over social media.

Even if it sometimes feels like LifeChurch.tv is not as hip as it would like to think, their slow-grow online empire of sermons, apps, and religious communities is one of the more successful innovations to come out of American evangelism in years. Christianity, and religion in general, continues to decline in the U.S.: a 2012 Pew Research poll found a third of adults under 30 have no religious affiliation, compared to 10 percent of Americans 65 and up. LifeChurch.tv manages to thrive in this increasingly unaffiliated landscape because it makes itself far more accessible to young people in the wired places where they spend so much time.

But LifeChurch.tv is most conspicuous as an emerging paradigm, both to be envied and looked upon with wariness, in the multisite-church movement. No longer just videotaping services on a Saturday and playing them on Sunday, Groeschel's sermons air live via satellite at all of LifeChurch.tv's campuses. As Kevin Henry, operational leader, says in one of LifeChurch.tv's YouTube videos, "It wasn't this idea as to, gee, 'a multisite sounds neat let's do that.' It was born out of constraint." LifeChurch.tv was growing so fast in the early 2000s that they simply couldn't fit everyone in their Oklahoma City facility, forcing them to temporarily hold services in a movie theater before eventually merging with MetroChurch and officially going multisite. Now with 23 campuses and counting, LifeChurch.tv seems intent on taking the satellite sermon as far as it can go.

But some of the deficiencies of having sermons led by a television screen seem inescapable. Congregants lose the immediacy of standing a few feet from their pastor, waiting with bated breath for that paroxysm of spiritual insight that might shoot from him to them like a bolt of lightning. Can we really imagine the Azusa Street Revival, the tidal of glossolalia, and the birth of Pentecostalism brought on by video sermons? What about laying hands on the sick, handling serpents, administering water baptisms? The great irony of video sermons is that, in an effort to spread the magnetism and charisma of a single gifted pastor, churches are sacrificing the spontaneity inherent in the house of worship itself, its potential for charisma and collective electricity and the inexplicable currents of faith and abandon running between a pastor and his ardent followers.

In what's now known as the Toronto Blessing of 1994, a small church near Toronto Pearson International Airport housed hundreds of followers, night after night, as they reported healings, were slain in the spirit,[1] roared like wild animals, and fell into fits of uncontrollable holy laughter. That's the stuff of physical connection, unscripted and visceral like a sucker

1 A term describing followers collapsing onto the ground after the Holy Spirit passes through or anoints them. The swoon is often followed by ecstatic convulsions and/or blackouts.

punch or a crying jag. It was surely a manic, unsettling spectacle, but as Dr. James Beverley told *Christianity Today* on the 20th anniversary last year, "There is no doubt that the vast majority of people [at the Toronto Blessing] have been helped, and there have been radical conversion experiences and radical renewal in many lives." It's one thing to lead a church, sustain a following, hold weekend services. It's quite another to capture the spirit of revivalism, to watch people dry-heaving Satan and laughing in silly spells of ecstasy and crumbling onto the floor like God's marionettes. A revival like that sucks out time; the faithful suddenly look and act no differently than their 19th-century counterparts. It's possible that the multisite model, bolstered by satellite sermons, will lose those coveted moments when the church is descended upon by the quicksilver spirit of revivalism, and the Holy Spirit rolls through like a wave swollen with storm, smacking a whole congregation into religious ecstasy.

In a 2008 article for *Outreach* magazine, "Questions for McChurch," Ed Stetzer wondered how multisites would be able to reproduce new leaders if so many are "relegated to hitting the play button." How is church leadership being cultivated when a single preacher conducts all the services, delivers all the messages? LifeChurch.tv certainly has other pastors, but it's Groeschel's likeness that graces the massive screens via satellite approximately 19 minutes into each service. Although there's a pastor on each campus—known (with unintended derision?) as "the face with the place"—he is more caretaker than architect, shepherding parishioners through each stage of worship services and ushering them into the satellite "experience." These LifeChurch.tv pastors, whose other primary responsibility is establishing relationships with their congregants and building each campus's parish, are far removed from the traditional ideas of priesthood. They are no longer principally focused on performing Christianity's rites—Eucharist, Baptism, Confession, and the rest of the holy sacraments. The multisites have drifted from the traditional, once-inviolable notion that a priest's chief role is to perform the Christian liturgy, to ensure that its rituals are flawlessly reproduced in his church. Part of this is simply a consequence of Protestantism, with its shift from ritualistic services to an increased focus on sermons. But the absent, or at least drastically reduced, physical presence of the ministry at LifeChurch.tv's campuses further diminishes the priest in contemporary churches.

In a country with more than twice as many Protestants as Catholics, and an increasingly perilous shortage of Catholic priests, the obsolescence of the priesthood has long been in the offing. Priests are vicars, representatives of higher Catholic authority that traces all the way back to Rome. From Southern Baptists to Lutherans to the Assemblies of God to nondenominational churches, America has long been championing the evangelical pastor over the punctilious priest. The impassioned, raving preacher, beholden to no one but God and his audience, is pure Americana, canonized not in Rome but in the wooden pews of Kentucky, Arkansas, Texas, and Oklahoma.

The problem is, multisites like LifeChurch.tv might be deadly to both Catholic priest and American pastor. LifeChurch.tv's leadership structure, which includes Senior Pastor Craig Groeschel and his four-person leadership team—Operations Leader Kevin Henry, Innovation Leader Bobby Gruenewald, Team Development Leader Jerry Hurley, and Sam Roberts, head of campus operations—functions as much like a business as it does a church. These men are responsible for elaborate logistics, campus operations, human resources, and technological innovations. With each LifeChurch.tv "experience" micromanaged practically down to the second, the church feels as much like a prominent tech company preserving the sanctity of its latest gleaming device as it does a Protestant church espousing the virtues of evangelicalism and salvation through Christ. Ten minutes before each service, the slick LifeChurch.tv logo appears on the video screen, accompanied by a countdown clock. When the service begins, it's meticulously choreographed, with worship songs and brief notes from the campus pastor flowing into the main event—Groeschel's sermon, flashed in from Edmond.

Congregants might get the very best of Groeschel, a talented minister, but the chances of the next Great Awakening taking place in front of celluloid are slim. The dramatic irony of LifeChurch.tv—it's easy to see from the fringes of spectatorship, but probably impossible from the inside—is that by consolidating and innovating the multisite model through satellite services, they are not only spreading the evangelism of one pastor but draining it from the church itself—that humble vessel ever-ready for the capricious whims of the Holy Spirit.

Originally published
May 2012

by Kiera Feldman

GRACE IN BROKEN ARROW

A cautionary tale of what happens when power goes unchecked and a pedophile infiltrates a private Christian school

Many are the afflictions of the righteous, but the Lord delivereth him out of them all. —Psalm 34

No more sleepovers. No more babysitting, or car rides home. No more being alone with children or "lingering hugs given to students (especially using your hands to stroke or fondle)." Aaron Thompson—Coach Thompson to his PE students—sat in the principal's office at Grace Fellowship Christian School as his bosses went through the four-page Corrective Action Plan point by point. It was October of 2001, the same month Aaron added "Teacher of the Week" to his résumé.

Grace's leader, Bob Yandian—"Pastor Bob" as everyone calls him—wasn't there: no need, he had people for this kind of thing. Pastor Bob's time was better spent sequestered in his study, writing books and radio broadcasts. His lieutenant, Associate Pastor Chip Olin, was a hardnosed guy, "ornery as heck," people said. Olin brought a *USA Today* article on the characteristics of child molesters to the meeting. At age 24, Olin explained, Aaron was acting immature and unprofessional, and someone might get the wrong idea.

The first two recommendations of what became known as the "do not fondle" agreement were prayer and "building relationships with young men and women of your age group in Sunday School and Singles group activities" at Grace Church, which ran the school. "Leaders in the kingdom are judged not so much by what they accomplish as by the character they reveal—who they *are* before what they *do*," the document continued. Aaron was to "live a lifestyle above reproach"—to act such that no one would question his character.

Associate Pastor Olin let head administrator John Dunlavey, Aaron's other boss, do much of the talking. Olin had only just read the Corrective Action Plan for the first time as he walked down the hall en route to the meeting. He was mostly there as an observer. It was Dunlavey's brainchild, after all.

Dunlavey didn't mean *that* kind of "fondle." He'd tacked it on, thinking it best described the overly affectionate hug-plus-hand-stroking he'd seen Aaron give a boy one day at lunch. With his big, square glasses and brow that furrowed in concentration, Dunlavey was more the earnest science teacher he once was than the administrator he'd become. He'd looked up "fondle" in the dictionary, and it seemed the most precise. Science guys love precision.

Dunlavey didn't think babysitting and all the rest were problems, just symptoms: Aaron had become too close to Grace families. Misplaced loyalties. That was the real issue.

Young boys were leaving Grace over the past few years, and no one knew why. One boy moved a full 1,200 miles away. He still skateboarded with friends and did normal kid stuff, but he was having horrible nightmares and failing classes, unable to contain his inexplicable fury at teachers. At one point, he told his mother he couldn't stand how he felt and no longer wished to live. But Grace's leaders would not know or would not admit such things about their flock until much later.

Grace Church sits atop a hill just south of Tulsa, off a two-lane country road with a speed limit of 50. The boxy, tan bunker of a building has flagpoles at the entrance, making the church look like a fortified post office. Eighty acres of grassy fields spread out below. Houses in the area range from spacious to McMansion, and new developments get names like Ridgewood or Shannondale. In the incorporated suburb known as Broken Arrow, Oklahoma, the ratio of car dealerships to churches is about 1:1. The nearest strip mall to Grace has a drive-thru Starbucks, a Wal-Mart, and a fast food chicken restaurant that pipes soft Christian rock over speakers into the parking lot. Such is the way of Tulsa geography: blacks to the north, Latinos and Asians to the east, miscellany in midtown, and evangelicals and big box stores in the south.

Fall of 2001 was the grand opening for Grace's new children's building, a real beauty, the pride and joy of the whole church. "Grace is the place for kids" was the church's slogan back then. The new, 56,000-square-foot building had two stories of classrooms, plus amenities like a Chuck-E-Cheese-style room with tubing and a ball pit, "Bob and Loretta's Soda Shoppe" (an old-fashioned ice cream parlor named after Pastor Bob and his wife), and the crowning glory: an antique carousel beneath a vaulted glass pyramidal ceiling. Bejeweled with big amusement park light bulbs, the carousel's gold and aqua paneling positively glowed: $125,000 well spent. Grace took out a $7.5 million loan to finance construction of the children's building, and when all was said and done, the whole thing was worth nearly $10 million—over half the value of all their buildings combined. In time, a new auditorium would be built, too, which would connect the children's building to Grace's main wing.

They'd begun a fundraising campaign back in 1998: "Investing in Eternity." That was the year Pastor Bob published his book *Righteousness: God's Gift to You*. "You don't need to crawl on your knees or do any 'good works' to try to earn God's approval," Pastor Bob promised.

Aaron Thompson was the teacher all the girls had crushes on and all the boys idolized. The younger kids mobbed him around campus and clamored for hugs. His smile was radiant, his Believer's pedigree sterling. Aaron had grown up at Grace Church. In high school, he was senior class president and a star basketball player, before heading to nearby Oral Roberts University. Parents frequently had Aaron over for dinner, asked him to babysit, or hoped he could stay with the kids for a week while they went on vacation. Aaron fielded invites for family outings big and small, from camping trips to ice cream at Braum's after church. Parents were delighted to have a young man like Aaron in their children's lives. He was the golden boy of Grace Church.

And yet, in August of 2001, prior to the signing of the "do not fondle" agreement, Grace received an unsigned letter. It read:

> This is a matter of life or death for a child or children. People have been known to commit suicide for this very reason ... Everything you need to know will be revealed if you will monitor the boy's locker room and private hallways or areas when no one is around, especially before and after the PE classes. Watch your staff when they are alone with young boys, even for two minutes. Ask yourself, "Why have certain boys left Grace?" and "Why are some boys tardy often?"

Olin didn't think the letter was about Aaron to begin with; Dunlavey came to agree as the meeting with Aaron wore on. Yet still, Dunlavey thought, perhaps Aaron's behavior was being misconstrued somehow, and so he read the letter aloud.

"Aaron, is this you?" Dunlavey asked. "Are you doing anything that might cause somebody to write this kind of a letter?" Aaron assured them he was doing no wrong. He was repentant, open to correction. Olin had high hopes for Aaron. Everyone did. For the remainder of the school year, Aaron was on probation. Violation of the agreement would mean termination. Olin, Dunlavey, and Pastor Bob would discuss Aaron's progress during their weekly meetings.

Aaron left Grace and headed to Cheddar's, a nearby restaurant, to meet with the teachers on his unit. They were the Specials Teachers, the "Special Ts," they called themselves, a tight-knit crew that taught subjects like PE, music, and Spanish—all women except for Aaron. Aaron plopped down in the booth, late and very upset. "What's wrong?" asked Laura Prochaska, the computers teacher. "We're your sisters. Talk to us."

Aaron swore them to secrecy, then confided that Grace had made him sign papers saying he could never take kids to the movies or babysit or hug them. "I can't be their big brother," he lamented.

"Just don't do anything questionable that they could get you for," Prochaska advised. "They must not think it's such a big deal, but they want to protect themselves by having you sign this contract."

"Maybe you should think about quitting," another teacher added, encouraging him to take the protest route.

"No, no. I'm not a quitter," Aaron told them. "I'm going to see this through."

The "Special Ts" didn't know he'd already been molesting children at Grace for years. From that day in October until his arrest on March 25, 2002, Aaron Thompson would sexually abuse four more boys. One of them was the son of a teacher sitting there in the restaurant booth.

• • •

This is a cautionary tale. It is about deference to authority, and denial, and the human cost of privileging an institution above people. According to Oklahoma law, anyone having "reason to believe" that a child is potentially being abused must make a report to the Department of Human Services or the police. Child abuse experts urge us to follow the law and not take it upon ourselves to evaluate or investigate allegations or suspicions of abuse. But that is exactly what Grace did. And they reaped what they sowed.

Grace Church was Oklahoma's Penn State of 2002. After such things come to light, we always wonder: how on earth did that ever happen?

Here is how it happened.

The public record is suspect when it comes to what was going on behind the scenes at Grace before Aaron's arrest. For starters, don't trust what I just told you about the signing of the "do not fondle" agreement on that day in October 2001. All that was reconstructed from the testimonies and depositions that head administrator John Dunlavey, Associate Pastor Chip Olin, Principal DeeAnn McKay, and Pastor Bob later gave during the negligence lawsuits in which Grace became mired. The only problem is that what they said under oath doesn't square with the recollections of two teachers who were sitting in the restaurant booth with Aaron immediately after he signed the agreement.

During the lawsuits, everyone at Grace said the Corrective Action Plan was Dunlavey's idea—they simply followed his lead. (Pastor Bob said he green lighted Dunlavey's idea in advance, got the executive summary of Dunlavey's text afterward from Olin verbally, and only read the actual document in the wake of Aaron's arrest.) And yet, Laura Prochaska and another Specials Teacher who spoke on condition of anonymity distinctly remembered Aaron telling the group, "Chip [Olin] made me sign this thing."

The second teacher had been a member of Grace Church for decades. "Knowing all the personalities as well as I do, John [Dunlavey] would not have come up with something like that. That was a Chip thing," she assured me. "If [Dunlavey] had had to write an agreement, it would've been dictated to him by Chip Olin," she added. "They liked puppets around there."

The Corrective Action Plan was just one plot point in the whole story. Who knows what else didn't quite happen as Grace said it happened? Conveniently, Grace's version of the story protects the man at the top.

Pastor Bob has long been a pillar of the national charismatic Pentecostal community. Colleagues describe him as "a pastor's pastor," a wingman for the megachurch pastors. Decades ago, Pastor Bob was Dean of Instructors at Rhema Bible Training Center while founder Kenneth Hagin Sr. pioneered the hugely influential Word of Faith movement, which teaches that the Lord blesses the faithful with healing and financial rewards (provided they tithe). Today Pastor Bob is a board member of Joyce Meyer Ministries, which brings in about $100 million in donations annually, affording Meyer the luxury of traveling by private jet.

At Grace, the stage is dark and bathed in soft pastel lights when the 11-member worship band leads the congregation in the gentle murmuring called talking in tongues, but when Pastor Bob takes to the pulpit, on come the harsh fluorescents: it's business time. Pastor Bob, ruddy faced and paunchy, preaches the prosperity gospel of health and wealth. His eyes narrow as his nasally voice rises. He even incorporates his love of fancy cars into sermons. He has owned several over the years, including a pair of his-and-hers BMWs: Pastor Bob bought his wife's Beamer, and Grace bought his. Pastor Bob is known for his "practical wisdom."

The first lawsuit, John Does 1–7 versus Grace, went to trial in September 2004.

"I don't really make 'Chip' decisions," Associate Pastor Chip Olin testified. "I'm an extension of Pastor Bob."

• • •

Maybe it began with the tittytwisters. Or the tousled hair, the hugs, the body slams.

"Older brother-type stuff," Josh[1] remembers. "He would slowly desensitize you."

Josh was Aaron's first victim, although of course he didn't know it back in 1996. Aaron would ask him to stay after gym class to help put away PE equipment.

Josh and I are sitting in a Mexican restaurant in downtown Tulsa, next to a mock-up boxing ring that has been incorporated into the décor. His bicycle is locked up outside. Josh wears a jean shirt with pearl buttons and rolled sleeves. He is quick to smile and has a little stubble, a handsome twentysomething. An autodidact since high school, Josh just sent off a round of out-of-state college applications. We compare notes on the arduous application process before hunkering down to talk about what we came here to talk about.

It was the end of fifth grade, and Josh was 11 years old. A cute, happy kid with a toothy grin and a center part in his hair, the 1990s style that made little arches on either side above the forehead. Josh's father had died a few years earlier. Now Josh wonders if it made him vulnerable, eager to latch onto a male figure, someone to connect to, hoping to please the golden boy of Grace Church.

"We had played dodgeball, and he asked me to bring in all the stuff with him," Josh begins to tell me. "When I was in the closet putting things away, he came up behind me and grabbed me and slid his hand down and touched me."

Afterward, Aaron told Josh to go to the nurse and get an Advil, a cover for being late. He spent all of the next class staring silently into space, trying to process what had happened. From there, it escalated. During Josh's fifth- and sixth-grade years, this became just about a weekly occurrence. In the supply closet by the gym, in the gym itself, in the coach's office that locked from the inside, in the boy's locker room that connected straight into the coach's office. Aaron's hand down Josh's pants, Aaron's hand putting Josh's hand down his own. Josh started to get used to it.

Josh became withdrawn, jumpy, moody. His parents didn't know what to make of his drastic personality change but assumed it was just a phase. He couldn't concentrate. That was the year he got misdiagnosed with Attention Deficit Disorder.

Like most abusers, Aaron was very skilled at coercing his victims into cooperating with their abuse. Josh felt guilty: he'd gone along with it. And Josh knew God knew.

For evangelicals, God is a personal God, there with you in every moment. Josh worried and worried: what did He think of him? It was a gut anxiety, ever-present. He hoped, desperately, that God would help him or guide him somehow. Josh did what he had been taught to do when he didn't know what to do: he prayed. He prayed constantly. But deliverance never came. He was 11, maybe 12. Josh found his mom's handgun and placed the barrel into his mouth. This way, he thought, he'd get to be with his dad again. When he finally got up the nerve to pull the trigger, nothing happened. It wasn't loaded. Josh took it as a sign. He didn't try again 'til years later.

The escalation continued. Before long, Aaron was having Josh perform oral sex on him and doing likewise to Josh. If it came out that this was going on, Josh knew he would be the talk of the school. Children are cruel, and Christian children no different. *He liked it*, they'd taunt. Walking down the hall, it felt like kids were staring at him. Surely they could tell, surely they knew that Josh had brought this on himself. Aaron had convinced Josh that *Aaron* was keeping *Josh's* secret.

Throughout it all, of course, Josh was still being asked to help put things away after gym class: he was needed and wanted and chosen. Abuse binds the abused to their abuser, power and control the engine driving all.

"He made you feel—" Josh pauses to find the word for the memory. "Special." Aaron treated him like the adult that he was not.

Sometime in seventh grade, Josh's face, neck, and back became covered with horrible, painful acne—in all likelihood a product of stress. But also puberty: it was 1998, and Josh was thirteen. The abuse tapered off.

Time passed. Josh drew into himself. Eventually, he started noticing younger boys coming out of the gym, late for their next class. Boys who seemed to have special friendships with Aaron. And that's when it hit him: there were others.

Aaron went way back with Grace's youth pastor and basketball coach, Mike Goolsbay, a big teddy bear of a man with spiky gelled hair who was always saying "bless you, kiddo" with gusto. Goolsbay had known Aaron since he was a 13-year-old in Grace's youth group. Aaron knew he could call Goolsbay late at night if he ever needed an ear, like the time his senior year of high school when he had some teenage angst to hash out, or the time in college when a girl broke his heart. Goolsbay was the one who asked Aaron to start helping out during Grace's summer camps. During the 1995–1996 school year, while Aaron was a freshman accounting student at Oral Roberts University, he volunteered as the assistant basketball coach/assistant youth pastor at Grace—Goolsbay's right-hand man.

By all accounts, the first failure to report child abuse at Grace came in early 1996, around the time Josh's molestation began. Dr. Mark Peterson and his

1. Names have been changed to protect the innocent.

wife brought Goolsbay a printout of emails Aaron had sent to their seventh-grade son, who was on Goolsbay's basketball team. One email described the son's genitalia and called him a "stud." The emails were all signed "Love, Aaron"—not, Peterson noted, "Love in Christ, Aaron." (Child abuse experts say that lewd emails constitute abuse.) Peterson insisted that the emails be made part of Aaron's permanent file. Goolsbay agreed to do so, using the exact same logic of denial and negligence that everyone at Grace would deploy in the years to come: Aaron is unprofessional, he's immature, I'll counsel him, and all will be well. (Had Goolsbay followed state law, he would have called DHS or the police.) Goolsbay says he didn't tell any of his superiors about the incident, and the emails were never found in Grace's files.

Meanwhile, Pastor Bob published *One Flesh: God's Gift of Passion—Love, Sex & Romance in Marriage.* "When you have a strong relationship with your mate's soul," the book advised, "the relationship with his or her body becomes something fantastic!"

Aaron became Grace's part-time assistant athletic director in 1997, and in late 1998, shortly before he graduated from ORU in the spring of 1999, he was hired as a fulltime PE teacher at Grace—on Goolsbay's recommendation.

After Aaron's arrest, Dr. Peterson called Goolsbay to remind him of the emails. Goolsbay was defensive, and the conversation grew heated, Peterson later testified. "CYA"—Cover Your Ass—was "the feeling I was getting," Peterson said.

• • •

Long before any sexual abuse came to light at Grace, Dr. Gene Reynolds, a Tulsa psychologist, remembered trekking out to the school on Garnett Road, asked by parents to evaluate this or that kid for issues unrelated to the abuse. He was struck that the administration and staff seemed totally unreceptive to professional recommendations.

"They had their own ideas about what needed to be done," Dr. Reynolds noted.

He ended up examining seven of the Grace boys Aaron had abused. In the boys' pre-teen and teenage years, the early effects of trauma were varied: the gamut ran from severe anger to depression, suicidal feelings and attempts, insomnia, fear of men, panic attacks, feeling like "damaged goods," shame, guilt, early sexual activity and promiscuity, incarceration, and drug abuse. "There were some boys who said they never wanted to set foot in a church again," Dr. Reynolds added.

Late effects of abuse vary individually, but the numbers are grim: victims of abuse are more likely to have trouble in school (a 50 percent chance); more likely to develop substance abuse or mental health problems (one study found 80 percent of 21-year-olds who'd been abused had one or more psychiatric disorders); and 5–8 times more likely to experience major depression in their lifetime. Both depression and substance abuse are associated with poor treatment outcomes when patients have histories of child abuse. Men who've been abused as children are 3.8 times more likely to perpetrate intimate partner violence as adults. Adults who've been abused as children are twice as likely to attempt suicide—and 12 times more likely to *commit* suicide. The sooner abuse is detected and treated, the better the child's prospects are in the long term.

The men who sexually abuse children—and they are mostly men—are often the last people on earth you'd ever imagine. About 90 percent of child sexual abusers are people the victim knows. About 30 percent of abusers are relatives—a father, older sibling, a favorite cousin or uncle, the people you trust most in this world. About 60 percent are outside the family—coaches, teachers, Scout leaders, ministers, neighbors, family friends, teenage sons of family friends: the authority figures children look up to. Abusers work their way into positions where they'll have access to children, so that they become the "not in a million years" people. This is exactly why state laws do not allow individuals or organizations to "handle" abuse complaints or suspicions on their own: these bonds of trust make it impossible to respond to potential abuse with anything but disbelief. Outside authorities, by comparison, don't have such preconceived notions.

Girls are victimized more often than boys, but boys are more likely to be victimized by a non-family member. Underreporting is common, making data hard to come by, but studies suggest 25 percent of women and 16 percent of men were sexually abused before age 18 (including peer abuse). According to the American Academy of Pediatrics, "The children most susceptible to these assaults have obedient, compliant, and respectful personalities."

At Penn State University, allegations of former assistant football coach Jerry Sandusky's sexual assault of a child traveled from graduate assistant to head coach Joe Paterno to athletic director and the university's vice president and president. Everyone, it seemed, was willing to report a coach up the chain of command and assume they'd done their due diligence.

For decades, Catholics moved their pedophile priests from one community to another, dumping them on unsuspecting parishes. The Catholic Church spent the '90s doling out cash settlements to sexual abuse victims, who were required to sign confidentiality agreements. The eruption of scandal was to be avoided at all costs. Defrocking was unheard of:

priests had repented, and that was that.

Then, a 2002 *Boston Globe* investigation blew the lid off of everything. Just as the Catholic clergy abuse scandal was breaking, Tulsa became likewise embroiled. While the Catholics shuffled their perpetrators from parish to parish, Grace harbored Aaron. In this way, the evangelicals of South Tulsa were much like the ultra-Orthodox Jews of Brooklyn, who have kept their abusers within the tight-knit community.

In the experience of Roy Van Tassell, an abuse specialist at Family and Children Services of Oklahoma, Grace was not all that unique among some kinds of religious institutions locally.

"They tend to be more autocratic, more cloistered," Tassell told me, "and there is some anecdotal evidence to say that those communities tend to be at somewhat greater risk."

"It happened because Aaron Thompson was a member of our family," the church's lawyer told the jury during the John Does 1-7 versus Grace trial. Family ties both bind and blind, the lawyer seemed to be saying—a truism that fits most all communities.

• • •

"The only assurance of our nation's safety is to lay our foundation in morality and religion [Christianity]."
—Abraham Lincoln, as quoted by the Grace elementary school handbook

At Grace Fellowship Christian School, everything from "the World"—that is, the secular world beyond South Tulsa—was suspect: Harry Potter, Tim Burton, whatever clothing happened to be in style that year. But students were led in prayer for the World: that the spiritual enemy known as Bill Clinton would be replaced with a godly leader; that Senator Jim Inhofe would be re-elected; that George Bush would lead our great Christian nation and glorify His kingdom.

Federal laws prohibit partisan political activity in churches and other tax-exempt organizations. Yet, Grace encouraged students to volunteer for Republican election campaigns, sometimes offering extra credit. One year, Grace students went on a field trip to hammer lawn signs for Representative Steve Largent, an original member of the C Street house in Washington, run by the powerful and secretive fundamentalist Christian group known as the Family (perhaps best known as the incubator for Uganda's "kill the gays" bill). Former Grace students and parishioners remembered that Largent and Senator Don Nickles, another Family member, were frequent guests at the school. Also a Family man, Inhofe has graced Grace's pulpit many times. For a number of years, Grace donated money to Christian Embassy, one of the Family's sister organizations that ministers to Washington elites. It was a Christian Embassy evangelist who led Inhofe to dedicate himself to Jesus in a congressional dining room in 1988.

In an email, the office of Winters & King, Inc., Grace's attorney, said the church "has no relationship with Steve Largent, past or present." The email continued, "Grace has no relationship with Senator Inhofe except to pray for him as mentioned in I Timothy 4:1-2"—the same answer they gave for District Attorney Tim Harris. The verse from Timothy reads, "In the latter times some shall depart from the faith, giving heed to seducing spirits, and doctrines of devils." *Stay the course*, Grace apparently prays for Christian conservative politicians.

"As we go we follow Jesus," went the Grace school song. "His Holy Spirit guides the way." The way was one of structure and discipline: wear pants the wrong color of blue, and you could end up with in-house suspension, be given a pair of headphones, and made to listen to tapes of Pastor Bob's lectures. Chewing gum as a repeat offense could mean a paddling in the principal's office; girls had to kneel in the entryway of the school to make sure their skirts touched the floor; only *one* What Would Jesus Do bracelet was allowed: excess was vanity.

At Grace, the bodies of the young were policed with the utmost of vigilance. When a ninth-grade girl kissed a seventh-grade boy on the cheek, he was suspended and banned from sports tryouts. Shaming was a teaching tool. When a 15-year-old girl got pregnant, her expulsion was announced to the whole school in chapel, with her younger sister sitting there in the pews. The infractions of children—major, minor, and everything in between—were punished swiftly and severely.

"It was definitely a dictatorship," remembered one Grace teacher who was a church member for over 30 years.

• • •

Grace had an application for volunteers to fill out, with a part that asked if they'd experienced sexual abuse as a child. An affirmative answer rendered a volunteer ineligible to work with children. Way back in 1995, Aaron answered "no." But one day toward the end of the summer of 2000 or 2001—Goolsbay couldn't remember which year—on a long car ride to a campground in Tahlequah where Grace held summer camp, Aaron confided in him. The real answer was "yes." Teenagers molested him when he was four. (Aaron later testified that he was molested again at age 16 by a youth pastor at a different church.)

The two talked the entire car ride, over an hour and a half. Goolsbay was relieved when Aaron told him

that his parents had found out about the abuse sometime in middle school—it hadn't remained a festering secret. But, at the same time, Goolsbay understood that victimization could be a cycle.

"Aaron, do you struggle with this in your life?" he asked. "Is this ever something that you've duplicated or acted out on?" Perhaps Goolsbay should have had thoughts along these lines back in 1996, when Aaron sent lewd emails to a seventh-grade boy.

"No, no, I would never, ever do that to a child," Aaron assured him.

Goolsbay thought about Aaron teaching every single child at Grace, preschool through eighth grade, including his own children.

"Are my kids safe, as well as every other kid safe?" Goolsbay wondered to himself.

"I felt like he gave me that assurance," Goolsbay later testified. He told Aaron he was there for him if he ever needed to talk. Goolsbay says he didn't bring up the lewd emails to the Peterson boy, and he didn't think to recommend professional help. After that, whenever they'd see each other around Grace, which was just about every day, Goolsbay would put his arm around him and ask, "How is your heart?"

Around this period, Aaron, as a counselor, molested two Grace students at Camp Dry Gulch, where many Grace kids went.

Despite Aaron's own history as a victim of sexual abuse, Grace continued to let Aaron work with children. Goolsbay claimed he never reported that conversation up the chain of command. Grace purged Aaron's volunteer file in 2001.

In 1998, Laura Prochaska became the computers teacher at Grace. She started noticing that certain boys used to arrive late. Again and again and again, the same boys. She'd ask them where they were, and they'd answer that they had been helping Coach Thompson put away equipment after PE—or at the nurse's office. Then they would sit the entire period, staring blankly at their computer screens without even turning the monitor on. After class, she'd pull them aside.

"What's wrong?" she'd ask them. "Are your mommy and daddy having trouble at home?" To no avail.

Prochaska went to Mary Ellen Hood, the elementary principal at the time. Hood was gung-ho about Christian education as a calling; Grace was her life. She wore a blue blazer emblazoned with the school crest.

"I said, 'I've got some kids who are coming late, they're sullen. I try to talk to them after class, they just stare down at the floor and don't say anything except, 'I'm OK, I'm OK,' " Prochaska remembered telling Hood. (When I called Hood in March 2012 and read her this quote, Hood paused a full five seconds, cleared her throat, thanked me with a "bye now," and hung up.)

At the time, Prochaska said, Hood apparently never followed up. This was all happening while rumors were circulating—malicious rumors, or so it seemed at the time, that Aaron was molesting boys. Without any formal complaints, Prochaska and the other teachers dismissed it as "just talk," she said. "We blew it off, thinking, 'Oh my gosh. What is this? A frustrated kid that wants to get back at his coach? Or a frustrated parent that wanted to attack the coach?' Because he was a man of integrity, as far as we knew."

Prochaska was the unit leader for the Specials Teachers. In retrospect, she marvels that the principal didn't have her monitor Aaron. "I guess Mrs. Hood gave Aaron the benefit of the doubt and thought she could handle it on her own," Prochaska said.

Prochaska didn't know reporting protocol because Grace hadn't trained her to know it: those rumors they'd been hearing of child sex abuse—"smack talk" about Aaron—were grounds enough for a call to outside authorities. Reports to DHS can even be made anonymously. But it was a culture in which the World was not to be trusted or called upon. One's responsibility was to the chain of command.

Under Oklahoma law, the Child Abuse Reporting and Prevention Act, it is a misdemeanor for anyone "having reason to believe" that a minor is potentially being abused to not report it to the Department of Human Services (DHS). (In at least three states, failure to report child abuse can result in a felony.) In some states, the legal requirements to report abuse are limited to certain professionals like health care workers and school employees, but Oklahoma is one of 18 states in which everyone is what's called a "mandatory reporter." The reporting obligation is individual, meaning that it's not enough to simply alert one's superiors and have *them* make a decision about whether or not to call outside authorities. DHS investigates abuse within the home and refers cases like that of Grace to the Tulsa Police Department (TPD) for investigation. When rumors were spreading at Grace, anyone could've alerted DHS or TPD. Then, hypothetically, TPD would've gone out to Grace to "turn over every stone, ask every question," said TPD spokesman Jason Willingham. "We're going to ask, 'Hey did you ever see anything unusual?' It's the little things that just didn't add up."

District Attorney Tim Harris handled Aaron's case. He never returned my phone calls. I left messages asking him to explain why he didn't prosecute Grace for failing to report child abuse. Harris once said, "As a criminal prosecutor, I look at the Ten Commandments." Harris and Mike King, Grace's lawyer, were classmates of Michele Bachmann's in law school at Oral Roberts University, which promotes a biblical interpretation of secular law in an effort to undo the separation of church and state.

Roy Van Tassell of Family and Children's Services of Oklahoma said failure to report prosecutions were "rare" in his experience. Nationally, successful failure-to-report prosecutions are few and far between. They typically result in a fine of a few hundred dollars, if that. "If any good would come out of any of this," one father of an abused boy at Grace told me, "it'd be that somehow, somewhere, laws would be changed." He suggested a fine of $10,000 for every day someone fails to report child abuse.

There is a big shortcoming in Oklahoma's current law: "reason to believe" can be read subjectively. The statute states, "Any person who knowingly and willfully fails to promptly report any incident" may be charged with a misdemeanor. "As a practical matter, unless someone made an admission ... that they knowingly and willfully failed to report as required by law," a DHS representative told me, "how would we know?"

According to the plaintiffs' lawyers, all Grace had to do to avoid prosecution was say they didn't have any "reason to believe" and didn't "knowingly" fail to report that Aaron was molesting boys. They didn't have any reason to believe it, because they chose not to believe it.

In a recent phone conversation, Grace's lawyer, Mike King, reiterated his interpretation of the law. When an organization receives an abuse complaint, King said, "If they have reason to believe that that report is true, they should report it [to DHS]." Yet, credibility is beside the point. That's for the World to discern.

At the time, Prochaska didn't know about all the parental complaints Grace was receiving. Sometime during the 1999–2000 school year, a father came to Mary Ellen Hood to complain that Aaron had showed up at his house one afternoon, wanting to treat his son to lunch. The family had just moved, and he had no idea how Aaron knew where they lived.

"I don't want my son around Aaron Thompson," he told her, asking for the boy's removal from Aaron's PE class. Hood refused, thinking his concerns irrational: teachers walk students to and from gym class, she said, and there was no way his son would be alone with Aaron. (Little did the father realize, his son was regularly late to Prochaska's omputers class. Which is to say he was among the victims.) Hood told the father not to worry: everyone at Grace had known Aaron for years and years and years.

Privately, however, Hood met with head administrator John Dunlavey—instead of going to the authorities. They told Aaron that under no circumstances was he allowed to be alone with children off-campus. None of the other teachers at Grace were informed, and no paperwork to this effect was ever found in Aaron's file.

In September of 2000, a mother called Grace to talk with Principal DeeAnn McKay, who had recently succeeded Mary Ellen Hood. After her son freaked out when asked to undress for a physical, a doctor wondered if there was sexual abuse in the child's past. McKay said she didn't know of anything. The boy was another one of Aaron's victims—also late to Prochaska's class.

Then, in early October, another mother contacted McKay, expressing concern that Aaron was giving her son special attention: an extra birthday cupcake, a kiss on the cheek during gym class to encourage him when he was struggling to finish laps; she'd also seen Aaron playfully swatting kids on the butt. Then, there was yet another mother who called McKay in October to inform her that Aaron had removed three boys from class, walked them toward the edge of Grace's property, told two of them to stay put, and led Jason Taylor alone into the woods.

Jason's father figure paid Principal McKay a visit in late October 2000. He wanted her to know that Aaron was planning to host a sleepover for a group of third-grade boys after Grace's annual Hallelujah Party. Plus, earlier that year, Aaron took Jason alone to the movies and back to his house afterward. McKay then talked with Mary Ellen Hood, the previous principal. Hood told her that she'd instructed Aaron not to be alone with students off-campus. Hood was surprised to learn that Aaron was now disobeying those orders.

After all this, on October 27, 2000, McKay and head administrator John Dunlavey sat Aaron down for a marathon two-and-a-half-hour meeting. (This was a year before the signing of the "do not fondle" agreement.) Dunlavey explained that good Christians often get falsely accused of things, giving examples of legal cases he'd learned about in grad school for Christian school administration at ORU. Dunlavey and McKay laid down the rules: no being alone with children off-campus (maintain "two-deep leadership" as they called it).

"What if I get invited to a swim party at someone's house?" Aaron asked. "Only where there would be numerous other adults present," Dunlavey answered. They instructed Aaron to stop babysitting and inviting students to his house. McKay would monitor Aaron's compliance with the babysitting stipulation by periodically asking him if he was babysitting. Grace ran on the honor system.

There was yet another incident in October of 2000. Zach Sweeney, a first grader, was on the merry-go-round one day at lunch. Aaron helped him off. Zach made a beeline for his teacher, telling her Aaron had touched his genitals. Aaron assured the teacher it must have been an accident; Zach insisted it was intentional. Later, the teacher called Zach's dad. He hung up the phone thinking it was an accident. The teacher said she never reported the incident to anyone else—not Grace, not the police.

Zach had done well in kindergarten at Grace, but something changed in first grade. He started getting in trouble at school, especially for sexually acting out—one of the more common indicators a child has been molested. (Yet, some victims don't have any noticeable behavior change.) Zach suddenly hated school and refused to give his mom, Julie, a reason. "What about PE? You get to run around and play," Julie asked him. "I hate going to PE," Zach answered. Until then, Aaron had been Zach's favorite teacher. He'd been Julie's favorite too. Aaron seemed like the only teacher at Grace who didn't look down on them for not living in a $1 million home. In fact, the Sweeneys could barely afford tuition, which was about $2,000 per year. Then, too, there were the monthly fundraisers students were required to participate in.

Julie met with Principal McKay, telling her Zach wasn't doing well at Grace, and the financial burden was overwhelming the family. "Have you thought about getting a second job?" McKay asked. Julie explained they'd still be short. "Well you and your husband could both get part-time jobs," McKay suggested. Both Julie and her husband were working 40-hour weeks already. She told McKay they had an eight-month-old baby at home, a boy they'd never see if they followed her advice. As Julie saw it, McKay only cared about Grace losing their tuition money. Colleagues say McKay was a real go-getter, determined to climb all the way from kindergarten teacher—where she began—to elementary school principal. Like Mary Ellen Hood before her, Grace was McKay's life. Blonde, always ready with a fake smile, she was one with the institution: "Grace personified," as one longtime teacher described McKay. To let a family leave the school was to admit Grace was not perfection upon a hill in Broken Arrow. "You should think about what is important to God," Julie remembers McKay adding.

Julie left the principal's office bawling. She withdrew Zach from Grace shortly thereafter. It was then that Zach told her, "There's someone there who is touching kids in their private area." It was Aaron, and Zach was one of those kids. It is painful for her to think back on it, but Julie didn't believe her son. Aaron? No way, not in a million years. It is a common misconception that children lie about sexual abuse. In reality, kids rarely ever do. But Julie consulted with her husband, who told her about the teacher's phone call, and they considered the matter settled. They should have but did not make a report to the authorities—like Grace, except without the whole body of additional knowledge Grace had.

During the whole 2000–2001 school year, Aaron would pop by Grace's after-school program, help himself to cookies, and ask to borrow a boy.

"May I borrow so-and-so?" he'd tell the after-school workers, and they'd go with Aaron and then come back alone an hour later with a piece of candy.

Head administrator Dunlavey and principal McKay hadn't told anyone else at Grace that Aaron was not to be alone with boys. At the end of the school year, Aaron decided to have a daycare in his house for Grace boys. This was after he'd been ordered to stop babysitting. McKay knew about it in advance and did nothing to stop it; Dunlavey found out after the fact. Four boys were molested at Aaron's home daycare during the summer of 2001.

"I'm glad to hear it," McKay gushed when another Grace employee remarked that he'd asked Aaron to serve as a counselor at Camp Dry Gulch, where Grace kids went. Two boys were molested at summer camp the summer of 2001.

FIRST ANONYMOUS LETTER

Josh made his parents promise not to tell a soul. They promised. He was in tenth grade. At school, he could not become The Kid Who Got Molested. Together, Josh and his parents drafted the first anonymous letter. Josh had a hunch he wasn't the only one who'd attempted or considered suicide. "This is a matter of life or death for a child or children," the letter urged. "We thank God every day that this did not go unrevealed any longer in our son's life ... [He] will not carry this experience and shame into his adult life, as others may." The letter was signed, "Your Brother & Sister in Christ."

Addressed to head administrator John Dunlavey, the letter arrived on August 16, 2001, by certified mail. Dunlavey opened it and prayed, "Lord, what do I do with this?"

Dunlavey photocopied the letter and took it straight to Pastor Bob and Associate Pastor Chip Olin. Instead of contacting the authorities, Olin and Pastor Bob went to their lawyers. That consultation did not lead Grace to go to the authorities, either. Instead, they took the law into their own hands, with Dunlavey as their detective.

Grace installed cameras in the hallways. Dunlavey and Principal McKay walked by the gym a little more often than usual, keeping an eye out. Every Tuesday afternoon, during his weekly meeting with Pastor Bob, Dunlavey would report back what he'd seen: a whole lot of nothing. Grace would later testify that they interpreted the letter as a generic warning: about what and about whom, they weren't sure, but they claimed nobody suspected sexual abuse. They latched onto the ending: "Watch, pray, open your eyes, be discreet, and above all use wisdom. God will reveal the truth!"

SECOND ANONYMOUS LETTER

By October 21, 2001, God had still not revealed the truth. Two days after the "do not fondle" agreement was signed, another anonymous letter arrived at Grace. It was addressed to Ron Palmer, the chief of the Tulsa Police Department, and CC-ed to Pastor Bob and Dunlavey.

"I am obligated by law and by integrity to inform you that I know PERSONALLY that Mr. Aaron Thompson ... sexually molested a boy at school." This, too, was written by Josh's parents. They were frustrated that nothing seemed to change after their first letter.

Upon the second letter's arrival, Dunlavey got called into Pastor Bob's office. Dunlavey asked Pastor Bob what they should do. Pastor Bob said he and Associate Pastor Olin would take care of it. Sometime after that, Pastor Bob and Olin discussed the letter with Dan Beirute, their lawyer at Winters & King, Inc.

Dunlavey and Olin called Aaron in for another meeting and handed him the letter.

"I don't know what to say," Aaron told them.

"Some encouraging words would be really good right about now," said Olin. "Like, 'I didn't do this,' or 'I've never done this before' and—or 'that is not me.'" Aaron simply nodded in agreement.

It was a short meeting. Dunlavey and Olin reminded Aaron about the guidelines of the Corrective Action Plan, and then he was dismissed.

TPD says they never received the letter. Later, Grace's lawyer explained to the jury that Pastor Bob and Olin figured they'd be hearing from the police if there was any reason to be concerned.

Dunlavey testified that contacting the authorities on his own prerogative was out of the question: Pastor Bob and Olin called the shots. Dunlavey explained, "I don't think I would have done it without them okaying it and putting their blessing on it."

THE ARREST

One Saturday, Lorrie Taylor was driving her son Jason, a fourth grader, home from a basketball game. Her cell phone rang. It was Aaron, and he asked to speak to Jason.

"I love you, too," Jason said to Aaron as he hung up the phone that day.

Lorrie spent the weekend grilling her son about those four words. Jason was defensive and angry. She knew something was not right. Recently, Jason had begged her not to have Aaron babysit him. On Monday, they were in the car again, stopped at a stoplight. She asked him flat out: "Has Aaron Thompson ever touched you in your privates?"

Jason answered yes.

On March 12, 2002, Lorrie met with school administrators in Jason's fourth-grade classroom. She told them what Jason had told her: Aaron had rubbed his genitals in chapel at Grace. Lorrie was beside herself: on the one hand, she didn't think Jason would lie about something like this; and on the other hand, she—like everyone else—didn't think Aaron could possibly have done anything of the sort. Jason's teacher told the group she had interviewed Jason herself, and she believed him. Lorrie watched the associate pastor, the principal, and the school's head administrator take it in. She was struck that none of them seemed the least bit surprised.

At the end of the meeting, they prayed together.

Lorrie had mentioned Aaron's ongoing babysitting of Jason, which meant Aaron violated Grace's Corrective Action Plan. This required a firm response. But Jason's molestation allegation was a separate matter—and one Dunlavey and Olin would later say they didn't actually believe. They decided to suspend Aaron. Olin then called Pastor Bob, who was traveling.

Rather than contact DHS or the Tulsa Police Department, Pastor Bob decided to confront Aaron upon his return. Olin made some phone calls—to Grace's attorneys at Winters & King, Inc.: Dan Beirute and Mike King. The next day, Olin announced that Grace employees were to bring him any and all documents pertaining to Aaron. (Youth pastor Mike Goolsbay, for his part, destroyed a photograph of Aaron.) Olin handed the cache over to the attorneys.

A meeting with Aaron was scheduled for Wednesday, March 20—a full eight days after Lorrie Taylor's confrontation—"in order to allow [him] to hear the allegation," Dunlavey later wrote in a letter to the International Christian Accrediting Association, detailing Grace's extra-judicial proceedings. During those intervening eight days, Dunlavey said, "All I did was pray."

Wednesday came around. Associate Pastor Chip Olin, head administrator John Dunlavey, attorney Dan Beirute, and Pastor Bob met with Aaron in the church's conference room. Olin told Aaron that they'd had a molestation report from a parent. Olin asked if it was true. There was a long pause. Finally, Aaron answered yes. They asked if there were others, and Aaron named two additional boys. Olin beseeched Aaron to report himself to the police. Aaron hesitated, so Olin called a Grace congregant who was a police officer. Then, another TPD child abuse detective called back.

At the end of the meeting, Olin, Dunlavey, and Beirute had Aaron call DHS to report himself. Pastor Bob had already left the room by this point.

"I think he had other responsibilities," Olin testified.

TPD arrested Aaron on March 25, 2002. Five days later, Pastor Bob wrote an open letter to the congregation and parents at the school.

"That such behavior may have occurred and caused injury to children is unthinkable," he noted. "Pray for the children and the families directly affected, especially for the children."

Pastor Bob's next letter to parents on April 5 began with an apology. "The time required to focus on these events has made it difficult to communicate with those who matter to me most—you and your family." Pastor Bob encouraged parents to be in touch. By proxy. "I have directed Chip Olin, Associate Pastor, with responding to you directly," wrote Pastor Bob. He assured the parents that Grace was "aggressively developing community resources that will give us guidance to ensure that this never again happens at our school." But, when Dunlavey and McKay testified nearly two years later, they said no changes had been made to Grace's child abuse reporting policies since then.

It should be noted that Dunlavey, along with Principals Hood and McKay, had certificates of completion from "Child Lures," a popular national sex abuse prevention program offered in conjunction with their law firm, Winters & King, Inc. At public schools in Oklahoma, staff are required to undergo yearly training on recognizing and reporting child abuse and neglect.

THE MONTHS AFTER THE ARREST (2002)

Over a lifetime, the monetary costs of caring for a sex-abuse victim can be sky high. Clergy sex abuse victims generally expect settlements of about a million dollars apiece. In lawsuits against the Catholic Church, attorney fees ate up about 40 percent of the settlements. In 2003, Aaron pleaded guilty to molesting nine boys between 1996 and 2002—16 counts of lewd molestation and two counts of sexual abuse of a minor. (Aaron's 25-year sentence ends in 2027, but he's up for parole in 2023.) Long after Aaron's plea agreement, a 10th and 11th boy came forward and successfully sued Grace for negligence. If Grace's settlements approximated those of Catholic churches, the Aaron Thompson ordeal could've cost them about $11 million, not including the defense's attorney fees.

In the aftermath of Aaron's arrest, faced with a spate of costly negligence lawsuits, Pastor Bob circled the wagons. In 2002, on the advice of their law firm Winters & King, Inc., Grace moved all of their assets into a dummy corporation. A $7.5 million mortgage, $1.2 million in cash, all of Grace's furniture and equipment—everything went into Grace Fellowship Title Holding Corporation. In a letter to Bank of the West, Grace board member and Financial Director John Ransdell explained that the board approved the corporate restructuring in hopes of "protecting the assets of the church in the event of a catastrophic event in the school that resulted in a momentary award exceeding insurance coverage." Ransdell is currently the president of Grace's Covenant Federal Credit Union, a position he's held since 1993.

In court filings, plaintiffs' lawyers alleged Grace had committed fraudulent conveyance, which is a civil offense. All the Grace lawsuits were settled before reaching the stage at which a court might have awarded damages for fraudulent conveyance. Several plaintiffs' lawyers told me Grace's financial maneuverings didn't impact their settlements. But it's the thought that counts. As attorney Clark Phipps explained, it "rubbed salt in the wounds" of the victims and their families.

Plaintiffs' lawyer Laurie Phillips remembered it took forever to assemble a jury for John Does 1–7 versus Grace. Potential jurists kept getting disqualified. As Phillips put it dryly, "Everybody in Tulsa has been molested in Tulsa County—or has a sister or a brother or a child who was." Each year, Oklahoma DHS has about 1,700 confirmed cases of child sex abuse, with underreporting a given.

After a grueling seven-week trial, in October 2004 the jury found that Grace had acted in "reckless disregard" and awarded the seven John Does a total of $845,000. The individual amounts ranged from $75,000 to $250,000. It was a pittance, given that each boy paid about $60,000 in lawyer fees that came out of their settlements. The jury found that Pastor Bob, Associate Pastor Chip Olin, head administrator John Dunlavey, Principal Dee Ann McKay, and former Principal Mary Ellen Hood had acted negligently. (According to plaintiffs' lawyers, Mike Goolsbay was not a defendant in the trial because his role with the lewd emails didn't come out until late in the discovery process. Goolsbay was named in two subsequent lawsuits.) "Reckless disregard" meant the jury could have awarded punitive damages in the next stage of the trial, but the lawyers settled out of court for an undisclosed amount before then. The court had capped the possible punitive damages amount at $870,000, so it's a fair bet that the plaintiffs settled for less than that.

Seven boys, less than $2 million in settlements. Grace got off cheap, especially considering that, as one boy's mother told the *Tulsa World*, the school had "turned and looked the other way and protected their reputation and not my son." Grace's new children's building almost certainly cost far more than the settlement.

On the Sunday after the settlement, Prochaska and the anonymous "Special T" said Pastor Bob announced the news to the congregation. Prochaska remembered punch and cookies at the end of church services; the anonymous "Special T" remembered a song with a pointed chorus: "freedom, freedom." Thinking back to that Sunday, Prochaska's colleague reflected, "Pastor Bob had the whole church rejoicing over them being free of [the lawsuit]—not praying for the families." Several victims' families confirmed that Pastor Bob never offered them an apology.

JOSH'S LAWSUIT

Josh and his family didn't want to sue. (Josh testified in the John Does 1-7 trial but wasn't one of the 1-7.) But, with his statute of limitations about to expire on his 19th birthday, Josh filed an extension protecting his right to sue—just in case. Sure enough, shortly thereafter, Grace stopped paying for his therapy.

Josh wanted something that Grace—as a corporate entity deeply vested in protecting its assets—would never give him: an apology; a recognition that he'd been wronged and hurt; an assurance that the people in charge were sorry for failing him. A court could tell him what Grace would not: the school hadn't protected him when they could have and should have. "If Bob had been kind and repentant and just a little heartbroken," Josh reflects, "I would have never sued Grace."

In February 2005, during the discovery period of the suit, Pastor Bob and his lawyer submitted a request for admission that tried to get Josh to "admit that you touched Aaron Thompson in a sexual manner before he first touched you in a sexual manner." Josh was 11 when the abuse started.

Grace also subpoenaed his therapist's notes, apparently trawling for material that would help make the case that Josh had somehow seduced Aaron as a fifth grader. After that, Josh could no longer trust the very person who was supposed to help him heal. He was just starting to get to the place where he didn't think the abuse was his fault. But that set him back. Way back.

While Pastor Bob engaged in victim blaming, surprisingly, no one at Grace retroactively labeled Aaron a gay child molester. This was remarkable for a deeply conservative megachurch that offered "Restoration by Grace," an in-house pray-away-the-gay counseling program.

Josh's entire middle school and teen years were taken up with his abuse—first with the molestation itself, and then with the criminal case against Aaron and the lawsuits and the endless depositions and hearings. It all blended together. The subpoenas were never-ending. He was forced to live it again and again and again. He said what many sexual assault survivors say: the protracted agony of the legal system was yet another assault. During one deposition, as he talked he could see his mom through a window in the door. She was sobbing.

After Aaron's arrest, Josh defected from Grace and spent the remainder of high school in homeschooling. Reading on his own, learning about things like evolution, he marveled at the realization that Bible class, science class, and history class had been pretty much interchangeable at Grace. Slowly, he began to cast off his biblical worldview. The only direct Grace contact Josh had was with John Dunlavey, who was always apologetic and kind when they'd run into each other. So Josh was surprised when Pastor Bob's lawyers contacted him with a message: Pastor Bob wanted to discuss a settlement with him over lunch at Marie Callender's, a home-style chain restaurant.

Josh thought Pastor Bob wanted to say he was sorry for what had happened. He also thought Pastor Bob was taking him to lunch. But it soon became clear that Josh was paying his own way, and Pastor Bob was not there to apologize. Josh ordered a glass of water and watched Pastor Bob eat.

"He quoted scriptures about how I was sinning against God for coming against his church, his ministry," Josh remembered. But Josh came prepared with scripture passages of his own, about the responsibility of a shepherd to protect his flock. The message fell on deaf ears. Josh drank his water. Pastor Bob ate a big meal and ordered dessert.

THE SCHOOL CLOSES

In the year after Aaron's arrest, Grace saw an exodus of students who headed for other Christian schools attached to Tulsa-area megachurches, like Victory Christian Center or Church on the Move. But before long, enrollment stabilized, more or less. Then the economy went bad. At the end of the 2008-2009 school year, Grace had 300 kids in grades K-12. The previous year it'd been 400.

In May 2009, Pastor Bob announced he was closing the high school. Nineteen employees lost their jobs. Everyone hoped it would be temporary—as soon as the economy got back on track. But in July 2010, Grace announced it was closing the elementary school, too. After 32 years in operation, the church was losing too much money on the school.

Josh's mother broke the news.

"Good riddance," he texted back.

THE LONG ARM OF GRACE

Jeff and Lynn wanted to send their son Gabe to a good Christian school. Gabe had always been an easygoing kid. But somewhere around first or second grade at Grace, he changed. Lynn would pick him up in the afternoon, and Gabe would beat on the dashboard, saying he hated school and didn't want to go back. He started acting out. Over the years, just about every counselor or doctor who looked at Gabe would tell his parents he had all the hallmarks of sexual abuse in his past. Jeff and Lynn guessed Gabe was in denial. Of course, they didn't realize Gabe was one of the boys who were late to Laura Prochaska's computers class.

"My son just got out of jail again," Jeff begins to tell me over the phone, his voice weary. "He got home and lasted two days before he was back on drugs." Jeff and Lynn are the kind of people who strive to keep their driving records spotless.

Once, Gabe threatened to slit his parents' throats.

"That night I found a box blade under his mattress," Jeff remembers. "At that point in life it didn't surprise me. We had been down the path with him so much. We were living with 30 or 40 holes in our walls from him kicking them in." To say Gabe was angry was an understatement.

One year shortly before Christmas, Jeff and Lynn were on yet another psych ward with Gabe. Something snapped, and Gabe threw a chair at a plate glass window, aiming for his mother. On Christmas Day, calling from another in-patient facility, Gabe finally broke down and admitted it.

"Mom," he said, "something did happen at Grace."

The stipulations of the settlement don't allow Jeff to name dollar figures, but he says it doesn't even begin to cover the cost of rehabs and detoxes and psych wards and halfway houses. A weekend on a psychiatric unit costs $12,000. Jeff and Lynn have paid Gabe's medical bills instead of putting away money for their retirement. Besides Gabe, several of Aaron's other victims have required in-patient treatment of one kind or another.

A lifetime ago, Jeff and Lynn had an account in Grace's Covenant Federal Credit Union. That was just the culture. "You're one for all and all for one, and you're trying to help each other," Jeff explains. "Why not keep it in the family?"

At some point in the phone call, Lynn comes home. She tells Jeff she brought some groceries over to Gabe that day. Gabe's doing well, for now at least, which is all they can hope for. During those times when she's scared of their son, or if Gabe's lashing out and calling her names, or if he's in one of his explosive rages, Jeff tells Lynn not answer the phone: he'll deal with Gabe. But, Jeff explains, she always caves in, wanting to help. His voice becomes soft. I get the feeling Lynn is standing nearby—that Jeff is talking to her now. "She's so tender, and so loving."

In November, Jeff and Lynn renewed their wedding vows and went on a second honeymoon to Hawaii. They love their son, they will be there for him, but now the next chapter of their lives is beginning. "He's *part* of life, but he's not all of life," Jeff says, determined to make this a reality.

Gabe met his girlfriend in rehab. Last year, Jeff and Lynn helped the couple get set up in an apartment, assembled donated furniture from friends, and paid for the first three months rent. Two weeks after moving in, Gabe was in police custody again: a domestic assault against his girlfriend. They're still together. In March, she gave birth to their son. Then, Gabe returned to jail, serving his sentence for last year's assault charge; mother and child just checked into court-ordered rehab and can't see visitors for a month. "Kinda takes the fun out of being a grandparent," Jeff wrote in an email shortly before this story went to press.

Julie Sweeney and her husband were not fated to have a second honeymoon. Who is to say what ends a marriage, but the life Julie and her husband had together for 14 years could only withstand so much. The pressures of the aftermath of Zach's molestation were not among the things they could bear—together, at least. Trusting one's own had been a basic fact of everyday life. Suddenly, everything they took for granted in this world was upended. Abuse is experienced by entire families, and it goes on long after the physical part is over. In the wake of Aaron's arrest, for the parents of the victims, at least two other marriages broke up.

It took Julie nearly a decade to be among Christians again, to conceive of church as a place where healing might be found. "I lost faith in people," Julie says. "I didn't lose faith in God."

If Gabe is one end of the sexual abuse spectrum, Josh is at the other. Of the two paths, child abuse experts say Gabe's is probably more common. The deck is stacked against abuse victims.

In his teens, Josh was angry: at Grace, Christianity, his parents, everything and everyone—but especially at Aaron and Pastor Bob. "I used to dream of beating Aaron and Bob with baseball bats," Josh remembers.

After settling his lawsuit, around the time he turned 20, a realization set in. All that bitterness wasn't making him the person he wanted to be. So he hit the road, crisscrossing the country, ending up at the 2006 Austin City Limits music festival. It was there that he got a tattoo across the underside of his left forearm: Hebrew letters that spell out "mechilah"—forgiveness. Forgiveness was what Josh wanted: not the Christian concept of forgiveness, but more a state of mind—of being at peace with the past.

Forgiveness was a goal, not an immediate reality. Josh returned to Tulsa and made a second suicide attempt. He swallowed two bottles of Tylenol PM and woke up in a hospital bed. "All my family and friends were huddled around me," Josh says. "I was so embarrassed and disappointed that I was still there." He spent the next few weeks on the psychiatric ward, wishing he'd been successful.

By the time he got the tattoo, life had settled down enough for him to mourn just how much of it he'd missed. 1996 to 2006 was Josh's lost decade. He was a little kid, and then, suddenly, he was an adult. Growing up, growing into one's own as a sexual being—Josh had been denied these things. "I couldn't imagine a future without something terrible happening to me."

In the years that followed, Josh worked at letting go. There on his arm, he bore *mechilah*, a daily reminder. That's what he wanted, especially for himself—for "letting it happen to me," as Josh puts it.

"For a long time I had the mentality of 'I am a child abuse victim,'" Josh says. "Now I have other things. It's not something that defines me like it once did."

At 27, Josh is ready to leave Tulsa. He has always felt years behind everyone else his age. But he's catching up. He was just accepted to a prestigious art school. He'll enroll in the fall. Meanwhile, Josh works a dayjob and makes art. That's what got him through his teens and into his 20s, and that's what will take him to whatever comes next.

. . .

Dick Thompson, Aaron's father, and I emailed back and forth for some time. I wanted to visit Aaron at the Joseph Harp Correctional Center, where he is said to have a thriving prison ministry. The Thompsons were deciding as a family whether they wanted to risk "going public" with their experiences. Christmas 2011 turned into the New Year. There was a much apologized for lull while the Thompsons remodeled their house. Then, I got this email:

> Aaron took a situation that could have destroyed him, but with God's help has received healing, rehabilitated himself, and moved on accepting responsibility and consequences for what he did. Our prayer is that all of the alleged victims have also received healing and moved on with their lives. However, we know that may not be true for all of them. Those who are stuck in the past and resisted God's healing and forgiveness will continue to blame Aaron and others for whatever failures they have in their lives. Being fondled or molested as a child, is a very bad thing, but many, many people who have gone through that have grown up to be very successful individuals and even role models for others, so it is not an experience that cannot be overcome. As with all things that happen in our lives, it's not what happens to us but how we respond that makes or breaks us and/or reveals our true character.

It turned out that Josh did not resent Dick Thompson's characterization of the long-term effects of abuse as personal failings on the part of the victims.

"Parents always want to see the best in their children," he replied. He was calm. I was baffled.

"You're not angry?" I asked.

"I guess I'm just all out of anger," he said.

PASTOR BOB'S PRACTICAL WISDOM

Photos of Corvettes are displayed on the bookshelf in Pastor Bob's office. One day shortly before Thanksgiving, Pastor Bob welcomed me into his domain. He held forth behind his big wooden desk, wearing jeans and a gray wool pullover that clung to his belly.

"We trusted this kid," Pastor Bob told me. "I'm not omniscient—I'm not like God," he noted. "The church is just people."

Up close, Pastor Bob's skin had a purplish putty quality. His bulbous pug nose was a few shades darker than the rest of his face. Pastor Bob continued, "You never quit trusting people. You just get wiser through the years."

Soon, our conversation turned to Penn State, which had recently been cast into the national spotlight over what appeared to be a child sex abuse cover-up. Pastor Bob hoped there were Believers on staff there to guide the university through the dark times to come. He identified with the school's predicament, he said, for he too had once been accused of turning a blind eye at Grace. He remembered the parents of the victims were particularly accusatory. "When we found out, we fired [Aaron] and called the police," Pastor Bob said. "But it's never early enough with them."

Every day during the seven-week John Does 1–7 versus Grace trial, Pastor Bob's wife, Loretta, made him a list of scripture to read. He drew spiritual strength from the Psalms on deliverance and protection, especially Psalm 91. "He'll protect you from arrow by day, the terror by night, the snare of the fowler," Pastor Bob recited, his own condensed version. When the jury came back with the verdict, Pastor Bob marveled at the low amount Grace had to pay the victims.

Before long, Grace got back to business as usual, as Pastor Bob always knew they would. He leaned forward slightly and bridged his hands. "Many are the afflictions of the righteous, but the lord brings you through *all* of them," Pastor Bob said. "So we came through."

Today, Pastor Bob estimated 50 or 60 percent of the congregation was unaware of what took place at Grace a decade ago. "The Lord moves on. He promises you that," Pastor Bob reflected, smiling broadly now. "The ability to forgive and forget is—" Here he paused. "Divine."

My time with Pastor Bob was up. On the way out, his secretary, Gwen Olin—Associate Pastor Chip Olin's widow—wished me a blessed day.

. . .

Back when the lawsuits were underway, Principal DeeAnn McKay was working toward her doctorate in Christian educational administration at Oral Roberts University. Associate Pastor Chip Olin died of cancer in 2007. Now retired, former Principal Mary Ellen Hood lives in Jenks. Since 2007, former head administrator John Dunlavey has been the principal of a private Christian school in South Korea. Dunlavey declined interview requests, saying he wanted others to learn from Grace's ordeal but was worried his words would be "taken out of context."

Mike Goolsbay, Grace's former youth pastor, has his own congregation now, Destiny, a massive stadium of a church with the motto "Loving People." By car, Destiny is about three miles northeast of Grace, a stone's throw as distances go in Broken Arrow. Goolsbay still refers to Pastor Bob as "my pastor." For financial guidance, Destiny's website recommends John Ransdell, the one who was tasked with maneuvering Grace's assets into the dummy corporation. Like Grace, Destiny is represented by Winters & King, Inc.

I asked Mike King how he'd hypothetically advise Destiny Church if they were to receive an anonymous letter exactly like the first one Josh's parents sent to Grace. King gave a little chuckle, answering, "Well, it would depend upon the facts and circumstances."

If anything, the lesson of Grace should be that it never depends.

Just before Thanksgiving, I went to Destiny's Saturday night church service. On stage, Goolsbay sat comfortably on a stool, against a backdrop of neon blue paneling and jumbotrons. A far cry from Pastor Bob's formal pulpit manner, Goolsbay ran his service like a call-in radio show, his speech peppered with "dude" and "sweet" and the occasional "ridonkulous." He videochatted a housebound congregant set to soft keyboard music; played for laughs with a call to his wife to see if she'd found his lost wallet; and gave a sermon in what he calls his "Perils of Power" series. The message: Accountability begins at home, top-down, from parents to children. King David must hold his son Ammon accountable for raping his daughter Tamar. Leaders went unmentioned.

• • •

Former parishioners say Grace's heyday was over three decades ago, at the old church building out on Memorial Drive, a few miles west of the citadel on Garnett Road, in the building that was later sold to Higher Dimensions church (where its pastor, Carlton Pearson, stopped believing in hell and all hell broke loose). It was standing-room only back then, with people crammed on a balcony that was really just a half story. That was the heyday of the Word movement, too, when a megachurch pastor could take to the pulpit and bring the house down and that's all anybody expected from him.

"Now people want somebody a little more personable," explains a former Grace member who'd been deeply rooted in the church for decades. Others were less charitable in their assessments of Pastor Bob: "no emotion" and "nothing behind the eyes." Tulsa, of course, is a city with ever-multiplying options.

On Sundays, Grace's parking lot is typically half full, if that. The church still offers a kids program, but attendance has dwindled. Peek into the children's building on a Sunday, and you'll find more building than children. Grace's membership appears to skew older, now, toward the retiree set. In the sanctuary/former gym, the big, padded seats are spread further apart, masking the emptiness. Basketball hoops are folded against the ceiling. The gym floor is still emblazoned with a maroon and gray decal of a basketball with the lettering "Grace Christian Eagles," a relic from another time.

Recently, Grace board members gave Pastor Bob a list of 30 things he could do to be more "people friendly."

"Why aren't things like they used to be?" he asked them. He was genuinely puzzled.

The Sunday before Rick Santorum won the Oklahoma primary on Super Tuesday, the former Pennsylvania Senator made a single campaign stop in Tulsa. Santorum spoke from the pulpit of Grace's gym/sanctuary, where he denounced liberals for thinking "the elite should decide what's best for those in flyover country." The crowd cheered and waved their Santorum placards, the word "COURAGE" projected upon the jumbotrons that flank the stage. It was a packed house.

Back in the day, Pastor Bob would say he'd preach 'til he died. But those close to the church board say he's announced he wants to step down soon. His son, Pastor Robb Yandian, will ascend the pulpit. Aaron has 15 more years to serve on his sentence. The boys are now men.

Grace never built the auditorium they'd planned, the one that would have connected the children's building with the main wing. They constructed what was to be the connecting wall of the children's building out of material that wasn't weatherproof, leaving it vulnerable to the elements. There are leakage problems now. There is also talk of perhaps selling the land in front of Garnett Road just to make ends meet. Then again, maybe things aren't so bad: Grace had a budget of nearly $5 million last year and ended 2011 in the black.

Heading toward the Mingo Valley Expressway on the way out of Broken Arrow, you can see, rising from the hillside, something that looks like a brand new airport hotel. It's stamped with rainbow-colored lettering large enough for passing cars along East 91st Street to read from across an immense grassy field: "Grace Kids."

Inside, a gilded carousel awaits.

Originally published
October 2011

by Denver Nicks

OKLAHOMA REVEALED!

Okie missionaries stir trouble in Armenia

In the spring of 2009, a cohort of evangelical Southern Baptists under the *nom du groupe* "The Singing Men of Oklahoma" traveled to the small Caucasian republic of Armenia to spread the gospel of Jesus Christ through their soaring choral music, and inserted themselves into the middle of an ancient but very urgent domestic crisis. The Okie missionaries were not warmly received by the Mother See of Holy Etchmiadzn, the central office of the Armenian Apostolic Church, to which 93 percent of the country's population is an adherent.

The Mother See, as its foreign press secretary explained to the American ambassador, "directed its ire not at the choir per se, but at those who misinformed it prior to its trip by characterizing Armenia as anti-Semitic and ineffective in delivering the gospel..."

The inside story of the Armenian evangelical crisis brought on by The Singing Men of Oklahoma is but one of thousands of diplomatic secrets exposed in August, when WikiLeaks released its entire cache of more than a quarter million communiqués sent between American diplomatic posts around the globe. The cables are mere snapshots—incomplete and unverified utterances of diplomats trying to do the knotty work of diplomacy. Nonetheless, rummaging through the newly leaked dispatches reveals that Oklahomans, in the great tradition of a state founded largely by dispossessed Indians and criminals, have been stirring up trouble all over the world.

When the revolution comes, it may be Okiefied. Oklahoma, as one cable revealed, is one of a handful of states playing host to a Bolivarian Circle, an activist cell the government of Venezuela operates as it "spreads the gospel of Chavez's Bolivarian Revolution." Chavez's interest in Oklahoma may stem from when the Venezuela-owned oil company CITGO called Tulsa home. The oil giant left for greener pastures south of the Red River in 2004, but Governor Brad Henry fought to keep the company in state, in what appears to have been a losing battle. Cables reveal allegations that CITGO's former president and CEO, Luís Marín, bought his "future Houston offices and then leased the space back to the company at an inflated rate." The company's vice president at the time was a major proponent of moving the company to Houston simply because he liked it better than Tulsa.

The Sooner State was not treated so rudely by all foreign dignitaries—in fact, Oklahoma may someday be the summer getaway of our future Chinese overlords. Li Keqiang, a man widely speculated to succeed Wen Jiabao as the premier of China's Politburo—that is, head honcho of the world's most populous country—has traveled widely in the United States, exploring both coasts and making daring forays into the wilds of the Middle West. But of all the corners of God's country he visited, "Li said he particularly liked Oklahoma." Portending a future crisis, diplomats noted that Li is an avid walker. The denizens of Oklahoma might consider making their two major cities more walkable, if it pleases his Eminence.

The Okies' cantankerous spirit, we find, is contagious. A citrus farmer in Najran, a remote town in southwestern Saudi Arabia along the Yemeni border, lost 1,000 trees in his orchard due to a water shortage and increasing salinity in the soil. The man, a graduate of the University of Oklahoma, called the Najran Chamber of Commerce "a lot of rich people with no idea about how to invest or spend their money." He then promptly disappeared.

Things could get interesting where the wind comes right behind the rain if Oklahoma passes a truly permissive open carry law. Oklahoma is one of several states where knock-off Kalashnikov's are manufactured, much to the consternation of Moscow, which is worried about Okies running guns to Russia's enemies, namely the Georgians. On the other hand, an AK-47 stamped "Made in Oklahoma" could come in handy for those Bolivarian Circles. ¡Hasta la victoria siempre!

It has been said that the art of diplomacy involves fucking someone over and then having them thank you for it. To be a diplomat is no easy task. Real and troubling deception on the part of the American government has been exposed in the leaked dispatches, but the image that reveals itself, like a pointillist painting, when one takes a step back and considers the picture in all of its parts, is one of men and women in the State Department working hard and faithfully to promote American interests in a complex and sometimes dangerous world.

One can understand, if not sympathize with, how The Mother See of Holy Etchmiadzn might have felt The Singing Men of Oklahoma were plowing a little close to the cotton. The Armenian Church was, legend has it, founded by no less than two of Jesus' 12 disciples and, early in fourth century *Anno Domini,* was the first Christian sect to become an official state religion. After a spate of arguments spanning several centuries over whether or not, or to what degree, or in what way Jesus Christ is, or was, divine, the Armenians took their proverbial marbles and told Rome to shove it—beating Protestants to the punch by about a thousand years.

When The Singing Men arrived, state-sponsored media went apeshit, declaring that the singers were "out to steal souls." Over half the group's appearances were canceled and the national security services issued threats to the tiny evangelical minority in the country, as well as to venues that hosted the traveling Okies. But the mess The Singing Men stepped into, cables released by WikiLeaks reveal, was entirely personal.

Annoyed by the missionaries from "cults and sects"—by which they meant "Jehova's Witnesses, Mormons, Adventists, etc."—Armenia criminalized proselytizing. Over the radio, the leader of the country's small evangelical community called The Mother See "an historical relic," and the comment enraged the Armenian Church. Once-cordial relations between the evangelicals and apostolics deteriorated—just in time for the arrival of a band of singing missionaries from Oklahoma. Not unlike the American diplomats, whose secret and mostly above-the-board dealings have been revealed to the world, when The Singing Men of Oklahoma entered a hotbed of ancient sectarian conflict, the crisis they seemed to have brought with them was, the cables reveal, waiting there for them when they arrived.

Originally published
December 2014

by David McGlynn

A PENTECOST OF BICYCLES

A father and son experience the wonderment of God—not in a church, but on two wheels, while navigating a leafy path near the river.

The attraction between a boy and his bike, as William Maxwell writes about the attraction between boys and dogs, can be taken for granted. One Sunday morning, I felt a moist hand touch my cheek. When I opened my eyes, the light through the window was gray and I could only see the shadow of a kid standing above me. The clock on the nightstand said 5:47. "Dad," Hayden whispered, his breath hot and foul. "I want to ride my bike."

"It's not even six o'clock."

"Can I ride at six?"

"Let me sleep," I said, rolling over. "You can ride later."

"Later when?"

"After church," I said. I reached for my glasses. "You can ride all afternoon."

"Ugh. Church." He bared his teeth. "Why do we have to go to church?"

I blinked at him in the silver half-light. I didn't have a good answer. I wasn't particularly eager to go myself, despite the fact I've been a churchgoer, regularly if not continuously, for most of my life.

• • •

I was Catholic, baptized and catechized until I was 12, when my parents divorced. Religion had never been a point of contention between my mother and father, but when their marriage began to falter, it had no power to hold them together. A few weeks after the papers were signed, my father left Texas for Southern California, where he soon married an evangelical children's pastor and became an evangelical himself. My mother, whose Catholic foothold had been tenuous at best, became nothing. Still, a Methodist minister married my mother and together we all attended his church for several years afterward. We were most regular in our attendance whenever my stepfather's son and daughter were in town, I think because my mother hoped that the six of us—my mother and stepfather, my stepbrother and stepsister, my sister, and me—lined up in the pew in our blazers and hot-rolled hair would cut the image of an intact family, unblemished by divorce. I never understood who might be looking or would have been able to spot us if they had. Most Sundays we sat in the back and were the first to shake the minister's hand on our way out the door.

When I visited my father and stepmother, the audience was clearer. The money people dropped in the offertory baskets paid my stepmother's salary. My father, sister, stepsister, and I sat in the front pew alongside the other pastoral families and lingered after the service on the plaza between the sanctuary and the fellowship hall while my father and stepmother kibitzed with the deacons and other members. The summer I turned 15, my stepmother presented me with a Bible, my name embossed in gold foil on the cover, and encouraged me to take notes during sermons. My father took me to a jewelry store to pick out a silver cross to wear around my neck, similar to the gold cross he wore around his own.

I resisted their pious overtures only at first. At the end of the summer, a few weeks after beginning my sophomore year of high school, my closest friend, his older brother, and their father were killed in a home invasion—a sudden, violent event that I'm still, decades later, trying to understand. But in the immediate aftermath of the murders, my father and stepmother's faith felt, with its effusive demonstrations, like an antidote to tragedy. A life raft in a tempest. I reached for it and clung to it, and the next June, while sitting beside a bonfire on the beach, I used the words my stepmother had taught me and, as the ritual goes, asked Jesus into my heart.

Almost immediately, as though I'd climbed inside a car that had been honking and revving in my driveway, I was driven into a world that revolved entirely around going to church. Freed from its erstwhile status as a Sunday morning gathering, church became the touchpoint of every day of the week. Bible studies met on Monday or Thursday evenings, fellowship meetings were on Tuesdays, my stepmother and father attended Bible Study Fellowship on Wednesdays. Even the Saturday morning, surf sessions began with a prayer on the beach, our boards staked upright in the sand, and ended with a scripture devotional over eggs at Denny's. I was so young, my initiation so swift and powerful, that several years would pass before I'd think to question it.

My father and stepmother's church was not Pentecostal in the contemporary sense of the term. Services did not involve spasmodic shaking or the casting out of demons or speaking in tongues. The church, however, skirted the fringes of that ecstatic realm. More importantly, the idea of Pentecost—that after Christ's ascension the Spirit of God descended to earth to abide in the Apostles, and that the Holy Spirit dwells in the heart of every true believer as an inner compass of joy and conviction—was central.

The enduring, ineradicable presence of the Holy Spirit was the message the church preached and propagated. Those mysteriously flaming words I uttered on the beach didn't merely reenact the moment Pentecost; they worked to literally bring forth God's spirit, as if unlocking the vault encasing the soul. Pentecostals express the presence of the Holy Spirit literally, with holy terror and a language spoken by angels. Evangelicals are subtler and more restrained, but not by much. For years I stood among believers (in some cases, thousands at a time) singing with their eyes clamped shut and their hands in the air, as if to gather in the spirit as it rained down from the rafters. I could never surmount my own self-consciousness enough to sing or pray this way, to allow myself to enter into the rapturous elation pouring forth around me, so I almost never tried.

In time I found the courage to leave the fold and to endure all the sundering and exile required of such a departure. If ever there was a time to give up the hocus pocus of religion, it was then. But though I could no longer believe as an evangelical nor assent to its politics or exhaustive litany of prohibitions, I couldn't help believing in God. In my quietest and most private moments, I still believed in a grand intelligence at the center of existence, and that whatever change had occurred in me while sitting on the beach that summer night had been real, even if I no longer trusted the vocabulary used to describe it. The bathwater had been drained, but at the bottom of the tub remained the baby, pink and kicking and demanding to be held.

So I hopscotched denominations, first to the Presbyterians with my future wife and future in-laws, then to the Episcopalians where I was married and my sons were baptized, and most recently, to the Congregationalists—a politically progressive, liturgically moderate congregation with a brick-and-glass church overlooking the river, a quasi-professional choir, and a robust Sunday School. I'm not as involved as I once was, but I'm still involved. I sometimes lead the scripture readings during the service. My wife takes her turn teaching Sunday School, and our two sons sing in the youth choir. We've baked plenty of lasagnas for plenty of potlucks and have ladled our share of soup to the homeless men and women who sleep in the fellowship hall during the coldest months of the year.

And yet, for all the countless hours I've spent inside churches, I can't recall a single Sunday—either now or in the past, as a Catholic, an evangelical, or a mainline Protestant—when I've actually looked forward to going. Once uncomfortable among the jubilations of the evangelicals, I now find myself restless, struggling to concentrate on either the message or the art of its delivery. Part of the problem is that church is no longer a place of quiet, solemn reflection; it is now most typically the conclusion to a morning of screaming for the boys to hurry up in the shower, a cup of coffee swigged at the kitchen sink as we're running out the door, and a Super Mario Kart race across town. By the time we're squeezing ourselves into the pews, I'm harried and exhausted, and I spend the service simply waiting for it to end.

The temptation to avoid church is sometimes so great that most Sundays I can barely resist it. On many occasions, I have not resisted and have opted instead for a second cup of coffee, an old movie, or a long phone conversation with a friend. I've thought that if I could only give up believing then I could quit the enterprise of churchgoing altogether.

But faith no longer belongs to me alone. Long gone are the days when I anguished over the afterlives of my non-believing friends, but the boys . . . the boys upend my logic, my every resolution. The fear of perdition was implanted in me so deeply and at such a young age that, though my faith has changed in every other way, I cannot extricate this last remnant of it. It's hypocritical and hedging and theologically unsound; I can't determine the destinations of their souls any more than I can protect them from cancer or car accidents. I know it, yet I'm helpless to it anyway. As I watch them leave for Sunday School, I only hope their time there, despite its inconveniences and discomforts and boredoms, will one day prove meaningful. That I will one day see them in heaven, by God's grace many years from now.

. . .

When we got home from church, Hayden jumped out of the car before I pulled into the garage. "Careful!" my wife shouted, but he was already on his bike, without his helmet, still in his khakis and brogans. "Come inside and change," I said.

"In a minute," he shouted over his shoulder.

"I don't want you to ruin your clothes."

"I won't," he said.

I let him ride while I made lunch. I set his sandwich on the table, opened the backdoor, and called him to come in. "Hand it to me when I ride by," he said.

"I don't think you're that proficient a cyclist just yet," I said. He shrugged and kept pedaling. "How about you come inside, eat, and change your clothes. Then we'll all go for a ride together?"

Usually a finicky eater, given to horsing around the kitchen during meals, Hayden sat down to his plate like MacGyver before a bomb. The sandwich disappeared in less than a minute, and his chips and apple were dispatched shortly thereafter. Five minutes after entering the house, his plate was in the sink, he'd changed into his shorts, and was back outside, hollering *Come on! Come on!*

"If we could harness this hurry-up," my wife said, "school mornings would be much easier."

We rode past the post office and performing arts center, the appliance repair shop, our local congressional office until we reached the path that followed the river. The trees forking over the asphalt were more golden than yesterday and the leaves beneath our tires sounded like paper crinkling. The path crossed the railroad tracks and meandered beneath our church, the windows of the sanctuary visible above the trees. I could see silhouettes moving inside and felt relieved to be on this side of the glass.

I looked away from the church, toward the river, avocado green and passing beneath the trusses of a rusted railroad bridge, the buildings of the university along the opposite bank. And that's when I saw it: the change in Hayden's face as he leaned forward on his bike. I watched him take in his surroundings with an emotion I'm still working to name. Pentecost is the word I want to use—that holy, rapturous sensation of wonder—but the word's hoary baggage makes it difficult to wield.

Whatever name it goes by, Hayden seemed to glimpse, however briefly, his place among the hidden structures of the universe, and when he glanced over at me I felt we shared an understanding, perhaps even the Big Understanding I've been grappling toward all my life. I wanted to tell him, that's God you're feeling, or at least it's the feeling that I've always connected to God's echo moving through me. But I decided I didn't want to name it for him, not just yet. I wanted him to feel it first. I watched his spokes spin around, the wind flap the sleeves of his t-shirt, and stayed quiet.

Up ahead the trail dropped fast and sharp through the trees, a hairpin turn at the bottom that followed the river's bend. Lose control at the wrong time and you'll end up in the drink. I could smell the fish and algae blooming in the river, the fallen leaves turning to broth. Galen bombed the hill like an old pro, followed by Hayden, his elbows out and his head crouched over the handlebars, yelping the whole way down. *Woo hoo! Woo hoo!* Is there a better sound in the world?

Hayden zipped around the bend and out of sight. I listened for a crash, a splash, metal scraping over concrete. When I didn't hear anything, I started after him, certain I'd find him on the other side.

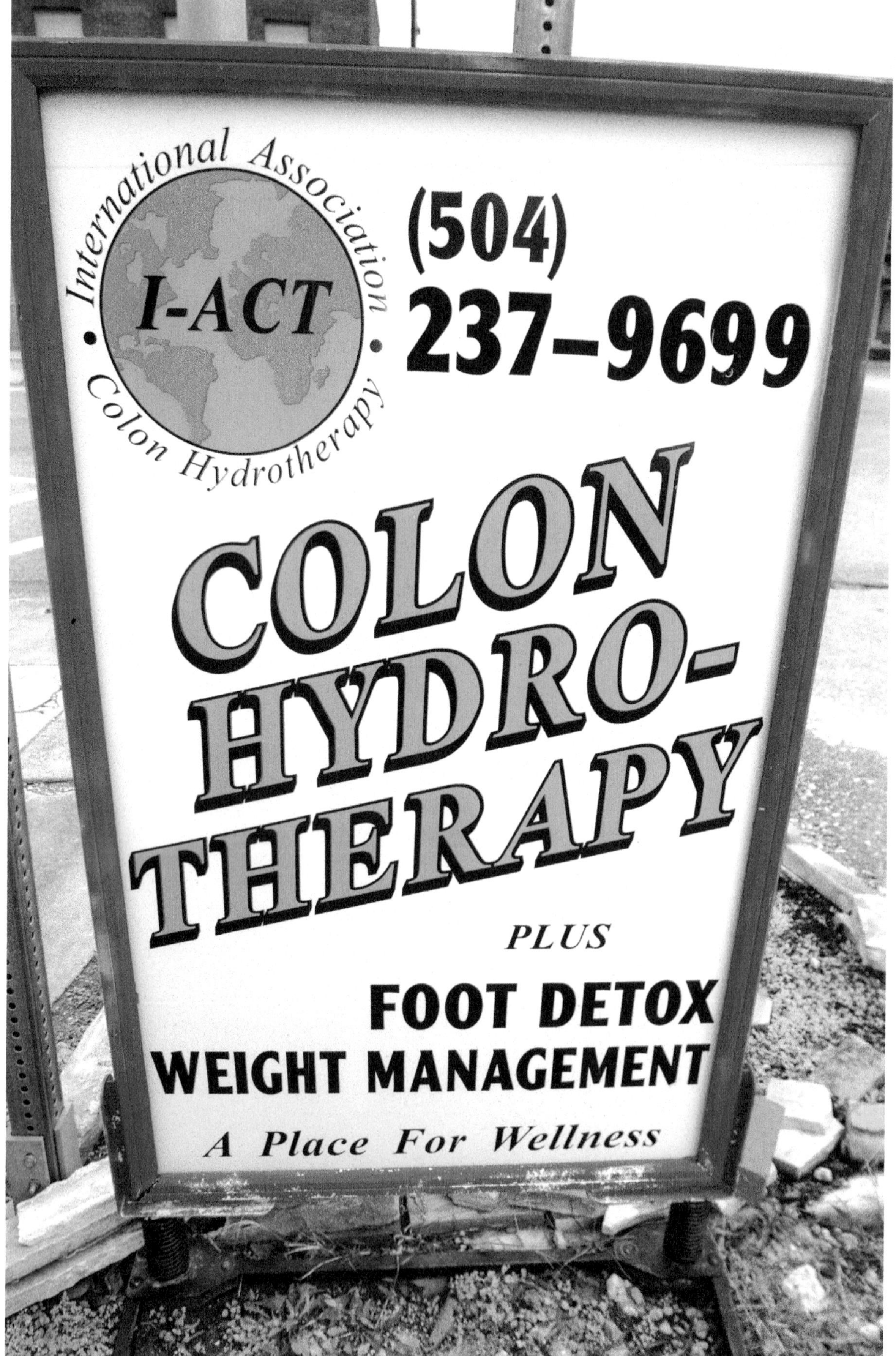
International Association
I-ACT
Colon Hydrotherapy
(504)
237-9699
COLON
HYDRO-
THERAPY
PLUS
FOOT DETOX
WEIGHT MANAGEMENT
A Place For Wellness

Originally published
June 2012

by Sheilah Bright

HOLY CRAP

A Talihina man is on a mission to clean up the town one gut at a time

Shit happens every day. At least, it should. When it doesn't, there's a Seventh-day Adventist in southeastern Oklahoma who can flush it out with a hydro-pressure machine and a few belly rubs.

Relax. Study the stool chart. Maybe reflect on the "The Cross Made the Difference For Me" wooden plaque hanging above pictures of poop. Do anything it takes to keep your mind off what's going in and what's, hopefully, coming out.

"I feel like I've been swimming upstream most of my life," says Emile Spalitta, owner of Oasis A Place for Wellness in Talihina, population 1,200. "This isn't something people around here tend to lean toward, but word is getting out about the health benefits."

The "COLON HYDRO-THERAPY PLUS FOOT DETOX" sign at the corner of Main and Second helps spread the message and stops traffic—especially since it sits at the town's only signal light. Spalitta's office is tucked onto the side street and packed with wellness books, natural health literature, and illustrations of internal organs. The music is peaceful. The candle smells clean. Overlook the Bristol Stool Chart—a giant poster of crap in every size and shape, though mainly just one color—and you can believe you're in a spa except that your nervous gut is starting to tense up and gurgle.

"I can tell what people's intestinal issues are just by looking at their faces," Spalitta says. "You eat late at night, don't you?"

Damn you, Hateful Hussy Diner cheeseburger, fries, and a hunk of pecan pie loitering there with two biscuits, sausage gravy, Snicker's, and some Cheetos.

"How much water do you drink? Do you drink alcohol?"

It's hard to lie to a man who deals with shit every day. He can practically see the vodka bubbling in your eyes.

Spalitta explains the ins and outs of his dredging process with the voice of a missionary. In fact, he and his wife, Pam, a registered nurse, spent several years abroad spreading the word and passing out literature through the Seventh-day Adventist Church.

These days, Spalitta is on a mission to help the people of Le Flore County redeem their health by what he believes is a fountain of youth: colon hydro-

therapy. He says too many people are living lives clogged with an overload of stress and processed foods that plaster intestinal corridors with thick toxic coatings. Oh, and we don't poop enough. Spalitta says if people would poop like babies—say, practically after every meal—they would feel years younger. Here's where you will likely start counting your daily deposits and realize your account is in arrears.

Spalitta has been preaching pure living and cleaner eating for years. At one time, he weighed 300 pounds. Today, he eats vegetables and fish. He doesn't ingest fat or blood. His diet is based on Genesis 1:29 (Then God said, "Behold, I have given you every plant yielding seed that is on the surface of all the earth, and every tree which has fruit yielding seed; it shall be food for you").

A few years back, he opened a health food store here and tried to steer folks toward vegetarian dishes and smoothies. He had some success but not enough to keep the doors open.

"People thought I was crazy for opening up a vegetarian restaurant in the middle of cattle country," he says. "People liked our food. Just not enough of them liked our food."

After that run, he didn't raise many eyebrows when he set up shop as a colon cleaner, massage therapist, and foot detox specialist in a town that doesn't have enough money to support its own fire department.

"Oh, I got a few odd looks, but gradually people started coming in to find out what was going on," says Spalitta, a former hair salon owner from New Orleans who moved to Oklahoma in search of a simpler life. "When they heard from people who tried it and were feeling better, my business began to grow."

Around the small mountain communities surrounding Talihina, health insurance isn't always part of the family budget. Many folks are self-employed or living off the land and filling income gaps by selling firewood or doing odd jobs. Some of Spalitta's regular customers are people who can't afford traditional medical care. He doesn't promise to cure anyone, but if he thinks he can help someone feel better, he helps them. Sometimes, they can pay the fee that day. Many times, they leave with a promise to pay later. Like small-town doctors of yesteryear, he gets his share of payment in vegetables and favors.

Here's the scoop on his "clean from the inside out" hydrotherapy straight from the Oasis website:

> A session is a comfortable experience for many people. It produces no toxicity. Techniques are utilized to allow a small amount of water to flow into the colon, gently stimulate the colon's natural peristaltio action to release softened waste. The inflow of a small amount of water and the release of waste is repeated several times. The removal of waste should encourage

better colon function and elimination. During the sessions, most clothing can be kept on and you will be draped, or a gown might be worn to ensure more modesty. Your dignity is always maintained.

Here are the questions that can bounce around your head as you gaze upon the Hydro-Sans Plus machine, which resembles something you could use to flush out your car's transmission:

Where does the shit go? Do you see the shit as it's coming out? Do you smell the shit as it's coming out? If you decide to go for it, can you be drunk?

Here are the answers:

The waste is sucked into the town's sewer system, a big relief to the neighboring businesses. You should keep your eyes closed as if in deep meditation. If you crane your neck to see shit going through the machine, you run the risk of bodily harm and possible spillage. There is no odor although there is a bottle of Febreze nearby. Alcohol is not recommended. "No fasting or special diet is required prior to your treatment although a large meal two hours prior is not advisable."

First visits take about 90 minutes. During this time, health questions will be asked, as well as important diagnostic inquiries like, "How much toilet paper do you use?"

The treatment takes 30 to 45 minutes. Spalitta says water is "introduced via the rectum into the colon." Your belly will be massaged during the process to "stimulate the release of stored fecal matter."

Jeanine, who lives down the road in Smithville and prefers not to use her last name, asked more questions than most before she became a believer. Now, she's practically a disciple.

"I must have called Emile 12 times on the phone before I decided to do it," says Jeanine, who suffers from Hashimoto's disease, an auto-immune disorder. "I was concerned because it's not like I'm a regular patient who just needs their bowels cleaned out."

She'd tried conventional medicine, threw back countless pills prescribed to take away her gut pain, jumpstart her digestive system, and make her stop losing weight. In the four years since her diagnosis, she's dropped 61 pounds—20 pounds in less than two weeks. It's not a diet plan that she wanted or would recommend. She used to work at a Home Depot and lifted heavy bags of building materials as if they were pillows. These days, she counts herself lucky if she can make it to town and back and not have to go to bed for the rest of the day.

When a health store owner in Mena, Arkansas, mentioned that she check into having her colon flushed out by a guy in Talihina, Jeanine thought it was about the craziest idea she'd heard in a while. Why would someone open a colon therapy joint in a town so far off the beaten path that the nearest turnpike was 50 miles away?

After several weeks, she softened to the idea. It impressed her that Spalitta took the time to research her medical issue and talk about things she might do to try to reclaim her life. Several gall bladder/liver flushes and weekly colon hydrotherapy sessions later, she started to feel something. It was herself, her old self. She was back.

"I'm optimistic about my health again," Jeanine says. "When I first started going, I was constipated and so sick. I don't like talking about my eliminations, but I'm blessed every morning now. When I started to eliminate properly, I was in seventh heaven."

From the minute she steps into Oasis, Jeanine says she goes into a state of meditation. The man who flushes toxins out of her insides has become a calming presence in her life. One day, she walked in with a shit-pleasing grin on her face: She'd achieved No. 4 on the Bristol Stool Chart. "Like a sausage or snake, smooth and soft."

"I believe he is a gifted healer. I feel like I receive a blessing every time that I go into his office," she says. "He's God-sent. I really believe it. Here is a man who lives his life in a moral way like Jesus Christ, and yet he's willing to clean the shit right out of you."

Gentle spoken and a bit reserved, Spalitta tends to shy from praise and the spotlight. If it weren't for the fact that his religion shapes so much of how he lives his life, he wouldn't bring it into his business at all. Sometimes, he asks people if he can say a prayer for them. He wants to help people as much as he wants to spread the word that alternative health practices can sometimes provide the answers people seek.

His patient list includes nurses, doctors, and other health professionals. Many of them travel miles to see him. When his wife and her hospital coworkers get sick, they often drop in to get their pipes checked. Spalitta spends a lot of time studying the benefits of colon therapy. He's a member of the International Association of Colon Hydrotherapy, which will hold its next convention in the Midwest on June 20–24 in Chicago. He sees it as a sign that colon hydrotherapy is catching on around these parts.

Morning, afternoons and some nights at Oasis, the Hydro-Sans Plus machine churns toxin butter into a free-flowing stream. Appointments are necessary. Information is free. If you are the least bit squeamish, try watching the DVDs with either Chinese or Korean narration.

Spalitta knows it's not for everyone. He doesn't take it personally when a stranger who obviously spends too much time eating greasy food late into the night decides to skip colon hydrotherapy and drink a few beers instead.

He saw it coming. He could see it in her eyes.

Originally published
March 2011

by Joel Vandiver

OKLAHOMA BABYLON

A Gnostic Mass on the prairie

Photo by Michael Cooper

The room is dark, despite the noonday sun. Thick curtains have been pulled across the windows. Several people are lined in two columns at the north and south. They comprise the only branch of the *Ordo Templi Orientis* in Oklahoma. I'm joining them for their Gnostic Mass, a ritual created by the infamous 20th century occultist Aleister Crowley. Some might call them Satanists. "We are categorically not Satanists," says the head of the Oklahoma City chapter of the OTO. "Neither was Crowley a Satanist. We do not 'worship the devil' or cast evil spells or any such nonsense."

The OTO, however, are certainly not Christians. For Christians, it is Easter Sunday; for this gathering, it is Sunday, April 9, 2001, *era vulgaris*.

In the center of the makeshift temple stands a small altar that bears the tools of magic: the wand of fire, the dagger of air, the cup of water and the disk of earth. To the east, an opalescent veil hangs between two black and white pillars, obscuring a throne on a black- and white-cubed dais and a large painting of a Tarot card above the altar. The deacon, a man in his fifties dressed in a long white and yellow robe, stands at the altar reciting the first section of the mass, invoking the esoteric deities of the order:

> I believe in one secret and ineffable LORD; and in one Star in the Company of Stars of whose fire we are created, and to which we shall return; and in one Father of Life, Mystery of Mystery, in His name CHAOS, the sole viceregent of the Sun upon the Earth; and in one Air the nourisher of all that breathes.
> And I believe in one Earth, the Mother of us all, and in one Womb wherein all men are begotten, and wherein they shall rest, Mystery of Mystery, in Her name BABALON.
> And I believe in the Serpent and the Lion, Mystery of Mystery, in His name BAPHOMET.

He chants in a forceful, barreling baritone that vibrates throughout the room, causing my chest to resonate like I'm leaning against a transformer.

When the deacon completes the first invocation, the priest and priestess enter from the west. The priest is plainly robed, his garments open at the chest to reveal a colorful tattoo of interlocking circles and a six-pointed star. The tattoo is etched directly above the thin skin of his sternum, and I try to imagine how much it hurt as raga music plays and the priestess begins a serpentine dance. She is festooned in bright jewels and veils, the costume of the infamous seductress Salome, her hips gyrating seductively. The priest remains motionless while the priestess places a red robe about his shoulders, a crown on his head and hands him a shining lance. By the end of her dance, he looks like a Babylonian king.

At this point, I realize I'm not in Kansas anymore. I don't even feel like I'm in the continental United States. It's like something out of an Edgar Rice Burroughs novel—I feel like John Carter, transported to Mars in the passing of an instant. All sense of rationality quickly escapes me as the priest escorts the priestess to the dais. The veil has been lifted momentarily, and, as she takes her place on the throne, she pulls it closed.

The priest and priestess perform a call and response play, acting the roles of the male and female principles of the universe. My head swims as I try to remember all the myths and symbols they invoke. As I focus on the ritual, I stop struggling to make sense of everything and just drink it in. The priest ascends the steps of the dais. When he reaches the top, he uses his lance to part the veil once again, revealing the priestess on the throne, looking positively feline. I'm somewhat shocked to see that all of her veils have fallen away, as well. Her milky breasts glisten with perspiration from her exertions, her nipples blushing and brazen. Her green eyes blaze under desultory brows and her hair is a sweeping auburn fire. A regal austerity, a selfless sense of presence in the moment, elevates her posture.

I'm reminded of the infamous sequence depicted in Stanley Kubrick's *Eyes Wide Shut*, when Dr. Bill Hartford steals into a secret ceremonial orgy, only to be discovered and forced to strip naked in front of the whole congregation for his subterfuge. Fortunately, I've gone through the proper channels, so there is no sense of illegitimacy on my part, just growing wonder. This is what happens when the veil is lifted. The ceremony culminates as first the priest, then the deacon, and then the other lodge members including myself approach the priestess and consume the Eucharist of the mass, the cakes of light.

These small baked morsels are made of flour, honey, red wine reduction, a combination of cinnamon, myrrh, galangal, and olive oils and a final, most controversial ingredient: human blood collected from the officiating priest and priestess. There is an entire dialogue among concerned people about the appropriateness of this last ingredient, and apparently there are those who use substitutions. In fact, the official recipe for the cakes of light requires that the blood be burned, the ashes rendered to powder, and finally added to the mixture. I have been assured prior to the ritual that there is no unrendered blood in the cakes, but it doesn't concern me much. I enjoy a medium rare steak, why should baked goods be a problem?

The only issue I have with the cakes of light is that they are extraordinarily chewy, or maybe it was just mine. It's very mealy and absorbs every drop of moisture in my mouth as I chew. I spend a good two minutes at the top of the dais, in front of the whole congregation, trying to swallow the host. I consider drinking the entire goblet of wine used in the ceremony to wash it down, but that would be rude. Someone stifles a laugh at my noticeable difficulty. But finally, the cake goes down and I recite, "There is no part of me that is not of the Gods," just as the rest of the members had.

The ritual is ended, and the temple is no longer a temple. It is the same unassuming one story suburban home that I had incredulously approached on my arrival roughly two hours ago. The drapes have been pulled from the windows, and the bright springtime sun shines into the breakfast nook, where I sit and chat with the others. The ritual chamber itself is actually the living room. All of the temple furniture is modular and quickly removable. This allows the two heads of the lodge to get back to doing what most others do—live a normal life.

The lodge members are, for the most part, financially successful and well-adjusted individuals. Among the participants that day, I meet an investment banker, a computer tech and a financial advisor, as well as a couple of students. Some of them hold positions in other orders, such as the Masons, and one of them talks excitedly about his attainment of a new degree.

I mention that it happens to be Easter Sunday and get some laughs. One woman makes light of it, completely comfortable with the schism.

"Oh, I have to make it to my mother's Easter dinner in an hour," she chuckles. "If she only knew..."

Speaking of Easter, I have my own family function to attend, so I say my thanks and goodbyes and head out into the sun. I pass the stone cherub in the front garden, which the priestess half-jokingly chided houses a protective spirit. I guess I'm in the clear, because I pass unscathed. The suburbs of Oklahoma City are quiet and calm. As I prepare for the drive back to Tulsa, I get a sense of vertigo. I get back in my car, driving back into the world of traffic cops, muffin tops, Big Macs, and box-office flops. It's mid-April, but the wind is biting and cold. Oklahoma spring never comes on time. The landscape is a brown and red blur outside.

Originally published February 2012

by Kelly Kurt

DEATH'S YELLOW DOOR

"We may be indifferent to the death penalty and not declare ourselves either way so long as we have not seen a guillotine with our own eyes. But when we do, the shock is violent, and we are compelled to choose sides, for or against."

—Victor Hugo, *Les Miserables*

Inside Oklahoma's death chamber

Within the maze of oppressive gray halls of the Oklahoma State Penitentiary's H Unit, the door that leads to the death chamber seems as out of place as a birthday balloon. It is yellow. Bright, daisy yellow. The color is unnerving.

It's almost 6:00 PM when I cross the threshold with six other media witnesses. Gary Roland Welch already lies strapped to a gurney a few feet away behind the window of the adjoining room. He's hidden from view by a closed shade. We take our seats on a row of metal folding chairs and listen for lingering signs of death row's sendoff. The sound began 10 minutes earlier, a forceful clanging and rhythmic tapping that echoed through the concrete corridors. CLANG. CLANG. Ping. CLANG. CLANG. Ping. This is how other condemned men pay their respects—by slamming their cell doors with their feet or tapping their commodes. Death row's goodbye sounds like someone trying to break out.

Six stone-faced men—prosecutors, law officers, and a state official—take seats in front of us. Behind us, behind one-way glass, sit three family members of the man Welch killed. No one is here on Welch's behalf. My stomach churns as we sit in silence, waiting for the mini blind to rise.

When the shade finally goes up, Welch is looking at us. His thick body is bound to the gurney—legs, arms, chest, shoulders. Tubes run from his arms and disappear into the wall behind him. I glimpse a colorful tattoo on a forearm. A graying ginger beard covers his jaw and chin. He turns his head and his eyes meet mine.

In a matter of minutes, the 49-year-old will choke on his last word and die, marking the nation's first execution of 2012. For now, he lifts his head, straining to see each witness through the glass. His eyes reach the row's end, and something unexpected happens.

The condemned man suddenly smiles.

And then, he winks.

I am here to witness a homicide. Not a murder, which is a crime. Even the governor is in on this death.

I've been here before and this is what I've seen every time: A brightly lit room. A clock on the wall. A warden standing with clasped hands. A prison official on a black wall phone with a long coiling cord, ready in case the governor hands down a last-second reprieve. What I've never seen: a reprieve. Or the three executioners hidden behind the wall. No one sees them. They arrive wearing hoods on their heads and faces to cloak their identities.

I am told that some people see the face of Jesus in the pattern of the concrete wall next to the yellow door, but I've never seen that either.

Sometime before Welch's January 5 execution date, I realize that I have lost track of how many men I've seen die here. Since 1915, Oklahoma has executed 177 men and three women. The oldest was 74. The youngest, 18. Ninety-seven died by lethal injection, 82 by electrocution, and one by hanging. Most of the executions I witnessed took place in the late 1990s and early 2000s, a time when Oklahoma's death chamber was one of the nation's busiest. Welch's execution, I later learn, is my 16th.

More than 60 percent of Americans favor the death penalty. But very few people actually have witnessed a modern execution.

At one time, executions in Oklahoma were public. A crowd of 30 or 40 onlookers crammed into the penitentiary known as Big Mac to watch the warden flip the switch on Old Sparky, the heavy wooden electric chair with its leather straps and helmet. Newsmen and sightseers, even children, were there, says Dale Cantrell, a 28-year Big Mac veteran who serves as the prison's de facto historian. A 1934 story by The Associated Press described what they heard and saw—"a sudden hum of a motor, a violent stiffening of the body." A crackdown on the circus-like atmosphere ultimately brought a section of law entitled "Persons Who May Witness," which largely slammed the door on public access. It did provide that "reporters from recognized members of the news media will be admitted upon proper identification, application, and approval of the warden."

Sister Helen Prejean, the death penalty abolitionist whose book *Dead Man Walking* spawned an Oscar-winning film and an opera that will open in Tulsa this month, predicts more Americans would turn against the death penalty if executions were more open. Responding to arguments that public executions could "coarsen" society, she wrote:

> An execution is ugly because the premeditated killing of a human being is ugly. Torture is ugly. Gassing, hanging, shooting, electrocuting or lethally injecting a person whose hands and feet are tied is ugly. And hiding the ugliness from view and rationalizing it numbs our minds to the horror of what is happening. This is what truly "coarsens" us.

Witnessing executions did start to feel like ugly business to me—but not at first.

It was part of my job as a reporter for The Associated Press, the one organization Corrections Department policy guarantees by name to claim one of the 12 seats reserved for the media. I was surprised to discover that I could witness a man's dying breath, write about it in detail, and later drive home, with my eyes on the road and my mind on dinner. Only once did a dead man haunt my sleep. I opened my eyes and saw him hanging by a meat hook above my bed. When I awoke fully, I was sitting up, staring at the ceiling fan.

With every execution, however, came a family's story of deep and lasting loss. The victim's survivors told me again and again how their lives had been shattered by a single act of violence. Dusty Miller, who was left to raise three children alone, marveled that a killer "could meet somebody like Gwen [his wife] and still make a decision that the world didn't need her anymore." The parents of Michael Houghton and Laura Lee Sanders, who were burned alive in the trunk of a car, endured more than 15 years of court proceedings before witnessing the lethal injection of one of the killers. The niece of Muskogee grocer Claude Wiley described his smile and kindness. He often delivered food to the poor and homebound, until the day he made a delivery to a home where a man was waiting for him behind the door with a baseball bat.

Sometimes an elderly woman, the mother of the condemned, sat in front me, clutching a tissue and weeping with loss, too. Jim Fowler, himself the son of a murder victim, saw his son executed for killing three people in a botched robbery, saying afterward in a shaking voice, "It makes your gut sick to see your boy die."

CRIME DOES NOT PAY!
ABSOLUTELY NO ENTRY INTO THIS AREA WITHOUT THE EXPRESSED WRITTEN CONSENT OF THE WARDEN

Some people call capital punishment justice. Others call it barbaric. In the death chamber, I feel a pervasive sadness and sense of futility. When people ask me what I've learned about the death penalty, I tell them the only thing I know conclusively: It doesn't take away the sadness or bring anyone back. But it does shut a person up.

What I have heard:

A cop's killer begging his victim's family, "Forgive me as the Lord has forgiven me."

A woman's weeping for her condemned son, whose crimes included the murder of his sister.

The warden announcing, "Let the execution begin."

Victims' families clapping after a five-time killer is declared dead.

What I have never heard: a condemned man cry.

Welch turns his scraggly bearded face toward the ceiling and speaks.

"I was just going to ask everybody if they could hear my brothers out there," he says, referring to death row's clanging. "I know it's kind of quiet now, but I want to acknowledge that my brothers are here for me to send me off on my journey. They are here on my behalf."

Welch claimed he killed Robert Hardcastle in self-defense on the evening of August 25, 1994. He said he went to the 35-year-old's Miami home in pursuit of drugs and ended up fighting for his life after Hardcastle came at him with a knife.

"My intentions were never to kill him," he told a *McAlester News-Capital* reporter during his clemency hearing in December. "But I also didn't intend for him to kill me either."

The jury believed the prosecution's story—that Welch assaulted Hardcastle in his home and then he and a co-conspirator, Claudie Conover, chased him into a ditch. There were multiple witnesses, including a family taking their 11-year-old to football practice, who saw Welch stab Hardcastle repeatedly with a knife and, when it broke, slash him with a broken beer bottle.

The first police officer on the scene, Officer Jim Gambill, found Hardcastle covered in blood sitting up in the ditch with his clothes in shreds. The officer recognized him. He and Hardcastle had grown up playing Little League ball together.

"Jim," Hardcastle said, "Gary Welch did this shit to me. Get that motherfucker."

Hardcastle then asked for some water and soon after fell on his back and died. He left behind 2-year-old twin sons.

"A big hole remains in our hearts that will never go away," Hardcastle's parents wrote to the Pardon and Parole Board, which rejected clemency by a vote of 3–2. "To know justice has been served gives us some closure to the agony we have had to endure."

"Closure" is a word that means different things to people whose lives have been turned upside down by crime. Grieving families after the Oklahoma City bombing described it as justice or, in some cases, vengeance. For some, it meant the end of round after round of court appeals or at least the silencing of the killer. Some described closure as relief from intense grief. Brooks Douglass, the man who authored Oklahoma's law allowing victims' families to watch executions, told me for an AP story that he did not find immediate solace after watching one of the men who killed his parents die for the crime. But, he said, the execution did restore his faith in the justice system.

The Supreme Court struck down the death penalty in 1972, finding that the power of juries to decide whether a defendant should live or die for a crime resulted in arbitrary and capricious sentencing. States brought capital punishment back, rewriting their statutes and giving judges and juries new sentencing guidelines.

But Lyn Entzeroth, who teaches a course on capital punishment at the University of Tulsa's law school, believes the system remains flawed.

"To me there is no way of discerning what murder case gets death and what murder case doesn't," she says. She notes a report by the Death Penalty Information Center that shows county-by-county discrepancies in how often the death penalty is sought.

Fifteen counties, including Oklahoma County, were responsible for 30 percent of the nation's total executions since 1976. Exclude Texas (with nine counties on that list), and Oklahoma County tops the list with prosecutions resulting in 36 executions since 1976. Tulsa County was 14th with eight executions.

"The discretion of that prosecutor in that county can have a huge effect," says Entzeroth, who also co-authored a death penalty casebook used in law schools. "When Bob Macy was the DA in Oklahoma County, there were a large number of death sentences sought. That's changed since then."

Support for the death penalty remains high—61 percent, according to a 2011 Gallup poll. But that number represents the lowest level of support since 1972 and a significant decline from an all-time high of 80 percent in 1994.

A spate of exonerations tied to DNA evidence may account in part for the decline. Evidence of innocence has brought the exonerations of 140 people on death row since 1973, with 66 of those occurring since 1999, according to the DPIC. Four states in four years—New Mexico, New York, New Jersey, and Illinois—have effectively abolished the death penalty.

And late last year, Oregon Governor John Kitzhaber declared a moratorium on the death penalty, saying he refused "to be a part of this compromised and inequitable system."

Along with concerns about wrongful convictions, the option of life without parole sentencing is changing the debate, Entzeroth says.

"Because someone has committed a horrible murder, we as a society would like that person incapacitated, not back out on the street some day," she says. "The option of life without parole gives that option, that security."

What no one saw (other than the robbers): Who pulled the trigger that fired the bullets into my friend, Michael Fifer.

Mike left college to stay home with his terminally ill mother. Years later, he ended up working the graveyard shift at a Circle K in Tulsa to pay the bills. He didn't get to choose his final words on November 30, 1991, the night the gunman pulled open the convenience store door. He died facedown on the floor, shot in the neck and back. Two teens, Johnny Davis and Eric Johnson, each accused the other of being the shooter. Both received no-parole life terms for the killing, though Johnson's was later reduced by an appeals court. A prosecutor said the jury gave then 17-year-old Davis the no-parole term to ensure he "didn't get out."

But he found a way out.

In 1996, Davis slid through 6-inch bars and climbed four stories down a homemade rope to escape the maximum-security floor of a private prison in Texas. He was on the run for four days.

Davis is now 37 years old. Mike died at age 25.

A murder that touches your life changes you forever. I still carry the weight of it. At some point, I stopped using the word "closure" in news stories.

Hours before I'm in the death chamber, I stand in the threshold of my closet. It sounds frivolous, but deciding what to wear to an execution is worse than deciding what to wear to a funeral. I reject the new black-and-white striped shirt that my kids dubbed "the burglar shirt." The sweater I got for Christmas seems too bright. I end up in a white shirt and black pants. When I stop for a soda to carry me to McAlester, the store clerk comments, "Black and white? You must be a waitress." I shake my head. He tries again. "Band leader?" I leave him squirming. How do you tell someone you dressed like this to watch a man be put to death?

Freedom meets its end on a long winding road at McAlester's edge before I even get to the Oklahoma State Penitentiary. If there's a road to perdition, it's this one.

I pass a minimum-security prison, the county jail, a juvenile detention center, an animal shelter, and a street named Electric Avenue on the way to the prison gate. Built in 1904, Big Mac rises like a medieval fortress behind 30-foot, whitewashed walls topped with coils of razor-tipped wire. I glimpse armed guards watching from a prison tower as I drive through the gate, past the warden's house where Christmas lights twinkled one December when I came here for two executions in seven days.

Executions used to take place at midnight. That meant that after the U.S. Supreme Court rejected an inmate's final appeal, we had time to eat dinner. While the condemned ate his last meal, journalists, photographers, prosecutors, and visiting law officers rushed to Pete's Place or some other Italian eatery in Krebs for heaping plates of pasta and lamb fries. In the late-night darkness, I scurried back to the lockup, burdened by too many carbs and the dread of what was to come.

I was at the prison as a student journalist on September 10, 1990, when Charles Troy Coleman became the first man executed in Oklahoma following the reinstatement of the death penalty. It was the inauguration of lethal injection, too. Reporters, TV crews, and photographers jammed the prison's visitation center—a one-room building that converts to a media center on execution nights. These days, often only two or three reporters come to witness. TV crews make rare appearances.

This time, when I pull open the door to the media center, more than six years have passed since I last saw an execution. Jerry Massie, the Corrections Department's public information officer, is inside waiting like always. He's been the media wrangler at every execution I've witnessed, and there's something comforting about finding him here, sitting in front of a tray of chocolate chip cookies and bottled waters. More than once after an execution, I've heard him quietly ask some reporter, "You doing okay?" But Massie is also the gatekeeper to getting inside and tends to give the impression that causing him trouble is a bad idea.

Tonight, there are seven media witnesses, four of whom have never seen an execution. Massie goes over the rules. We can't take anything in. No recorders. No notebooks. No pens. No cell phones. (The phones, we're later told by prison spokesman Terry Crenshaw, can sell for $1,000 inside the lockup.) And if we need to go to the bathroom, we better do it now "because once you get to the H Unit, it's almost impossible to use a facility," Crenshaw says. We pile into two vans that drive to the back of the prison where the modern H Unit crouches in the earth like a bunker. Inside, a female guard tells me to take off my shoes, turn around, spread my arms, and turn

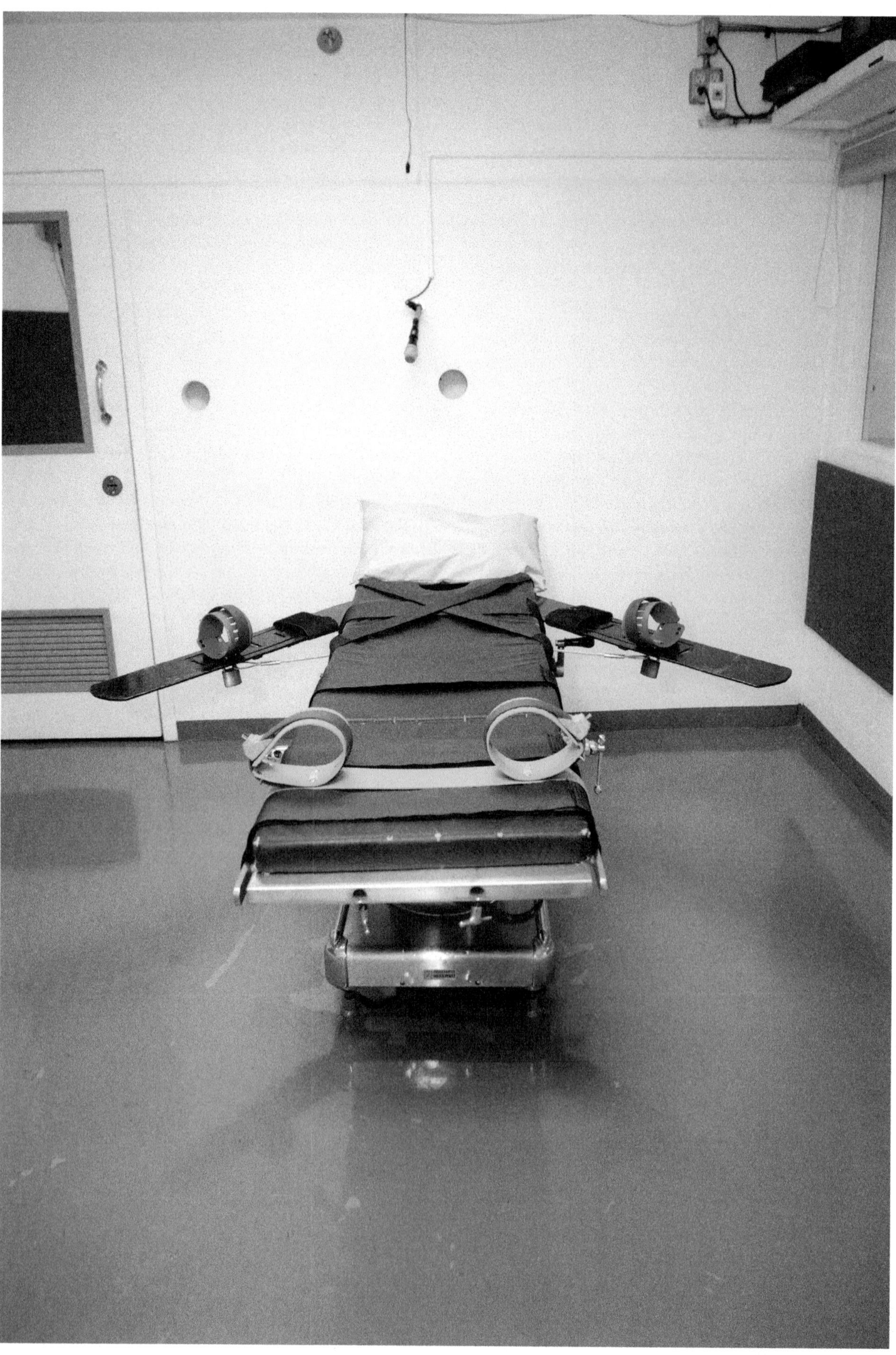

my palms up. She pats me down, first from the back. "Coming around," she says, as her hands glide over me searching for contraband.

We put on our shoes and enter a barred holding area. The heavy cell door behind us slowly rolls shut and locks with a reverberating KUH-CHUNG. In a prison, you wait for doors to open, and slowly the one in front of us does. We are led to the law library, a rectangular room where inmates can work on their cases enclosed in small cells with desks.

"Do you have the notebooks?" I ask Crenshaw.

The prison usually provides us with notebooks and pencils, but this time they're missing. He sends an officer in pursuit of them. The clanging from death row begins, and Crenshaw notes that it is louder than usual. The notebooks arrive. There's a knock at the library door. It's time.

What we report: No one says much of anything on the ride back to the media center after Welch is dead. I look out the window and notice the moon, a five-eighths moon, shining on prison buildings. The seven of us reassemble in the media center to piece together what we saw and heard.

Who did he wink at? "Was he winking at the DA?" I ask, thinking of the case's prosecutor who was sitting at the end of the row where Welch directed his smile.

"No," says the reporter from the McAlester paper, who had previously had a lengthy interview with Welch. "I smiled at him."

Massie, overhearing, puts his head in his hands.

"Should I not have done that?" she asks.

"Probably not," Massie sighs.

Over the next few minutes we scan our scribbled notes and contribute bits and pieces of Welch's last statement. None of us got it down in its entirety.

The reconstruction goes like this:

Me: "I had, 'I want to acknowledge ...' Um."

Second reporter: " '... that my brothers are here with me ...' "

Third reporter: " 'here with me to send me off on my journey. They've already given me my sendoff ...' "

Me: "I heard 'my little sendoff.' "

A fourth reporter questions the order of sentences. We re-examine our notes. We move a sentence.

Everyone works to get it just right, although it's doubtful anyone will ever question those final words. You can't libel a dead man.

The clock on the death chamber wall reads 6:04 PM. Welch finishes his last statement saying, "They've already given me my little sendoff. So let's get it on because that's what we're here for."

Each of the three executioners injects a different drug. The first, pentobarbital, is the same sedative used to euthanize pets. It causes unconsciousness. The second, vecuronium bromide, a paralyzing agent, halts respiration. The third, potassium chloride, stops the heart.

"Let the execution begin," says the warden, setting off the process.

Immediately, Welch launches into a chant, his chest heaving against the straps:

"Valhalla. Odin. Slay the beast!" he says rapidly, almost shouting. In Norse mythology, Valhalla is the great hall in which the one-eyed god Odin receives the souls of slain warriors. The hall has 540 doors. "Valhalla. Odin. Slay the beast! Valhalla. Odin. Slay ... the ... beast. Valhalla." He slurs and chokes. "O...."

The next several minutes are awkwardly silent as we stare into the sterile room. My thoughts turn to the details of the crime that was so heinous jurors thought a man should die for it. I picture Robert Hardcastle lying slashed along a road, bleeding from nine stab wounds and a dozen other serious cuts. He died eyes open, his head on green grass, no chance to say goodbye to his sons. I see Welch, his eyes closed, releasing a slight snore and then going still. His face slowly changes from pink to purple to gray. There is no terror in this quiet scene, except for the fact I know this man is tied to the bed and his life has just been taken.

The physician steps forward, checks for a pulse and finding none, looks at the clock. "Time of death," he pronounces, "6:10 PM."

The mini blind goes down. The door opens. We file out into the darkness.

I've walked through death's yellow door 16 times to see 16 men die. They were Benjamin Brewer, Michael Edward Long, Stephen Edward Wood, Scotty Lee Moore, Bobby Ross, Gary Alan Walker, Charles Adrian Foster, Gregg Francis Braun, Mark Andrew Fowler, Vincent Allen Johnson, Alvie James Hale, Daniel Juan Revilla, Scott Allen Hain, Robert Don Duckett, Kenneth Eugene Turrentine, and Gary Roland Welch. The crimes that brought them here claimed 30 innocent men, women, and children. Every story has two sides and, in the death chamber, I've sat sandwiched between them.

Here's what else I have seen: When the execution is over and the mini blind goes down, you still see a face looking at you from the window of the death chamber; the other part of the story.

That face is your own.

Originally published
May 2010

by Rivka Galchen

SEVERE STORM WATCH

We all thought the weather was god, didn't we?

Whether it was the golf-ball hailstorm that ruined the business plan of the magnificent mile of cars or the crepuscular rays of a rainstorm at the horizon. A striking tornado was something we really wanted, wasn't it? A gale of importance, beating pompous and ludicrous as a cape lined in purple satin, sending us to the basements of nearby churches or schools, not that we ever actually went there, to the shelters, but we thought about it, and in the thinking we imaged a mottled kind of festive underground, a noble sharing of crackers and peanut butter with the extended Mormon family from across the street, an oddly jovial game of cards—like a commercial for life insurance—might break out amongst diffident adults.

Yes the "severe storm" would sweep down and make our lives suddenly as important as a Greek tragedy, or at least an early Hollywood film now in Technicolor. Really. In reality, I remember, the few times when the emergency siren went off, no one in my family much cared. My dad would go and stand outside. It was nice, to be able to see in him an indifferent kind of bravery, or foolishness. It was almost a heroic stance, and one didn't get the chance to see him that way—he didn't get the chance to appear that way—in the negotiations of the McDonald's drive-thru or picking up a kid from swim practice.

But with the sirens it was suddenly the lost world of warrior kings. Turn on the wind machine. It was the nobly unwinnable battle. The white buffalo one might even say. Man v.s. Nature! I'd brave outside too, cinematically. Those wall clouds looked like an advancing army of spirits from 1,000 lost civilizations. Our land was one to be conquered; our destiny was hard, and welcome. Soon, if the scenes in one's mind gathered from movies and Channel Nine News were correct, roofs would lie on the ground, idle as an unreplaced flour jar lid.

A flour jar lid? Or: roofs were blown off as easily as the seeds of a granny dandelion? The cars and trailers would lie scattered like children's toys out of a trunk, one stuffed bunny missing its button eye, the understated note of tragedy. Or... was it that the sky darkened like drippy acrylic paint from fourth period weeping across the newsprint paper?

There had been a poem. The beautifully inscrutable radar images of Crayola green and purple molds advanced across the state in the petri dish round of radar signal data. Meanwhile, the rain finally broke. It built and then didn't. That was the storm, now headed South to Ada. Another storm soon enough. Yes: the storms were wild molds or melodramas or armies or gods or ghosts or historic wraths or good times as had only on screens. The storms were all sorts of things.

But the one thing those storms were not—unlike the 11 items or less express checkout lane, or the pollen count, or the snapped shoelace, or the current price of oil, or the rate of bank foreclosures, or the Girl Scout cookie time of year, or the way the dryer never quite fully dried denim—yes, in distinction to all that, the one thing those storms weren't—not the really strong ones, not the scary ones, the beautiful ones, the majestic ones—was real. Or, at least, that wasn't the part most worth noticing.

Originally published
November 2013

by Gordon Grice

STILLER GROUND

A father's lament

"Reaching" by Western Doughty

... 1 ...

I walked in graveyards, gathering trash and fallen branches. I pulled weeds that obscured the names on old headstones, and, when I was through, most of the names I'd revealed meant nothing to me. I took special care with the graves of children. I put the ceramic animal caricatures back on the stones they'd fallen off of. After a rain, I thumbed mud from the Lucite-covered photographs set in stones. I took the time to read a turn-of-the-century marker made of crudely hand-lettered cement. On it was an asymmetric heart pieced from small stones. I subtracted compulsively; death year minus birth year equals age, give or take one.

I started, almost always, with the graves of my own ancestors and cousins. My mother's mother, dead before I was born. Carved next to her name was my grandfather's. He was still alive, though his name had been written in the city of the dead for 34 years. My cousin, a suicide at 21. His epitaph declared his heart too big to last in this world. I read his stone with double vision: the disdain I'd always had for such sentiments; the tolerance I had now for anything, anything at all, to ease the pain. I walked along the rows, taking care of people past caring.

That was my daily routine. Sometimes the woman I loved would come with me. I envied her. She seemed to know how to grieve. To let herself feel things, to take time. She wrote letters to our stillborn daughter. She ordered photographs from the hospital and put them in a scrapbook. She talked. Most of these activities were strange to me, though I clumsily tried to emulate her for the sake of my mental health. I wanted to have my private scene at the cemetery, unwitnessed, and be cured for good, or at least for a little while.

Usually the last grave we visited was Abby's, on the western edge of the cemetery, a new section where shade trees were forbidden and the buffalo grass grew sparse. Around the temporary steel marker clustered a miniature rose bush and a petunia, both recently planted and probably doomed by the heat, and an assortment of artificial flowers. I rinsed the fake flowers every day. Despite my care, mud splashed them and became a coat of dust by the following day. Their brilliance evaporated. My mind crawled sluggishly into the groove of trite symbols—life is transitory as a spring rose, and that sort of thing. I despised such easy comparisons even as I dredged them from my stock of clichés.

One day the petunia bore the marks of some small nibbling animal. The next day the entire plant had been devoured, and rabbit scat lay among the artificial flowers. I cleaned things up. A black string lay on the ground, and as I knelt closer the string resolved itself into a trail of ants. They came out of a small hole in the ground, traveled a few inches, and vanished into another hole.

The ants reminded me of a long dream I'd had the night before. It ended with bullies throwing black ants on my daughter. She looked about four years old. I couldn't protect her. I was a bad father. The dream had clung for hours, souring the morning.

Now I knew what it meant. Ants eat dead things.

· · · 2 · · ·

At the hospital the day Abby was born, a nurse handed me a booklet about being the parent of a dead child. What's the cost of a funeral for a newborn? Can you take a tax deduction? What should you name a dead child? Is it OK to build the coffin yourself? The booklet plainly answered such questions. It was my introduction to a realm of knowledge I had never known existed.

The answers run like this:

You can build the coffin if you want. It might make you feel better.

Name the child what you meant to name him. Don't save the name for someone else.

You can claim the baby as a dependent on your taxes if he drew a breath.

General practice in the funeral industry is to charge low for a baby. In Guymon we had two mortuaries to choose from, and I chose the one that had buried my grandmother. The man at the funeral home appeared well-muscled and athletic, out of place in his gray suit. He sold me a baby-sized Styrofoam coffin not unlike a picnic cooler. I paid $250 for it, and that was all I paid for the whole job. The athletic man asked me if anyone would view the body, and I said no. He asked me if I was sure, and I said I was. I thought it was a strange thing to ask. No one would want to look at a stillborn child. The last look is for someone you've seen before, and no one had seen Abby except Tracy and me and some strangers.

When Tracy's grandmother asked if she could see the body, I felt overwhelmed with gratitude. Abby was a real person, and now someone besides Tracy and me was saying so, however indirectly. Others had given us words of comfort that cut to the bone: *When this happens, it means something was really wrong with them. It's for the best. You'll have others. At least it happened before you got to know her*. All of which seemed to say Abby was not worthy of the grief.

I called the athlete to ask if it was too late to look at Abby, and it was.

"I'll tell you what," he said. "The casket's glued shut, but I can try to pry it open." That seemed a violation of the dead. I declined his offer. Later, when I saw the ants at the grave, I remembered the sealed Styrofoam. Maybe the ants weren't getting in. But something was happening to her, by whatever physical agent. Her decomposition was inexorable.

· · · 3 · · ·

We were living in Arkansas, where we were in grad school, when Tracy got pregnant. It was a long drive from our hometown in the Oklahoma Panhandle. We had planned the pregnancy, and in October it happened. Not long after conception, Tracy bled, and we feared we'd lose the baby. Tracy had to stay in bed a while. Then everything smoothed out. In December I landed a teaching job back home in Oklahoma. The higher pay meant Tracy could stay home with the baby. We moved to Oklahoma in January.

Near the end of April, the pregnancy was 30 weeks along. Tracy hadn't felt the baby kick for a day or two, which worried me. I dismissed that fear, as I had many others over the months.

Tracy couldn't dismiss it, though she wasn't ready to press me with her worry. She remembered feeling the baby kick the previous Saturday, several fast kicks. She put her sister's hand on the place to let her feel, but there was no more movement. Later Tracy would wonder if those movements were caused by fear or pain. She would be haunted by the thought that those kicks marked the moment of death.

On Tuesday morning, Tracy was asleep when I left for work. When she woke, she tried to remind herself that babies sometimes don't move for long periods late in a pregnancy. Her sister Corey told her our nephew Cody had laid still in the womb for two days just before he was born. Tracy's stomach felt different, softer, and she tried to explain that away. And down deep, she knew the baby was dead.

Corey and Cody went with her to the doctor's office, where an experienced nurse failed to find a heartbeat. The nurse, an old family friend, didn't state the obvious conclusion. Tracy didn't say the words either. The nurse sent her to the hospital, where she waited with Corey and 14-month-old Cody.

Tracy held Cody and sang to him. She sang "Me and Bobby McGee," a song she'd sung to him many times before. She always meant for her own baby to hear it

Photo by Gaylord Oscar Herron
From The *Signal Tree Series*

too. Somewhere she'd read that babies are soothed by songs they first learned in the womb. After an hour's wait, the hospital technicians were ready for her. She submitted to an array of machines—fetal monitor, X-ray, sonogram. The technicians said nothing about the baby. Each technician did his work, patted her on the arm, and left the room without a word.

When I got home from work, no one was there. I had a snack and turned on the TV. Then I saw a blinking light on the answering machine, and somehow I knew everything. The telephone rang. It was Corey. She told me to come to the hospital. Before I left, I listened to the message on the answering machine, and of course it only said the same thing my sister-in-law had just told me.

At the hospital I found Tracy getting a sonogram. The room was dim, its fluorescent lights shaded by wooden blinds, the monitor casting a green light. The technician moved the probe soundlessly across Tracy's body, making furrows in the green lubricating jelly. The look on Tracy's face when she saw me was almost an apology: Surely this is nothing and it's a shame you had to worry about it, I hope. Corey yielded her position at the bedside and slipped out. The green shapes on the monitor moved with the motion of the technician's hand, forming pictures like those the weather people show on TV, storms forming, detected by shifting velocities, painted in thicknesses of a single shade. I couldn't see any image in the shifting green. The technician said nothing.

We went to a waiting room, where Tracy's family had gathered. It was a long wait. We saw the doctor arrive. He walked past the door of the waiting room to the sonogram room, and a minute later he was with us.

"It doesn't look good," he said. He hardly paused after that sentence, but for both of us the little pause was filled with frantic silent interpretation. He continued: "We've lost the baby."

··· 4 ···

"Here we see a double outline of the skull, and this is another indication of fetal loss," said the obstetrician we'd driven 40 miles to see. Our family doctor had sent us. The obstetrician traced the double outline with the blunt end of a pen on the sonogram screen.

"Is it a girl?" Tracy said.

"I don't see any indication of a boy," the obstetrician said.

It was Wednesday, the day after we found out. Everything was confirmed. He outlined the options: Wait for the baby to come to term, which could be two more months. A hard two months to go through, he said. Or take the baby out by cesarean. Hard on the mother's body; and you're robbed of everything about your baby, even the birth itself. Or induce labor. We chose the last. There was a rustling of papers as a nurse came in and out, offering us choices for an appointment at the hospital.

The obstetrician inserted some sticks made of seaweed into Tracy's cervix. The idea was that they would absorb moisture overnight, expanding, dilating the cervix. Then, early in the morning, they'd give Tracy a drug to start contractions.

··· 5 ···

At the hospital the next day, a nurse took the booklet from me and turned to a certain page and pointed. "This is a list of what some people like to keep. If you two will circle what you want, I'll see you get it. Also, if you'll look at this other list and tell me what you want to do with the baby. I'll check with you later."

The baby was not yet born. Tracy lay in a hospital bed, clutching a sort of joystick with a button that coaxed morphine through an IV drip. A machine with red liquid digits rationed out the drug, keeping her from getting too much.

The suggested keepsakes included a lock of hair, inked footprints and handprints, a birth certificate, the plastic hospital bracelet, the receiving blanket, various bits of paperwork. And photographs.

I didn't want the photographs. The very thought of having such a thing repulsed me. A dead baby. You wouldn't want it, I reasoned—it seemed like reasoning—because someone else might come across it, might without preparation or desire see a dead baby. Where would you keep such a picture?

"In a photo album," Tracy said. She lay on her side, her hair clinging to the sweat of her neck, occasionally whimpering with pain—something I'd never heard her do. She lay there with her fist wrapped around the morphine button, her eyes almost closed against the pain, and knew exactly what she would want later. I stood there feeling embarrassed at the thought of photographs of the dead, but my embarrassment, I would decide later, was really shame. The shame of a failed father.

I massaged Tracy's back, because they'd said in childbirth class that relaxing was supposed to lessen pain, and because I had nothing else to do.

··· 6 ···

Eight hours after the IV drip started to convulse her body, Tracy said she had to urinate. The nurse asked her how long it had been and threatened to run a catheter. As she sat up, Tracy said, "Oh!" She pushed away the nurse who was still trying to help her stand. "I think my water broke."

Minutes later the obstetrician was back, and other nurses, and the pushing started. Tracy screamed. After the hours of helpless inertia, she was sitting up, straining her muscles, her eyes wide and bright.

"Don't scream, honey," the head nurse said.

Tracy thought she had to be kidding. "It seemed like a stupid thing to say," she told me later. "I thought I should get to scream if I wanted to." She screamed again, and her whole body seemed to strain into that primal sound. It seemed closer to anger than pain.

"Don't scream, honey," the head nurse insisted quietly. "Use that strength to push."

"Really?" Tracy said, as if someone had just dropped an interesting fact in casual conversation. She didn't scream again.

I stood holding Tracy's hand, and I cried as I never had before. The day had seemed long and tense and irritating, and now all the tense irritation unmasked itself as grief and overwhelmed me with tears. I was trying to help. Nothing we'd learned in childbirth class, nothing I'd read in the books held any relevance here. The head nurse told Tracy what to do, speaking in a compassionate whisper that Tracy could hear in spite of my blubbering. I was supposed to let Tracy squeeze my hand when she needed to. With the other hand I continually wiped my eyes so I could see what was going on.

Beneath the foot of the bed lay a pool of blood, shimmering in the fluorescent light. Most of it had fallen there when the water broke, but there was still a steady drip from the bed. I marveled at the sloppiness of it. You'd think they'd have a way to keep it from getting in the works of the bed and all, I thought. The obstetrician sat on a swivel stool, crouched like a watchmaker going about some routine task at the work bench. He stuck his finger in to stretch the opening. It seemed to me he had nothing better to do. The baby's head appeared, dark curls plastered to bright red skin, pushing through a little wave of slimy fluid.

"It's crowning," the doctor said. What a useless son of a bitch you are, I thought.

"Jesus, that hurts," Tracy said, without any particular intensity. The baby came out surprisingly fast, falling audibly on the padded shelf the doctor had pulled out of the bed. Her entire body was bright red, as if she were blushing deeply, and covered with the waxy white substance called vernix. Otherwise, she looked like any other baby. The cord trailed out with her, fleshy and also blushing. It was tied in a red knot.

"That might explain something," the doctor remarked mildly.

"There's a knot in the cord," I sobbed.

"Oh," Tracy said.

"Could that have killed her?" I said.

"Yes," the doctor said. "It could have." He poked at the knot with some surgical instrument. "Not very tight, really."

Shut up, you useless son of a bitch, I thought. This is an explanation. Don't ruin it.

... 7 ...

Tracy's mother was in the room, but she didn't want to see Abby. She looked at Tracy's face throughout the labor, and never saw the body. When a nurse mentioned holding Abby, Tracy's mother left the room.

The booklet the nurse had given me suggested things to do. Hold the body; bathe it; rock it; take pictures; dress it; talk to it; invite the family in to see it. Touching was supposed to make it easier to heal because you have to have a tactile sense of somebody to remember. All of these struck me as weird and disturbing at first mention. But the book said I'd be sorry if I never held her, and that sounded plausible.

A nurse took Abby out to clean her up a bit. Shortly she was back, carrying Abby in a white receiving blanket with a few stripes on it. She made a ridiculously small bundle, which the nurse handed to Tracy.

"She's beautiful," Tracy said, pulling the blanket away from her face to see her better. We made inventory. One foot was cramped into an odd position, and the nurse said that would have straightened out in a little while. Tracy claimed her ears looked like mine.

I was still crying and not saying too much. "Can we open the eyes?" I finally choked out.

"No, it's better if we don't," said the nurse with the hushed but strangely audible voice. I wanted to know what color her eyes were, and I didn't know a newborn's eyes may not settle on a color for several months.

When it was my turn I sat and rocked Abby. An errant smudge of blood stained my shirt cuff. It was not really Abby's blood, but placental blood. Still, I thought of it as hers. I'd been meaning to return the shirt because of its shoddy workmanship, but now I realized I never would. A corner of her right eye had worked itself open, and the crescent of color I saw was dark.

... 8 ...

That night I lay beside Tracy's bed in a reclining chair. I wrapped myself in a sheet and a thin blanket and lay there sweaty and cold, my neck crimping. I slept a little. What kept waking me was baby-sound. The nursery was nearby. The cries would come, thin as wet slivers of rosewood, and I would wake. They sounded less than real, like cries on TV do. I liked to hear them.

Glass vases with thin necks lined the windowsill. A rank of white irises traced cloud-shapes against the dark of the real clouds behind them. The moon was bright. I fell in and out of dreams. In one dream the doctor suddenly realized we had two children, and he took Tracy into surgery to cut out the unborn twin. It was a boy, monstrously large, and instead of his sister's fatal softness he had a hard skull and great predatory teeth. But he cried, helpless as a human child. His eyes were wild, ape's eyes, nothing human in them except the need to be fed, and Tracy and I would have an unrelenting lifetime of hunger and screams.

When I woke I was not scared, only lonely. I lay awake listening to Tracy's breathing and the cries of the distant children.

... 9 ...

It was 40 miles from hospital to home. Tracy sat quietly. After the long labor with its violent artificial contractions, they'd taken her into surgery to scrape out the recalcitrant placenta. She was in considerable pain.

A snowstorm had blown up that morning. Its gusts danced on the highway like white dresses on a wash line. On the car stereo, which had been a birthday present to me the week before, we had Billie Holiday, and she was singing "Summertime." In the song a mother is singing to her baby. She says the living is easy. She says one day the baby will rise up singing and spread his wings and take to the sky, but till then he's safe with his father and mother.

Illustration by Henrik Uldalen

When we got home I took two days' worth of mail from the box. All of it was damp along the edge where snow had blown in. There were bills and business and letters from friends, as if nothing had happened.

· · · 10 · · ·

I didn't sit and brood about Abby all the time. I thought of her often, many times in a day. Sometimes I thought of her with nothing but pleasure. Tracy and I both found the memory of her birth profoundly beautiful, despite everything. But the grief returned frequently. It would start as an irritable feeling, hardly noticeable to me, though no doubt others found me harder than usual to get along with. Over the course of a week or so, my irritability would blossom into a restless insomnia and an unfocused anger. Eventually I'd find myself up long past midnight, pawing through the months-old sympathy cards and the toys people had sent in anticipation and the photos and the birth certificate and the footprints and handprints.

I was happy if I could draw tears. Tears would make me feel sane for a few days or a few weeks. But everything would start over, the grief cycling in unpredictable intervals. Sometimes it came as a sudden catch in my voice, or as a craving for hard-driving rock and roll, or as a suspicion that I had somehow killed her. Sometimes it came as a diffuse hunger that seemed to have no object, an almost subliminal feeling that I could satisfy myself with a meal or a drink or a sudden insight.

Sometimes it was a daydream. In one of them I found myself holding her in some realm outside of time, and I was telling her everything would be all right.

· · · 11 · · ·

My mother admitted she was mad at God. She would go to the grave and sing lullabies and check on the flowers. If the flowers faded, she'd ask Tracy's permission before she took them up. Before she left the cemetery she always traced the name on the iron marker with her finger.

One day, not long after Oklahoma's fitful spring returned, Tracy and my mother went to the cemetery together. They found the deep gouge of a tire across the grave. The tire had bent the iron marker. Tracy had a habit of putting a pretty rock on the grave every time she visited. The rocks were scattered, and one of them, a rough cluster of quartz crystals, had broken. It lay scattered on the road like rock salt.

The tire track guided them to another grave nearby, freshly dug, heaped up with wet clods of earth the color of unripe peaches. Some workers had run over the older grave on the way to digging the new.

"It felt like they had hurt her," Tracy told me later.

The two women took up the trash of ruined flowers and salvaged what they could. They raked the grave level. They even wrestled the marker back into shape.

When they told me what had happened, I went to look for myself. Then I went home and started making phone calls. A man in charge of the cemetery agreed to meet me there.

"This is my daughter's grave," I said. When he saw the tracks he apologized repeatedly. He shook my hand in an unchallenging grip and said he would personally see that everything was put right. He gave me his personal phone number and assured me he would instantly resolve any problem for me, though, he hastened to add, he would see to it that no other problem ever arose.

I said, "All right," and drove home. I was angry because the man had given me no chance to start a fight. When I got home I took a handsaw up a tree and worked at a branch, my strokes frantic and ineffectual, the saw continually jumping out of its groove to start a new cut. Soon I was tired and sweaty. The bark was scored in a dozen places, but the heartwood remained unscathed. I climbed down and sat on the porch drinking iced tea. Tracy joined me.

"Caring for a grave is a lousy substitute," she said.

· · · 12 · · ·

Someone told me my dead grandmother would watch over her in heaven. I took comfort in that, even though heaven struck me as implausible. I pictured my grandmother in the dress they buried her in, which she'd never worn in life. I pictured Abby on her lap. But I couldn't see Abby's face, because I had forgotten it.

I got out the photos the hospital had sent us, the disturbing Polaroids with the blood-red lips and the better ones with her the way I remembered, or would have remembered if everything weren't slipping away from me. You don't remember her face, I told myself. Now you remember the photos of her face. You held her for half an hour; you've held the photos longer than that. I found I had an idea of her personality, which I based on nothing but the face in the photos. She was a serious little girl, given to wrinkling her brow irritably at the silliness of others. The sort of person who listens closely when you speak and then asks blunt questions.

· · · 13 · · ·

One morning in April I lay in bed hoping the phone wouldn't ring. I needed work, but hoped nobody

would call to give me any that day. It was two days until my birthday, and after that it would be one more week to Abby's birthday: one year old.

The day was misty and cold. I warmed some vegetable soup and sat on the couch in front of the TV. When the picture came on I saw an aerial shot of a building from which a section seemed to have been bitten. After a while I gathered that the building was in the capital city of my own state, and that people were dead and others bloody on the street. The dead were numerous, and many of them children.

In the ensuing weeks, one of those children came to stand for all of them in the newspapers and magazines. She was one year old. An often-printed image showed her, newly dead, in the arms of a fireman. A single idea came to dominate captions of her image: the heroism of the rescuers.

That's not what it means, I thought. That's not it at all.

··· 14 ···

To the east, where most of the graves lay, were a few stands of pine. One day, in a pause between rains, I watched a flight of birds wheel above gray puddles, and reflected in the puddles were multiples of the sky: the jagged line of pines, the stacked clouds solid as cut limestone, the dark birds arcing. The birds made tight turns—how did they synchronize?—and suddenly were absorbed in the still trees. It took my eyes a moment to pick out the individual birds standing silent in the boughs.

As our car crept along the narrow lanes of the cemetery toward the exit, Tracy and I discussed the birds. They seemed to always be there. I thought they were crows. I had once seen crows picking through the rubble of a car wreck, the windshield broken into blood-smeared gravel and gleaming under their delicate iron feet. I'd seen them at the carcasses of mule deer and coyote on the highway. They should roost in a cemetery, I thought. It would be a nice symbol.

Tracy thought they were grackles. "They're smaller than crows," she said. "And look how their heads are midnight blue instead of black."

I will never forget her, I found myself thinking. I will never forget, I will never forget. But I will, won't I? When I die.

That thought had been hurting me like a fresh bruise all day. When Tracy and I are dead, no one will remember that a girl named Abby ever was. I thought of my youth slipping away from me, of the fact that I too would one day be buried in a cemetery—maybe this one—among the ants and the murder of birds in the pines. It was the old but always fresh insight that the death of the child is also the death of the parent, and that nothing taken by the ants can ever come back.

"These never seem to make any noise," I said aloud. "If they said something, you could tell whether they're crows."

Just then one of the birds came up from the ground, flapping at an indolent pace. It seemed as if it should crash, but instead it cruised at four feet, crossing in front of our windshield. Grasped in its blue-black feet, complete, as yet unmutilated, almost surreal in the crisp perfection of its details, was a cottontail rabbit kit. The bird curved its flight to the ground in front of a red-granite headstone.

"Drive on," Tracy said. "Fast." She was pregnant again, and easily made sick.

··· 15 ···

The spring warmed up, and every night on the news they numbered the dead from the Murrah Building in Oklahoma City. Friends and relatives who'd been in the city on business recounted their stories, except for one man who'd helped dig out the children. He kept silent about it.

One night the news was interrupted every few minutes with tornado warnings. I didn't much care. We had a lot of tornado warnings in Oklahoma, and who has time to run for shelter with every warning? Outside the air was muggy and gray and smelled as if it might break into lightning. I had a backache. Not the kind that really hurts, just the kind that tells you there's weather out. I walked in the yard, watching a scatter of ants scramble against the coming of the rain. What were they in such a hurry to do? Probably they meant to seal themselves in against the storm. So why were they all outside their den?

I had recently read about the Torajan people of Indonesia. They inter dead children in cavities hewn in trees. The tree slowly closes its wound around the child. The tree keeps growing in the child's place.

I watched the clouds and the ground by turns. The storm stacked up. The ants vanished, as if absorbed into the dry ground about to take the rain.

"A State of Silence" by Sean Ball

Originally published
July 2015

by Russell Cobb

SHALOM, ARDMORE

The long goodbye to Oklahoma's small-town Jews

I went down to Ardmore looking for the last Jews in a town that could—if it were so inclined—lay claim to the title of "The Birthplace of Judaism in Oklahoma." Even before the first land run, Jewish peddlers had established themselves in fledgling towns across Indian Territory. Early towns like Boggy Depot were set up by Jewish merchants to trade between Indians and white settlers. Until a few years after statehood, though, it was Ardmore that boasted the largest population of Jews in the Territory.

According to an encyclopedia entry from the Institute for Southern Jewish Life in 2014, Ardmore's Jewish population has shrunk to two people in this once distinctly Yiddish-flavored town. Here, I should confess a certain morbid curiosity about populations in decline. I've always been attracted to cemeteries, ghost towns, and failed expeditions. And although I'm a *goy*, my family is mixed. So, I had to get down there. I wanted to meet these two Jews before they joined their brethren in eternal rest at Mount Zion Cemetery.

The day was miserable; snow was blowing sideways and flakes were hitting my cheeks like tiny little darts. I got off the Turner Turnpike and wandered down Highway 18, where the entire town of Meeker stopped for a Baptist funeral. Cell phone coverage was spotty. The phlegmatic tones of NPR on FM 89.5 gave way to something called *American Family Radio*. While I waited for the funeral procession to pass, I heard that America was under siege. Socialists, terrorists, and "illegals" were undermining the very fabric of our Christian civilization. The president wasn't a Christian; he didn't even love his own country. The air of paranoia and miserable weather had me in a strange mood.

When I finally made it to Stephanie's Beautique on Main Street in Ardmore, I was relieved to be in a place whose motto on Facebook is "keep calm and stay classy." The place was packed to the rafters with a seemingly unending collection of women's dresses, formal wear, and accessories. The store's namesake, Stephanie Baker, was supposedly one of the last two Jews in town. Stephanie and her best friend from high school, Phyllis Chandler, were happy to talk to me, but wanted to get something straight right off the bat: there were not only two Jews left in Ardmore. That was bunk. There were at least five. Maybe even nine or ten.

It really depended on how you defined who was Jewish. There was a guy in town born Jewish, but his stepfather raised him as a Baptist. There were the Daubes, who had a Jewish father but a Gentile mother who took them to the Episcopal church. "But they're going to be buried in the Jewish cemetery," Phyllis said. So, maybe we could count them as half.

Then there was Phyllis's husband, Burke, a bit of an amateur historian and a self-described "closeted Jew." A guy named Boomer, an Army veteran and groundskeeper for the now-defunct Temple Emeth who wore a muscle shirt in this awful weather, "had some Jew" in him. "German and Jewish," he clarified. "Go figure."

Phyllis and Burke escorted me around Ardmore. As we cruised Main Street, Phyllis pointed to an empty storefront that had once served as a Jewish bakery. That payday loan place used to be another Jewish-run clothing store. There had been a Jewish restaurant where you could get latkes and brisket. It was now a rib joint. Stephanie and Phyllis remember a time when all the businesses on Main Street would close down at sundown on Friday to observe *Shabbat*.

At the end of Main Street was Ardmore's first department store, Westheimer & Daube, begun by Jewish pioneers. The exterior of the building, which had once held Ardmore's most ornate Christmas displays, was now mostly boarded up, although it had been partially converted into an antique mall. Beyond that was a section of town suffering from typical small-town rot. One venerable old building had collapsed when a car ran into it.

We drove down a street that flourished for a brief time when the Carter County oil fields were discovered, and Ardmore could boast that it had more millionaires per capita than any town in America. Even it looked a little run down. "I don't know what happened," Phyllis said. "Ardmore used to be a lot nicer."

Why did I care so much about the Jews anyway? They all wanted to know. That was a good question. I wondered that myself. I was living in California, and enjoying a pretty sweet phase of life with a paid sabbatical from my job as a professor. I still had family in Tulsa, but driving down to Ardmore during a Winter Weather Advisory—that was pretty odd.

I wondered, I told them, what happens when a once-thriving community disappears. What happens when there are no more Italians in Little Italy or Germans in Germantown? How does our sense of place change when the population changes? And does it even matter?

• • •

At the beginning of the 20th century, parts of New York City had become transplantations of Jewish *shtetls* in the Old Country. Immigrants on the Lower East Side were so densely packed that the place's unhygienic conditions provoked a rallying cry for Congress to restrict Eastern European immigration. New York's German Jewish population, which had assimilated quickly and prospered in the financial industry, became concerned about a possible anti-Semitic backlash. The financier Baron de Hirsch thought Russian Jews should be sent to Argentina, Africa, or Canada—anywhere but New York. A banker named Jacob Schiff worried that the waves of Jewish immigrants from Russia would lead to a repeat of the pogroms—this time in the New World.

Schiff came up with a plan to reroute Jewish immigration from Ellis Island to the American South and Southwest, where land was plentiful and Jews were few and far between. He sunk at least half a million of his own dollars into a scheme to make Galveston, Texas, the new hub for Eastern-European Jewish immigration. For a while, the Galveston Plan seemed to work. The first steamer to arrive in the port was greeted by the mayor and a brass band. Rabbis came from Houston and Fort Worth to help the newcomers find a place to live.

Many stayed in Texas, but others caught the Santa Fe Railroad north to Oklahoma. Phyllis Chandler's grandfather, Ike Fishman, got off at Ardmore and started peddling bananas from a cart in the booming town. He later started a scrap metal business, which proved to be extremely lucrative when oil was discovered in southern Oklahoma in the 1920s. Two of Coleman Robison's grandparents—Romanian Jews whose last name was changed from Rabinowitz at the port of entry—came over as part of the Galveston Plan.

But by and large, the plan failed. Immigration officials in the conservative South started to judge Jews—and Catholics as well—as "morally defective." The deportation rate was four times higher at the Port of Galveston than at Ellis Island. And word of a swampy land run by bigoted *goyim* circulated back to the Old Country. By 1914, the Galveston Plan was done.

For most of its history, Oklahoma has been a remarkably hospitable place for Jews. Even the poor Yiddish speakers from Russia—those "great unwashed" that Schiff so feared—quickly worked their way into the mainstream of Oklahoma life, especially in small towns like Ardmore and Muskogee. According to Burke Chandler, some of the Old World tension between German and Russian Jews survived in southern Oklahoma for a while. Some of the German and French Jews—yes, there were even French Jews in Ardmore—had sprung for first-class tickets on their steamships, while the Russians came over crammed into third class.

Western European immigrants were largely Reform Jews who might do a little work on *Shabbat*, marry Gentiles, and not keep kosher. The majority of Orthodox Jews were from Eastern Europe and held fast to the Torah as the direct word of God. Some Orthodox immigrants, such as Phyllis's grandfather, never totally assimilated. She was raised in the nearby town of

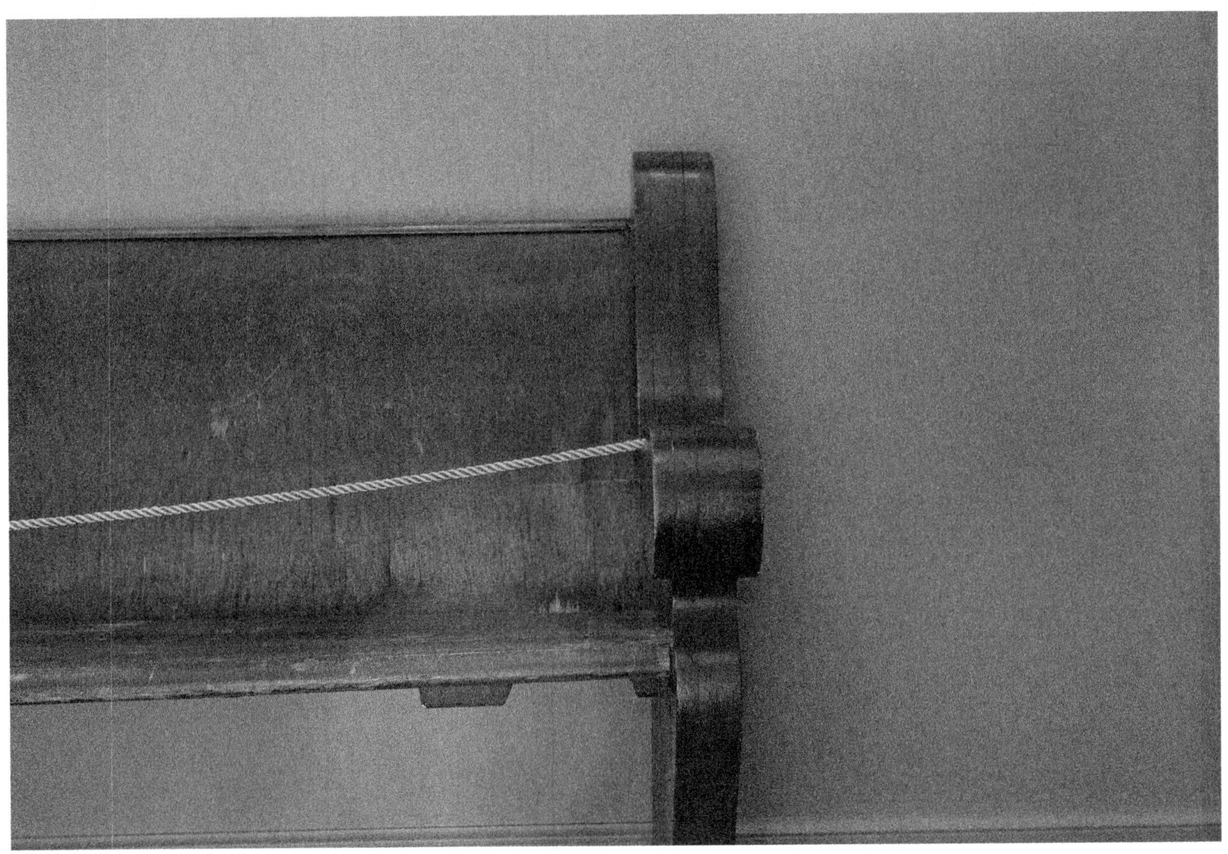

Decalogue that originally hung in Ardmore, now on display at Sherwin Miller Museum of Jewish Art in Tulsa

Healdton, where her grandfather tried to keep kosher, driving to Oklahoma City to buy matzo and kosher meat. "This place wasn't good enough for him," she says.

Although Phyllis also married a Gentile, she keeps up connections with her Orthodox heritage. Rabbinical students come visit her from Oklahoma City to bring her matzo.

"And the matzo's always stale," Phyllis chimes in. "They [the Orthodox students] are so annoying. They won't shake women's hands, and you have to walk behind them. I go hide when they come to town."

Since the 1960s, many of the old ways have disappeared. When Burke moved from Tulsa in the late 1970s, he was "shocked" to see one Jewish Ardmoreite, Harry Galoob, eating a ham sandwich. He ended up marrying Galoob's sister, Phyllis, to the delight of his mother back in Tulsa. "She thought I should marry a Jewish woman," he says.

Jews became the town's scrap-metal dealers and tailors, dry goods merchants and dressmakers. "Growing up here, I was never excluded from anything," Phyllis tells me.

"And Phyllis was in everything," Stephanie quips.

This, at least, is the story Oklahoma likes to tell itself: we are still a young state where newcomers can pull themselves up by their own bootstraps and worship whatever god they want. And there's plenty of truth to that. Rabbi Jeremy Simons, who has spent some time traveling around Oklahoma and other parts of the South, said he's faced more anti-Semitism in California than he has in the Bible Belt. "Religion is so important here," he says. "Because I wear a *kippa*, people stop me on the street to ask me about Judaism."

In reality, though, there have been some dark moments of anti-Semitism in Oklahoma, starting with the very beginnings of statehood. In 1910, Oklahomans voted to move the capital from Guthrie to Oklahoma City. The night after the vote, Assistant Secretary of State Leo Meyer took the official state seal out of Guthrie, catching the attention of the *Guthrie Daily Leader*, which proclaimed in a headline, "Shylocks of Oklahoma City have the state by the throat." Meyer, himself Jewish, was part of an "unparalleled conspiracy on the part of Jews and Gentiles of a rotten town to loot the State for twenty-five years."

This supposed conspiracy did little to damage the state's reputation as a haven. Only two years after the Guthrie incident, *The Daily Ardmoreite* ran a glowing article about the arrival of a commissioner from a Jewish Industrial and Agricultural Aid Society in New York. "Thousands of progressive and scientific Hebrew farmers may settle in the state in the present year," the article stated. News about Ardmore spread far and wide. Even as Oklahoma City and Tulsa grew, Ardmore still counted as the second-largest Jewish town in the state.

Its distinctly Yiddish flavor grew when a World War I fighter pilot showed up in town in the early 1920s. Bill Krohn spoke Yiddish while growing up in eastern Pennsylvania and came to Oklahoma for a new adventure. He settled into life in Ardmore, writing a column in the *Daily Ardmoreite* about oil news. He didn't reveal his Jewish identity to the many oilmen he met, but he greeted everyone downtown with the phrase *sholem alechem*, Hebrew for "peace be upon you."

The perhaps apocryphal story goes that Krohn ingratiated himself to wildcatters, who took him along to discovery wells where he hoped to get the scoop about Oklahoma's next big oil field. One night, on a rig floor, he witnessed oil spouting straight into the air. "Sholem alechem!" he shouted to all the roughnecks, who had no idea what the expression meant. The name stuck, and Sholem Alechem became the name of an entire oil field between Duncan and Ardmore.

Krohn started a club—also called Sholem Alechem—that met in the lobby of the Ardmore Hotel. Technically, it was a "benevolent society," but in reality it was little more than an excuse to smoke cigars, drink booze, and play cards. The club counted among its members another Jewish Ardmore oilman, Walter Neustadt, the benefactor of a literary prize at OU sometimes called "America's Nobel Prize." David Halpern, a Tulsa photographer who spent years documenting rural Oklahoma Jewry in a project called "Prairie Landsmen," heard the outsize stories about Krohn's club and decided to track down the old Mobil Oil sign for Sholem Alechem. He says that the few locals who still know about the oil field assume its name derives from the Chickasaw language.

Even as oilmen like Neustadt and Krohn prospered, peace was not always upon Oklahoma's Jews. Krohn's rise in fame paralleled the rise of one of the state's most notorious anti-Semites, Governor "Alfalfa Bill" Murray. Curiously, Krohn was, at first, a booster for Murray. They were both colorful characters: the walrus-mustachioed Murray would deliver a stump speech standing on his head. Krohn published the first account of the governor's life. In it, he acknowledged that the governor "ain't much for looks. But what a man! He's got the guts and what it takes mentally and otherwise to literally translate the meaning of the title 'Governor.' " Rumor has it that Krohn helped convince Murray to build the lake just south of town that now bears his name: Lake Murray.

At the time, Murray had his sights on the Democratic Party's nomination for president as a Dixiecrat challenger to Franklin Delano Roosevelt. After a resounding defeat, though, Murray started to rant about a Jewish conspiracy against him. Krohn left the state for other prospects in Illinois around the same time Murray produced tracts like "Palestine, Shall Arabs or Jews Control It, or America Admit 100,000 Communist Jews from Behind the Iron Curtain?" Murray, who by this time was fortunately retired to a hotel in Tishomingo, argued for adoption of Adolf Eichmann's "Madagascar Plan." This was a plan to force much of the Jewish population to relocate to the African island.

Here's the thing: as a secular urban-dweller who cringes whenever an Oklahoma politician speaks, I came to Ardmore expecting to hear tales of suffering and discrimination. Curiously, though, most anti-Semitism in Oklahoma has happened in the cities, not in the smaller towns. The Silver Legion of America, a fascist group active in the 1930s, considered Tulsa, not small towns or even Oklahoma City, for its headquarters. The Sherwin Miller Museum of Jewish Art in Tulsa has in its collections a label reading "Communism is Jewish. Boycott Jew Stores," which briefly appeared on Tulsa Jewish storefronts in 1986.

In the past 20 years or so, though, even the most conservative Christians across the South have come to embrace Jews. Rabbi Simons says he fields calls from Gentiles anytime there's a crisis in the Middle East. He's become a de-facto representative of Israel. "The challenge," he says, "is to talk about it in a way that is holy but still respects different opinions while having a conversation." It's harder for him to talk to Jews than to Christians about Israel. "There's an old saying: you have two Jews and three opinions," he says.

The reason for the embrace of Jews, however, probably has more to do with a resurgence in Christian Zionism than a newly tolerant Oklahoma. According to this movement (supported by worthies such as Pat Robertson), Jews must be allowed to reconstruct the Temple Mount in Jerusalem, where a mosque now stands. This will be a signal to God that the Second Coming of Jesus is at hand. Jews, in other words, are pawns in a game of biblical apocalypse.

• • •

After World War II, Ardmore built a new modernist synagogue in preparation for a bright future. The architect of the temple, Ludwig Isenberg, was also its lay rabbi. Isenberg and his parents had come over on one of the last passenger steamships out of Hamburg before the Nazis started sending Jews to concentration camps. Isenberg's parents were cattle farmers who had a distant relative in Stillwater. Five years after applying for an exit visa, the Isenbergs were allowed to leave Germany in 1938. The elder Isenberg took a small Torah from the local synagogue. He wrapped it in dirty clothes and stuffed it in a trunk. The Nazis confiscated everything of value, but they missed the Torah, which found a home in Ardmore's Temple Emeth for over half a century.

Despite a huge oil boom in the 1950s and another wave of Post-World War II Jewish immigrants, the community started to decline by the 1960s. There was a feud between the two most prominent families (the Daubes and the Neustadts) over the fate of Ardmore's most important department store that went all the way to the Oklahoma Supreme Court. It's a feud that some may take to the grave. At the same time, Rabbi Isenberg would travel to Las Vegas to play poker without designating a replacement rabbi to hold services. Numbers slowly dwindled until the Temple was forced to close in 2003, only to briefly reopen for Isenberg's funeral a year later.

Temple Emeth now sits empty in downtown Ardmore. It was almost bulldozed over its asbestos insulation, and later was sold to a local businessman who eventually ended up giving it to the Goddard Center.

The center's groundskeeper, Boomer, shows me around the Temple. Phyllis won't come with me: "It's like going to a funeral, going in there. I prefer to remember it during better days."

There is something creepy about it. There's a stack of old playing cards in the kitchen, some of them burned at the edges (an errant cigarette?). There's a room full of vintage beauty chairs with hair-drying domes crammed into an old classroom. While the asbestos has been removed and the building appears structurally sound, some rooms look like they were abandoned in a hurry decades ago. Boomer and I marvel over an unopened package of paper straws. "Did you have these growing up?" he asks me.

"Nope," I say. "That was before my time." There are other condiments in the kitchen with expiration dates from 20 years ago.

Coleman Robison was one of the first boys—and perhaps the only—to be bar mitzvahed at Temple Emeth in 1956. Robison is a Tulsa lawyer who left Ardmore in 1964, only returning for the occasional visit. He remembers the town fondly. "It was a good place to grow up," Robison told me. But he always felt a little bit like an outsider. "We weren't in the mainstream."

Robison's mother had to pull him out of Christmas plays, and Jews were still excluded from the country club. "That was before the separation of church and state was recognized in Oklahoma," he says. By the time of Robison's youth, the Jewish community was already in decline. By the 1960s, the prospect of selling scrap metal or dry goods to cowboys didn't seem as appealing as it once did. Most of the post-war generation moved to nearby cities: Dallas, Tulsa, Oklahoma City.

• • •

On the second floor of the Sherwin Miller Museum, you can see a model synagogue put together with artifacts from a number of now-defunct Oklahoma synagogues, including Temple Emeth in Ardmore and Temple Beth Ahabah in Muskogee, which closed in 2010. There's a bema from Ardmore and a Torah from Muskogee. There is a wall describing a dozen or so Jewish communities in small Oklahoma towns. In some, a once-sizable Jewish population has disappeared entirely. In others, like Ardmore and Seminole, there are only a few Jews left, most in their 60s and 70s. They are people like Phyllis and Stephanie, whose task has been to assure their "perpetual care" at Mount Zion. "When there is nobody left here," Phyllis says, "we now have a trust that will mow us and keep us clean out there. They'll rake the leaves and trim our trees."

A famous rabbi, Simon Rawidowicz, once wrote that Jews see themselves as the "ever-dying people." It is precisely this fear—that the present generation may be the last—that paradoxically keeps Judaism alive. That's what Rabbi Simons tells me by way of context when I ask him if it makes him sad to see Judaism disappear from small towns. "Jews have been a minority religion for at least 2,000 years," he says. "Of course it's sad. It's sad for everyone, especially the last members of a community. But it's just like the human life cycle." We are born, we grow and thrive, and then we get old and die.

Jews thrived in small-town Oklahoma. They were *machers*: an untranslatable Yiddish term for someone who gets stuff done. A *macher* is a person who brokers deals or works as a "fixer"—mostly for good, but occasionally for ill. Half a century ago, you would have had a few *machers* at the chambers of commerce in Muskogee, Ardmore, and Ponca City.

I pick up the day's copy of the *Daily Ardmorite*. It has a fancy pullout brochure about the town's economic revival and thumbnail photos of all the members of the Chamber of Commerce. Nary a Jew there. But the guy who runs the brand-new La Quinta Inn off I-35, Mitesh Patel, is an hotelier looking to expand his Ardmore-based Apollo Hospitality Group into North Texas. Now, that man seems like a *macher*. Indeed, it's often said in 21st-century America that immigrants from India are the new Jews, but that's another story.

Back in Tulsa, I ask Coleman Robison if he's saddened by the prospect of a purely Gentile Ardmore. "It is what it is," Robison says. He has a poster of a coffee mug in his well-appointed law office: "Oy freakin' vey," the mug reads. Robison speaks with some difficulty and walks with a cane, but his eyes still gleam with vitality and a sense of humor bordering on the macabre—he's also on the board of the Mount Zion Cemetery Association.

Robison goes back home occasionally to visit the graves of his parents, but now he's more concerned about the future of the Jewish community in Tulsa than he is about Ardmore. "The same pattern is repeating itself here," he says. Most of it boils down to economics. "I saw the bright lights of the city and never wanted to go back," he says. Now all his children have moved to Connecticut with no intention of coming back to Tulsa. "The opportunities just aren't here," he says.

On the surface, Tulsa appears to have the most prosperous Jewish community in Oklahoma. Its Jewish population is larger than that of Oklahoma City. The Sherwin Miller Museum gleams with a new brass exterior on the south Tulsa Zarrow Campus, next to a swanky new retirement community and a robust Jewish Community Center. Names like Kaiser, Schusterman, and Kravis are inextricably linked to the city's redevelopment.

But Tulsa's Jewish population, too, is shrinking. According to the Institute for Southern Jewish Life, "About two-thirds of the Jewish children raised in Tulsa don't come back after college; while the city continues to attract new Jewish families, they are unable to offset this loss." Many Jewish Tulsans quietly speculate that the community has built up an infrastructure—an expanded museum, community center, retirement villas—that won't be supported by a declining population.

What this means and whether it even matters depends on how you see the state's identity. Oklahoma has been, at various times, a destination for displaced Native Americans, white sharecroppers, black freedman, and Jewish merchants, among others. All these populations have evolved. Some have moved on entirely.

More recently, the state's Latino population has quadrupled, and its Asian population has doubled since 1990, giving rise to a new nativist movement that has more in common with Alfalfa Bill Murray than it would like to admit. So, as Oklahoma says its long goodbye to its Jews, it might also want to consider how it says hello to its newcomers: Muslims, Latinos, and Hindus.

Originally published July 2016

by Annie Heartfield Hartzog

THE OLD WAYS

In one of the stars I shall be living. In one of them I shall be laughing. And so it will be as if all the stars were laughing, when you look at the sky at night... You, only you, will have stars that can laugh!

—*Antoine de Saint-Exupéry,* The Little Prince

Barely audible words came from the man as he began the cedar blessing.

"*Maheo. Wakanda,* I come to you again like this, pitiful," the man began. "I don't know what to say, Creator, I don't know how to say it."

A ponytail hung down his back—black strands laced with iron-grey, held in place with an elastic band. He bent over the altar, speaking softly, eagle fan in one hand, the other hand touching and arranging objects.

About 60 of us sat in the meeting room of Fellowship Congregational Church. As Clark Inkanish went about his ministrations, papers rustled, throats cleared, and people shifted in their seats. A leader from the Cheyenne-Caddo-Wichita tribes of Oklahoma, Clark wore a traditional wool vest, calling up memories of beautiful old horse blankets. A bolo fashioned of a large, oblong turquoise hung just above his heart, the stone and silver-tipped leather braid rocking forward as he leaned down. The altar he'd built for the ceremony was a wooden box, covered with a vibrant Pendleton: rainbow stripes. He'd once looked in my eyes and said, "Indian people like colorful things. Always remember that."

A few minutes before people arrived, Clark took me aside and asked me to assist him with the blessing. I explained I'd never done it before, but he waved my protests off, looked me in the eye, and said that the most important part of the job was sincerity. I nodded my agreement, and he handed me a lighter and inclined his head toward the altar with a gesture that let me know to go ahead. I lit the small bowl-shaped puck of black carbon, a tiny basin that, once covered in white ash, hid a red-hot center that became the sprinkling ground. Dried sage, sweetgrass, tobacco, and cedar would be instantly converted to rising smoke, prayers carried up to Creator. Clark checked the disk with the middle finger of his right hand, tapping it a couple of times right in its glowing center. He fanned the smoke with eagle feathers, out, toward the congregation, and up. He lifted a smoldering bundle of cedar greens he'd gathered and neatly bound with colored string, and raised it slowly to the four directions, and then straight up; his eyes and face looked toward the center above him, toward Creator.

I had seen Clark do these things before, but by his side, today, I was close enough, for the first time, to actually hear his words.

"Please guide us like this," he continued. "And if I left anything or anyone out, forgive me, Creator, and take care of that in a good way."

I had never heard anyone pray in such a plain, modest, and reverent way. Without agenda. Nothing for God to *do*. I felt the smoke carry the words up. As he said "pitiful" my right arm and shoulder twitched, and I sensed a pressure behind and between my eyes. The prayer landed in my gut, resonated, then vibrated upwards. Horizontal membranes in my body felt as if they were humming, like a finger thumping on the taut skin of a drum. As he spoke, my heart felt tender and I went shivery in my core, resisting the urge to go down on my knees. I hadn't felt anything like that since a certain kind of church, a low kind of church, many years ago.

• • •

A refugee from the fundamentalist Christianity of my childhood, I had been drawn to philosophies that had taken me beyond Western culture: Buddhism from India, East Asian Taoism, and the mystical Sufi Way. I was enamored of shamanic healing practices, the magico-religious traditions of the ancient Amazonian Yanomami, and wanted to experience the Native American sweat lodge and peyote ceremonies.

"We shall not cease from exploration," T.S. Eliot wrote toward the end of his poem "Little Gidding." "And the end of all our exploring / Will be to arrive where we started / And know the place for the first time." My weak-kneed experience with Grandfather, as Clark allowed me to call him, was part of a bigger circle, a wheel I had been attempting to turn for some time.

Clark's blessing lasted only a few moments, yet I ended up with salty streaks down my face and my gut quivering. He finished, and I helped him pack up the artifacts of his ceremony: herbs tucked into antique drawstring bags he'd beaded himself, long ago, tiny red, blue, and green glass slivers neatly sewn into deerskin; a silvery shell for catching ash, black charcoal pucks wrapped in foil to keep them dry; a Bic lighter; the eagle feather fan with its beaded handle. It all went away, back into his attendant "briefcase," a weathered, slender wooden box with a carrying handle on its side.

After a few minutes of not listening to the next speaker, I spotted Clark watching things from the rear of the room, watching over things, his back to the wall, where he had gone after the ceremonial duties were complete. I wanted to go to him, be near him, ask him to explain what had happened to me, even though I didn't think he would. He had an uncanny ability to ignore certain kinds of stories and questions, and one should rarely question one's elder on these things. Sometimes, even after long conversations that involved many queries from those seeking his wisdom, and with very few words coming back their way from him, Clark would end a "dialogue" with two simple words: "We'll see," and with that, he would gather his things and rise. He'd often make a joke or say, "Time for a nap," (even after several cups of strong coffee) before leaving and holler, "See you folks later," over his shoulder, tossing up a wave of his hand as he turned and walked away. Clark was expedient when it came to saying goodbye.

That day, as we stacked chairs, folded tablecloths, and swept up, Clark came to me and said there would be a sweat out south next Sunday.

"It would be good for you to be there," Clark said. "We'll need your help building the lodge."

And just like that, the answers, which were no-answers, came in response to my questions, which were no-questions.

• • •

"Welcome, relatives! *Mitakuye oyasin*!"

We were on a hill south of Tulsa, a good-sized blaze burning on top of a pile of chunky, New Mexican volcanic rock. Friends and family circled the morning flames and stood together without speaking, nods for greetings, some holding hands. After his welcome, Clark made a blessing, this time without words: arm, face, and smoke lifted to the four directions.

Our first job involved gathering young willow trees from Polecat Creek, so we piled into the back of someone's pickup truck for the short ride. The truck trundled through on bumpy terrain next to the creek. We stopped close to a thick stand of green stalks at the water's edge. It was a bright spring-into-summer day. Sunlight mirrored against the sky, grass, trees, and dirt of northeastern Oklahoma, where our earth is rich and brown—an antediluvian river bottom studded with limestone rock, pockmarked with the imprints of plants and animals from another time. We found young willow trees crowded into a living wall some 20 feet high, waving us over with fluttery arms of translucent green. Clark thanked the river and the tender trees and leaned back, right hand behind hip, face to sky. He confirmed the presence of a bald eagle, which was slowly circling far above, tipping spread wings against current, claws outstretched, head turned, eyeball a glint in the brightness.

"The eagles come to hear us pray for blessings of healing and protection, for all of God's creation," Clark said to us. Looking up, he said more loudly, "Welcome, relative! Greetings!" and with that, he headed toward the creek, ready to show us which young saplings would be best for building the lodge.

One woman watched him move toward the water with his machete, marveling at his determination and vigor. All of a sudden, he slipped on the scree of the bank and went down, laughing as he rolled down the hillside, toward the river. She saw him as a little bear in that moment, rascally and frolicsome, part of the earth, constant and robust, and when he stopped rolling, she yelled to him, "You are a bear!"

"Yes," he replied, "that is what some people call me."

Bear liked the trees that were strong and straight. We took our time finding the right ones, enjoying the beauty of the clear-lighted day and the coolness of the water. Clark thanked the trees for their sacrifice as he moved among them. He taught us to leave certain young to grow another day, and old ones to show them how. It was important, in everything we did, to be stewards of this earth, to leave behind enough resources to provide for the future. To Clark, the earth was an extension of his own family and loved ones.

"Because of some things it's been easy for the old ways to get lost. It's good to keep them alive," Clark said. "By you knowing them, others will, too. This way the old ways will not be lost forever."

We cut about 50 or so of the right-sized willows and hauled them back to the lodge site by pickup. We felt lucky to stay out of sight of the local police. (It wouldn't have been the first time for Clark to have a run-in with the law over his beliefs, over doing things in the old ways.) We slipped in and out, free of restraint, *aho*!

Back on the hill, we stripped the outer skin from the willows, preparing them to be bent in the shape of the dome that would become our lodge. We learned that sap ran under the willow skin in the spring, like maple syrup, and that it contained medicine—salicin, a precursor to aspirin—for treating arthritis and other maladies. So we rubbed the slick inner bark on the parts of our bodies that needed healing. With Clark as our elder, we worked as a tribe, singing and praying, teasing one another and sharing stories. In this way, we became each other's relations, family, each person carrying an important gift to contribute to the whole.

After the willows were prepared we continued our work. We created medicine bundles from tiny cubes of red, blue, and yellow cloth that we wrapped around pinches of tobacco, cedar, or sweetgrass, tied like tiny gift boxes. We left the scarlet ribbon long enough to hang in the branches of nearby trees, and to fasten onto the curved poles of the lodge. Clark told us that we were putting our prayers in there, and reminded us that the medicine was for all: "That's why we say, *'Mitakuye oyasin.'* "

We stayed outside after our morning and afternoon work. All throughout the day, the fire burned, fed by seasoned scrub oak that was dry, hard, and dense enough to hold the heat a long time. Sometimes we gathered around the fire and at other times we went to walk the medicine wheel or sit under a tree. We prayed each to our Creator as we moved about the land. We chanted and sang traditional melodies: sweet voices lifting high on Oklahoma breezes, old songs floating up and hanging in the sky. We sipped water (but didn't eat), shared hugs, sat close, held hands. Clark mostly kept to himself after his lodge-building duties, sometimes sitting near the fire, periodically holding his palms toward the flames, muttering a word or two or just a sound. He strolled the medicine wheel, hands behind his back, eyes at times on the ground, then looking up.

The sun's retreat west painted the wide sky in bluesy purples; it was finally time. The fire was burning low as we entered the small lodge on hands and knees through an opening in the blankets and tarps that draped its shell. Crawling blindly into the inky interior, we felt for the wall around to the left. The first person crawled all the way around to the other side of the door frame so we could fit, all wedged in closely together. Clark clambered in easily on all fours, settling into his place across from the door, facing east. Flickering light moved across faces and scattered around the lodge's interior, illuminating the bent hoop frame. Prayer bundles dangled like ornaments from branches, dancing and bobbing in response to our movements. There was no heat yet and the pit at our feet was empty and dry. Men scooted their backs against willow spines, and women tucked our legs up close under our skirts to make room. When the first few rocks came in, Clark doused them with water. Steam rolled into the small space and the soft heat rose.

Clark shepherded us through the sweat, praying, making the rounds to the four directions. Our fire woman responded to his calls for more rocks. Each time the door was thrown open, night air rushed in to mix with the ashen, wet closeness on the inside. Just outside the lodge, with the shadowy light of the waning fire reflected on her face, the fire woman reached into the low flames with the pitchfork and scooped, balancing each blistering hot chunk of lava on the fork's tines, then carried it our direction: quiet, strong, steady. As she reached in through the low door, she slipped the rock into the pit at our feet.

"Welcome, relative!" Clark said enthusiastically to each new arrival, patting the bright red lava lightly with his hand, "*Mitakuye oyasin*! Thank you!" As each glowing rock transformed water, sage, tobacco, and sweetgrass into heated steam, smoke, and ash, it faded to black and disappeared. As the stone's light got smaller, Clark's shone, a preternatural part of his constitution.

It was hot in the lodge, but not too hot. I'd been in sweats so fierce I scrabbled in the dirt just trying to find one tiny breath of air. But not so with Clark. He led sweats as the gentle patriarch of those in his care, with a refinement I'd not experienced at the hands of other guides. We rested between directions, threw open the door, some climbing out to wander a few steps away, breathing deeply. Someone told a joke. The water bucket with its gourd dipper moved frequently between us, no one going thirsty for long. Clark's prayers remained simple and we followed his lead, heat rising with the spare words in a way that was agreeably elemental, a baptism in smoke, soot, steam, and sweat. Each person had strength for their journey from neighbors on either side, bodies close, sweat mixing. Songs came, spontaneously, sweet-tempered ardor, and then faded. Sometimes a little suffering was necessary, and the only thing you could do was to lay your face as close to the earth as possible and breathe, hard, with your lips in the mud, your thirsty tongue tasting metallic tang, snot running from your nose and water from your eyes. Conviction causes the heart and mind to submit, submit, let go, love better, for real this time.

We remained in our prayers for a long time, finally crawling out of the lodge into the small hours, a tiny haze of pale purpley-blue way off in the east, the first inklings of this day's new colors. Covered in salty ashes and redolent with smoke, we laughed, reveling in hilarity's release. We were energized by the night, radiant and hungry after a day of fasting, and ready to feast.

That day, Bear called me Granddaughter, one of the great honors of my life. He became my Grandfather, earthly and spiritual, an act made possible because of who he was, and simply because I was there, willing and desirous of practicing these old, kindly ways.

• • •

Clark was raised by his maternal grandmother, Mary Little Bear Inkanish, whose own mother was a *Mah-hee-yuna*, a Sacred Woman of the Sun Dance of the Southern Cheyenne. It is his lineage, and part of his legacy, that some of the old ways will be practiced and not forgotten. Because he lived them, he showed us how. Because he believed that the teachings of the medicine hoop were given for all people, it allowed me to let go of my need to understand why I was drawn to them, and only turn in practice toward these ways, doing them wholeheartedly for one reason and one reason alone: to enter the presence of our Creator. There were times I observed Grandfather walk away from the frantic productions of human process and stand tranquilly outside, in any weather, gazing up, face impassive, eyes on the sky, or beyond. I made up a story that he had gone away from all our efforts, gone to be more intimate with God. In those hushed moments, I took something from watching him just be. In those moments he was, for me, quintessentially spirit, essence, *élan vital*. All meaning, intention, understanding, and analysis were carried up and away with the smoke. For that and so many other things he showed me, I am grateful.

Clark's nephew Jason Caddo is a fireman and can run a sweat. He has always known the old ways, as taught to him by Clark and others, and acknowledges that it can be tricky to connect these ancient practices to 21st century life. In his youth, Jason learned them like instructions in a textbook, and now he sometimes longs for a more visceral connection to the traditions. I asked him, is it possible that it only matters to do these old ways, and not to understand?

When Clark's dear friend and spiritual brother Luis Carlos Sanchez was ordained to the Christian ministry the midst of a thunderous Oklahoma storm, he heard these words from Clark: "That thunder is the great Spirit, clearing the tracks, so that new ones may be made." Luis Carlos saw the hard, slanting rain and the lightning, and he saw that they were all parts of the whole—like that day Clark was settled comfortably in my tipi and a big spark flew from the fire, spit sideways and landed somewhere on or near him. Unshaken, he said, "Thank you for that confirmation." I had no idea for what; I was learning not to ask.

"I knew Clark Inkanish, and it was sweet," Luis Carlos told me. "He just went along, like Johnny Appleseed, spreading the seeds, blessing this life as he went by."

We buried Clark's body on December 3, 2015, when his spirit was gone long enough from flesh that we could share stories of messages and mischief from that far side. It turned out quite a few of us had heard from Clark in the days since his death. In the chapel, people came to the front of the room and stood at the lectern to share:

"Clark saved my life. I would not be here if it were

Clark Inkanish with his family, date unknown

not for that man there."

"When he was mischievous, I knew I had a lesson coming."

"Bear helped me remember we are one with our environment, inseparable."

"This man lived beyond the limitations of mind and body."

"Head on home, brother."

A man with a lilting, sonorous voice sang the old Wichita-Caddo hymns. People standing in a long line to approach Grandfather's coffin took sharp inward breaths at the sight of him: so lively, so knowing, and now laying so still.

At the Broken Arrow burial ground with family and friends, we witnessed his body lowered into a deep hole in the earth and made our offerings of tobacco and other gifts to go with our elder on that good journey. Reverend Anne Clement commented, "Well, the granddaughters picked the right spot, here by the road, where he can wave at all the people passing by," and we laughed, again, through the sadness of our goodbye. We knew that would have been just where he wanted to be, right in the middle of everything. She said, "Clark's just hanging around, mischievously, saying, 'Finally, now you guys are getting it!' "

Later, as we drove away from the place we'd laid his body, I called out to him. I wondered out loud when, and where, we would be with him next, and I distinctly heard the sound of his voice in response. Immediately, I heard that constant and true expression. In an undimmed voice laced with the gently swinging rhythm of his barely suppressed grin, I heard Grandfather say: "We shall see..."

Originally published
July 2011

by Larry Guthrie

WOODY GUTHRIE'S SOCIAL GOSPEL ROOTS

Woodrow Wilson Guthrie was named in the summer of 1912 on a hope that his namesake would become president, and he did. So, Woody carried a presidential message. In the future formation of that message, Christianity and Catholicism played significant roles in the entire tapestry of the life of Woody Guthrie.

First, Woody was broad-minded, or "catholic," in his consideration of world religions. This curiosity exhibited a universal ecumenism that is the definition of catholic. Woody married Catholic. His Dust Bowl darling and first wife was a Pampa, Texas, Catholic named Mary Esta Lee Jennings. According to their Certificate of Marriage, Woody and Mary were lawfully married on October 28, 1933, according to the Rite of the Roman Catholic Church at Holy Souls Church in Pampa, now St. Vincent de Paul Parish. The priest, Father Wanderly, made Mary promise to raise her future children—Gwen, Will Rogers (Bill), and Sue—as Catholics.

Woody's father-in-law Harry Jennings had two sisters who were Catholic nuns. Although Harry disapproved at first of his daughter marrying Woody because he was not a Catholic, a couple of days later Woody's and Mary's fathers celebrated together.

As a youth, Woody studied Kahlil Gibran and considered converting to Catholicism and possibly taking holy orders and becoming a priest.

Matt Jennings, Woody's friend and brother-in-law, in 1935 prodded Woody towards social justice through reading Catholic newspaper ***The Sunday Visitor***. In it, then-Monsignor Fulton J. Sheen condemned the evils of communism.

In the desperately hard times of the Dust Bowl days, many Oklahomans explored socialism as an avenue of social justice. The strongest state expression of socialism in the United States occurred in Oklahoma between 1914 and 1917 when Woody was 2–5 years old.

In Oklahoma, low crop prices and high credit costs drove farmers to socialism.

Woody's father, Charlie, watched the rise of the Socialist Party in Oklahoma with concern. The Socialist vote had steadily grown until Oklahoma had the largest membership of any state in the union. In Okfuskee County, the Socialists had skimmed off 15 percent of the votes in the 1908 presidential election.

The Socialist Party in Oklahoma in 1914 elected six members to the state legislature.

Jim Bissett, in his book ***Agrarian Socialism in America: Marx, Jefferson, and Jesus in the Oklahoma Countryside, 1904–1920***, notes that former Sequoyah County Judge L.C. McNabb sued bankers and landlords for violations of an anti-usury law passed at a special session of the Oklahoma Legislature in February 1916. It set 6 percent as the maximum legal interest rate.

The Catholic Church also condemns usury. "Although the quest for equitable profit is acceptable in economic and financial activity, recourse to usury is to be morally condemned."

Woody's words were a social gospel. Although Woody did not seem to like participating regularly in organized religion, he did develop a great concern for social justice. Social justice evolved from the "Social Gospel," a movement in the early 20th century, which developed from Protestant to Baptist to Episcopal and on to Catholic. It believed that all Christians should work to improve social conditions for the poor, the sick, and the downtrodden. Many of those who supported the Social Gospel supported the New Deal of Franklin Roosevelt in 1933, and later the civil rights movements of the 1950s and 1960s.

Like the Socialists of pre-statehood Oklahoma, Guthrie remained a bedrock Christian, un-churched, undisciplined, but certain of his faith. "I seldom worship in or around churches, but always had a deep love for people who go there," he explained.

Woody supported labor unions, a cause championed by the Catholic Church, as described by Greg Guthrie in his Georgetown University thesis, in which he lists the four papal encyclicals that support labor unions: Rerum Novarum (Leo XIII, 1891), Quadragesimo Anno (Pius XI, 1931), Laborem Exercens (John Paul II, 1981), and Centesimus Annus (John Paul II, 1991).

"The Magisterium recognizes the fundamental role played by labor unions, whose existence is connected with the right to form associations or unions to defend the vital interests of workers employed in the various professions," according to the 2005 Compendium of the Social Doctrine of the (Catholic) Church, by the Pontifical Council for Justice and Peace states.

On March 23, 1946, Woody, Pete Seeger, and Lee Hays flew to Pittsburgh to perform for 10,000 striking Westinghouse workers. Seeger felt that every union should have a choir, just like every church. "We went to union halls and sang... 'Union Maid,' 'Talking Union,' 'I Don't Want Your Millions, Mister,' 'Get Thee Behind Me, Satan,' 'Union Train a' Comin'.'"

In Woody's song "Tom Joad" (referring to the character in Steinbeck's *Grapes of Wrath*), he said, "Everybody might be just one big soul." Later, Woody said in an interview, "We wasn't in that class that John Steinbeck called the Okies because my dad was worth $35,000 to $40,000 and everything was hunky-dory an' he started havin' a little bit of bad luck..."

Oklahoma has come a long way, Arlo Guthrie says, from the days when it all but disowned his father Woody Guthrie. Woody has also been vindicated through Charles Banks Wilson's portrait of him in the Hall of Fame beneath the Oklahoma Capitol dome, and through his 1943 book, *Bound for Glory*, which received the Oklahoma Center for the Book Ralph Ellison Award in 2004.

Woody was described as one of the "American rebels" in *The Nation* in 2003, along with Dorothy Day, whose social justice fervor gained her a nomination for sainthood in the Catholic Church.

Woody's married his second wife, Marjorie Greenblatt Mazia, from New York, in 1945. She was Jewish, and the mother of his children, Arlo and Nora.

Eventually, Woody said, "Love is the only God I'll ever believe in."

Originally published
October 2015

by Faith Phillips

WOODY'S JESUS

Listening for traces of the gospel in modern folk music

Now as I look around, it's mighty plain to me
This world is such a great and a funny place to be
The gamblin' man is rich, the workin' man is poor
And I ain't got no home in this world anymore.
—"I Ain't Got No Home," written by Woody Guthrie and adapted by Bob Dylan

Just this past July, a rambling throng caravanned across the asphalt byway of I-40 to the sleepy town of Okemah. These travelers defied oppressive humidity, torrential rain, and the resultant mire to sit at the feet of musicians carrying on in various form the rich inheritance bestowed by Oklahoma's Woody Guthrie. From Wink Burcham's devastatingly heavy performance in the dark enclave of The Brick to John Fullbright's heart-rending delivery of "Deportee (Plane Wreck at Los Gatos)" on the final night, the five-day festival proved the social issues that smoldered in Woody's day remain: the plight of the immigrant, the struggle of those born into poverty, the systemic unequal administrations of justice, and the vast overreach of consumerism.

Folk singer-songwriters continue to echo the red-letter words of the New Testament and gospel music influences; its allusions infiltrate contemporary rock and roll/folk even now. Joe Baxter, an Oklahoma singer-songwriter from Midwest City, recalls, "I grew up in a real lower-class neighborhood. These poor people were moving in and needed help bringing their piano into the living room. The notes were written on the keys in lipstick. They had nothing else in the house, literally didn't have a pot to pee in. Kids dressed in rags and dirty faces gathered around, and their mother started hammering out gospel tunes. I was just amazed," Baxter said. "Here are these poor people that don't have nothing—instead of worrying about getting everything moved into this house or where the next meal might come from, this lady was pounding out gospel tunes."

Baxter recalled a particular era when gospel had a resurgence in popular music. "It could just be two or three words that opened the door for people like Roger McGuinn and other mid-60s folk-rock genre people to use those references. It was an era of rebellion before the '70s Jesus freaks. Turn on, tune in, and drop out—that didn't involve Jesus. Sixties people were looking for something, and Jesus fit the bill. The fact that Dylan and Gram Parsons did that lent it some credibility."

The most famous example of the Oklahoma gospel–Woody Guthrie connection is Bob Dylan. Dylan cut his songwriting teeth at the foot of Guthrie's sickbed as he lay suffering from Huntington's disease in Brooklyn State Hospital. Dylan later declared that he had begun his career by "writing like I thought Woody would write." Bob Dylan's spiritual inclinations in song are most often associated with the trio of albums released in the late '70s and early '80s—*Slow Train Coming, Saved,* and *Shot of Love*—a collection of songs rife with spiritual fervor, biblical imagery, and obvious gospel intonations. Those albums were met with an uproar from fans who, having previously pledged their undying devotion, howled in protest that the songwriter dare proclaim religious loyalties in song. But from the beginning, Dylan's collective work contained a consistent thread of death and eternal preoccupation, the apocalypse, judgment, and biblical imagery. His debut album in 1962 was peppered with songs like "In My Time of Dyin' " ("Jesus gonna make up my dyin' bed"), "Gospel Plow" ("All them prophets so good and gone / Keep your hand on that plow, hold on"), and a cover of Blind Lemon Jefferson's plea to "See That My Grave Is Kept Clean" ("Now I believe what the Bible told"). It is no wonder, since Guthrie was Dylan's hero, that ideas spawned from biblical verbiage and instruction would have bled into Dylan's burgeoning artistic quiver.

Although Woody didn't necessarily sing old-time gospel music as it is traditionally recognized, he touted the word and deeds of Jesus Christ as depicted in the New Testament and decried the perversion of that message by a society riddled by greed and corruption. Oklahoma is widely known as the buckle of the Bible Belt, and over time struggling families clung to the Gospel as their last shred of hope. That cultural and spiritual inheritance has been passed down through generations of Oklahoma families.

But Woody Guthrie consistently called out Christians in song for the social injustices he witnessed that spat in the eye of Gospel teachings. He made no secret of it, blatantly singing in "Jesus Christ":

> Jesus Christ was a man who traveled through the land
> A hard-working man and brave
> He said to the rich, "Give Your Money to the Poor"
> But they laid Jesus Christ in His grave...
>
> But the bankers and the preachers, they nailed him on the cross
> And they laid Jesus Christ in His grave.
>
> This song was written in New York City
> Of rich man, preacher, and slave
> If He was to preach what He preached in Galilee
> They would lay Jesus Christ in His grave.

The account of Jesus Christ and the money-changers at the temple echoes in the brutal indictment of greed and the oppression of the working class in "I Ain't Got No Home."

Recently, a vote went up in the Oklahoma legislature to secure funding for historical archives that would, in part, memorialize Woody Guthrie and his prolific contributions to Oklahoma music and culture. One argument in the Oklahoma State Senate debate used to rail against funding was that Guthrie was a communist and an atheist—despite the portrait of Guthrie that hangs pointing and chiding on the fourth-floor rotunda of the Oklahoma State Senate. Regardless of religious proclivities or lack thereof, Guthrie's writings make clear that he admired and sang the teachings of Jesus Christ. The Woody Guthrie Festival in Okemah evidenced an Okie legacy of musicians carrying on in that vein.

CPSIA information can be obtained
at www.ICGtesting.com
Printed in the USA
FSOW04n2241031217
41725FS

9 780996 251631